Rethinking TESOL in Diverse Global Settings

ALSO AVAILABLE FROM BLOOMSBURY

Reflective Language Teaching, Thomas S. C. Farrell
Teaching and Learning the English Language, Richard Badger
Teaching English to Young Learners, edited by Janice Bland
Why Do Linguistics?, Fiona English and Tim Marr

Rethinking TESOL in Diverse Global Settings

The Language and the Teacher in a Time of Change

Tim Marr and Fiona English

BLOOMSBURY ACADEMIC
LONDON · NEW YORK · OXFORD · NEW DELHI · SYDNEY

BLOOMSBURY ACADEMIC
Bloomsbury Publishing Plc
50 Bedford Square, London, WC1B 3DP, UK
1385 Broadway, New York, NY 10018, USA

BLOOMSBURY, BLOOMSBURY ACADEMIC and the Diana logo are trademarks of
Bloomsbury Publishing Plc

First published in Great Britain 2019

A catalogue record for this book is available from the British Library.

A catalog record for this book is available from the Library of Congress.

ISBN: HB: 978-1-3500-3346-7
PB: 978-1-3500-3345-0
ePDF: 978-1-3500-3348-1
eBook: 978-1-3500-3347-4

Typeset by Newgen KnowledgeWorks Pvt. Ltd., Chennai, India
Printed and bound in Great Britain

To find out more about our authors and books visit www.bloomsbury.com
and sign up for our newsletters.

To Ana, Mark and Stanley

Contents

Figures

Abbreviations and Acronyms

ASEAN	Association of Southeast Asian Nations
BANA	Britain, North America, Australasia (UK, United States, Canada, Australia, New Zealand)
CertTESOL	Certificate in Teaching English to Speakers of Other Languages (also CELTA)
CLT	Communicative language teaching
EAL	English as an Additional Language
EAP	English for Academic Purposes
EFL	English as a Foreign Language
ELF	English as a lingua franca
ELT	English Language Teaching
EMI	English as medium of instruction
ESL	English as a Second Language (i.e. English as used in countries where it is not the native language of most, but where it has some official status)
ESP	English for Specific Purposes
GCSE	General Certificate of Secondary Education: public examination taken by school pupils at age sixteen in most of the UK
INSET	In-service training: INSET days are particular days devoted to teacher development in UK schools
IPA	International Phonetic Alphabet
L1	First or native language
L2	Second language
LF	Lingua franca
LWC	Language of wider communication
MFLs	Modern foreign languages
NEST	Native English-speaking teacher
NNEST	Non-native English-speaking teacher
NNS	Non-native speaker (of English)
NS	Native speaker (of English)
RP	Received Pronunciation

TEMI	Teaching with English as medium of instruction
TESOL	Teaching English to Speaker of Other Languages
TPD	Teacher professional development

Acknowledgements

We would like to say thank you to our present and former students, as well as to everyone who was kind enough to give us their views or help us in other ways. We're particularly grateful to Policarpio Bulloker, Ben Coulthard, Markus Davis, Stefanie Hehner, Chayan Mallick, María Fernanda Reyes, Martin Stark, Stephany Torres and Matt White for providing us with insightful comments and textual nuggets. Thanks, too, to Maria Giovanna Brauzzi of Bloomsbury and to our anonymous reviewers who helped us hone our ideas.

1

Introduction: What Is It About Language Teachers and Language?

1.1 Three snapshots

- *In southern China, a group of Chinese university lecturers from various academic disciplines are on a training course to help prepare them for the shift from teaching their subjects in Chinese to teaching them with English as the medium of instruction (EMI). As a preliminary microteaching exercise, they are asked to identify two specialist terms in their own discipline and then teach these words to their colleagues. After a while, one woman puts her hand up: 'I don't know what I should do.' Asked what she is finding difficult, she replies: 'I'm an English teacher – we don't have any words.'*

- *First day of another in-country training course, this one for university teachers of English for Academic Purposes (EAP). We, the trainers, have been talking about the lingua franca context in which English is used in international universities, filling in some sociolinguistic background and introducing some of the core concepts of EAP such as genre, register and disciplinary discourses (Hyland 2000, 2007). During the coffee break, we are approached by an Australian teacher of pre-sessional EAP at an Australian university. He is unhappy about the content of the course thus far and anxious to get on to something 'more practical'. We try to persuade him of the relevance of these topics and terms to the practice of teaching EAP, but he is adamant. 'Aw, look, fellas,' he says, finally, 'we're going to have to agree to disagree. I know language is your thing, but it's not my thing. I just want to help my students to learn better.'*

- From an internet advertisement for EFL teachers: *'Have you heard that you can go live in South Korea and get paid to do so? The main requirement is that you have to be born. That's right. If you are from a native English-speaking country, you can get paid to live in the country for a year teaching school children how to speak better the very language of your birth.'*[1]

These snapshots will not, we suspect, be altogether unfamiliar to anyone who has spent any time around ELT (or TESOL – we use the terms interchangeably), almost anywhere in the world. It is our contention that a thread joins these three takes on ELT, and that between them they suggest something profound and worrying about the relationship between large parts of the ELT profession, or industry, and language itself (or the discipline of language study). In order to demonstrate what that something is, and why we think it so important, it is perhaps worth trying to unpick them a little.

In the first snapshot, the confusion of the teacher, when faced with the task of identifying core terminology in her field, seems to suggest confusion about what her field actually *is*. Language teaching is of course a broad, interdisciplinary pursuit, which draws on, for example, psychology, education and sociology as well as the study of language. However, restricting ourselves to language-related disciplines only, we might suggest that she could have chosen specialist terms from at least three or four different areas. At the most obvious and basic level, she might have chosen terms from the area of traditional grammar, or grammatical analysis, which as a Chinese teacher of English, she would certainly be comfortable with. (A native speaker, admittedly, might have been on less secure ground.) She might have chosen to teach *subordinate clause*, for example, or *past participle*, or *subjunctive*, if she had wanted to set herself a sterner challenge. If she were more inclined towards literature, as some English teachers of course are, she might have picked on some of the technical language of literary stylistics: traditional terms like *metaphor* and *synecdoche*, perhaps, or more contemporary ones such as *deviation* and *foregrounding*, if she had wanted to move towards the area where modern literary and linguistic analysis meet. We would have thought it perfectly appropriate if she had decided to teach a couple of words from the general field of linguistics – *phonetics* and *phonology*, say – or applied linguistics: how about *corpus*, or *register* or *domain*? If her interest, reasonably enough, lay principally in the direction of language learning and teaching, rather than language as such, then why not terms used routinely in the relevant academic literature, such as *backwash*, or *natural order hypothesis* or *CLT*? Applied linguistics is of course a very broad field in itself. In the United States, it has often been understood to be restricted largely to issues of language learning and teaching, while in the UK and Australia, for instance, it has a wider ambit, also encompassing areas such as sociolinguistics.

What she eventually said, though, was that in English teaching there are no 'words'. We take this to mean that as far as she was concerned, ELT or TESOL does not have a specialist terminology of its own, and that she did not regard it as forming part of a legitimate academic discipline, let alone standing as an academic discipline in its own right. The possession of a specialist lexis is, of course, one of the fundamental, defining characteristics of an academic discipline. The strong sense we got from her was that she had never thought of ELT as a discipline: the idea was entirely new to her. Her job as she saw it – prior to the training course at least – was to help lecturers and students in properly academic disciplines such as microbiology or engineering with their English. She was to all intents and purposes positioning herself as an assistant to real academics, rather than as an academic herself.

The second example we give here throws an even sharper light on how some English teachers regard the subject of their daily practice. Our Australian EAP teacher not only disowned the disciplinary identity of linguist ('*it's not my thing*') but was quite unable to see how the discipline of language study, or applied linguistics, might link to the day-to-day practice of language teaching: '*I just want to help my students to learn better*.' Perhaps the most startling aspect of this conversation was the airy suggestion that we should '*agree to disagree*' – on whether language teachers should be interested in language or not! It is genuinely difficult to imagine the circumstances in which a teacher or lecturer in any other discipline, at any level, would profess such a lack of interest in the subject they teach – indeed, would *refuse to recognize that it is their subject at all*. For what links these two examples, of course, is that in neither of them did the teacher actually consider her or himself to be a *language* specialist. Rather, they each seemed to think of themselves essentially as a skills trainer (Gray 2000), someone who happens to be a competent user of English, whether by accident of birth or by undertaking an active learning process, and who has some ability to pass this skill on to others. The third snapshot, the TEFL advertisement, follows naturally from this: no training or skill required *at all* – you just have to be born an English speaker.

We might equate this conception of the English teacher to that of a driving instructor. Driving instructors can obviously be good or bad, but as a general rule they share a common skill set. They are technically very competent drivers, they are (we trust) patient and calm with learners of all kinds, they understand the rules of the road and the requirements of the test that their learners will eventually have to take, and they have the requisite social and communicative skills to be able to convey their knowledge to the learner. They are not expected to know anything much about how the car works or what is under the bonnet. It is not required that they have an interest in automotive design, or an opinion on the development of electric or self-driving cars (though of course they might well have one). Other than semi-technical terms like *clutch* or *yellow box junction*, they do not need to use a particular professional vocabulary. In fact, and crucially, their being able to deploy the specialist vocabulary of mechanical engineering or fluid dynamics would not help their learners learn to drive any more effectively. Driving instruction, in short, has no university departments, no degree courses, no peer-reviewed journals, no glossaries of terms and no international conferences on theory and practice.

It is therefore telling that in many institutions around the world, and especially where there has historically been a strong American influence, language teachers are professionally classified and routinely referred to as language *instructors*. Employers who use this epithet – they include BAE Systems, Berlitz and the CIA[2] – are making a statement, whether they intend to or not, about what they regard as the disciplinary status of language teaching. We will argue here that language teachers who themselves subscribe implicitly to that view of language teaching by claiming that they are 'just English teachers' and don't lay claim, or even *wish* to lay claim, to any disciplinary knowledge, specialist lexis or professional/academic standing, help to facilitate this reductive and ill-founded view of their own profession. As for language teachers who are simply not interested in language, or aver that language is not their 'thing' – how could this even be conceived of in any other academic area? And yet in the case of ELT, it is so common as to be unremarkable. Indeed, we contend that it fits into a generalized discourse about language teaching that is taken to an extraordinary extreme in quite large segments of the commercialized, globalized activity of TESOL, and has its echo in mainstream education, too. Let's examine this contention in more detail.

1.2 'Anyone can do it': ELT and disciplinary specialization

We noted in a previous book (English and Marr 2015) that language typically occupies an odd and rather elusive place (or rather, places) in schools. We called the relevant chapter of the book 'The Subject That Isn't A Subject', in order to highlight the fact that while language is obviously studied in schools in various ways, there is no subject called 'language', let alone 'linguistics' on the curriculum. In the Anglophone academic tradition, 'English' stands both for the study of the language and the study of the literature written in that language. Mainstream English and modern foreign languages (MFL) teachers in many countries are often literary specialists or just happen to be proficient speakers of the language concerned, with an interest in its related culture(s). They may be very comfortable with the traditional terms of grammatical analysis, or (especially in English-speaking countries), they may not. Certainly, in most cases they can qualify as teachers of English, or whatever language it may be, without necessarily knowing about even the most basic elements of linguistics, such as the phonetic alphabet. We commented then that this 'leads to a very curious state of affairs. History teachers are obliged to be specialists in history, maths teachers to be specialists in maths, physics teachers to be specialists in physics and so on; *but language teachers are not required to be specialists in the discipline of language itself*' (2015: 233; italics in the original).

In the staffrooms of educational institutions worldwide, it is perfectly easy to find language teachers who not only have little awareness of how language works but relatively little interest in the matter, either – though they think of themselves and are thought of as competent teachers, with a genuine commitment to academic excellence and the welfare and progress of their students. Most egregiously, teachers of EFL who happen to be native speakers of English are routinely employed even though they may have little or no knowledge even of English grammar, let alone linguistics, and often very little formal training of any kind. As Stanley (2013) comments on the subjects of her (sympathetic) ethnography of EFL teachers in Shanghai, 'these are "teachers" who would not necessarily be considered teachers elsewhere' and whose 'only qualification for the job is a degree of enthusiasm' (2013: 2). This still goes on all over the world, despite repeated attempts at professionalization, bringing the whole of the practice of English language teaching into disrepute and contributing to what Thornbury (2001: 391) calls the 'unbearable lightness of EFL'. As we will argue later, one reason why it continues to happen is because many stakeholders in the practice of ELT – language centre managers, head teachers, academic administrators, government policymakers, schoolchildren and their parents, among others – do not really see language teaching as a true academic discipline, any more than do the teachers with whose words we began this chapter. One

PhD-qualified Moroccan teacher, who wrote to us as we prepared this book, referred wearily to the 'anyone can do it' attitude – that is, a deeply rooted belief, 'widespread and often unquestioned', according to Bunce (2016: 1), that 'anyone can teach English'. It of course leads logically to a host of other, related and similarly intractable problems, as he explained when asked to list what he most disliked about his job in a Gulf state university:

> *The at times 'anyone can do it' attitude by managers. Uninformed education leaders, managers or administrators setting goals that are not realistic and therefore unachievable. The discriminatory attitude that exists in the Gulf countries to favour passport and citizenship over experience and academic qualifications.*

Unqualified and uninformed managers are a recurring theme when one spends time talking to global English teachers (we'll see another prime example in just a moment). But this is not to say they are all malicious or charlatans, though some certainly are. Rather, the problem lies at the deeper level of conceptions of disciplinary knowledge: if you believe language teaching is best done by American or British native speakers and needs no specialist knowledge, why would academic qualifications matter? Or to put it in the terms we used above, if you just want to employ a driving instructor, why on earth would you insist on them having a training in mechanics or automotive engineering?

It is a regrettable fact that the absence of – sometimes even the *active denial of* – any need for disciplinary specialism is firmly established as a dominant discourse within many English language teaching contexts. There exist, for example, reams of often seriously meant careers advice online for would-be EFL teachers, which make no reference at all to knowledge of, or interest in, language. Take this 2011 extract from the BBC/British Council website www.teachingenglish.org.uk[3] on the topic 'Characteristics of highly effective teachers of English'. The writer reports that, having reflected on his experience as a teacher and teacher trainer, and consulted his students and fellow teachers, he can define an effective teacher of English as 'someone who possesses 5 I's'. These turn out to be *imagination, innovativeness, interaction, independent thinking* and *interdependence*. Now, there is nothing wrong with this in itself, and we are not setting out to criticize this author (indeed, his classroom sounds like a rather stimulating environment). But the implicit consolidation of the prevailing discourse is as unfortunate as it is familiar. Where is the L for language? There is no mention of disciplinary expertise here – in fact, there is no mention of *any disciplinary content at all*. And predictably, in short order, someone who is presumably a practising teacher posts on the website an enthusiastic comment: 'The five "I's" you've listed are very interesting and quite relevant to the teaching profession. Language classrooms cannot be like content ones and should reflect the life that is there in language.' That is to say, language teaching, unlike physics or history or literature, *does not have content*. This discourse is extraordinarily pervasive; and this approach is echoed again and again in teacher development websites, courses and other resources. It is routinely counselled that the main priority for TESOL teachers is to develop such things as 'a willingness to connect' and 'understanding of a student's cultural background' along with 'understanding [of] the individual needs of students'.[4] It's not only as if these things were somehow peculiar to the English language classroom, but as if the discipline of language study simply did not exist, leaving a vacuum that needs to be filled by fun and games, empathy and cultural sensitivity, formalized in the shape of methodological approaches that are supposedly 'humanistic' or 'creative', or whatever the fashion of the moment might be.

The discourse that holds that language teaching has no need of an identifiable academic or specialist core extends even to the sphere of formal training. One well-known institution offering ELT teacher training courses in the UK holds academic applied linguistics in such disdain that it cannot refrain from trumpeting this disdain on its website. Prospective trainees will not, boasts the course director, have to come into contact with figures like the 'woolly-headed "applied" linguist', the 'researcher who cannot teach', the 'person whose self-esteem depends on her place in a university pecking order', or the 'person who has lost all touch with the language teaching classroom'. Not content with this idle and contemptuous stereotyping, he goes on to announce proudly that his team of teacher trainers draw on their experience in such fields as business training, cinema and video, as well as counselling, therapy and 'exercise choreography'. Curiously, the webpage ends with an approving mention of an eminent British academic, noting cheerfully, if repetitively, that he is 'a real linguist, not a woolly headed "applied" linguist!' It is hard to resist the suspicion that there is some history here.[5]

Or consider the following, taken from the introduction to a textbook on ELT methodology, which is aimed at people training to become teachers:

> This book is handy reading for pre-service teachers enrolled for courses at University, Teachers' Training Colleges and ELT Institutions. It is also great as a point of reference throughout your teaching career. By no means the definitive guide to English Language Teaching, 'English to The World' offers a simple yet easy to follow overview of English Language Teaching. It is

precisely the simplistic nature of this book which allows you the reader to gain a clear understanding of the fundamentals of this exciting and diverse industry. Some scholars and academics might argue that the approach and style of this book is too simplistic, but I'm not writing for specialists. Explanations and ideas are presented, as far as possible, in simple everyday English. Where it has been necessary to use ELT terminology, I have generally used more traditional terms that are well known and easy to understand. (Geyser 2006: iii)

The assertion 'I'm not writing for specialists' patently demands a question: so who *are* you writing for? Such an approach, in any other area of pedagogy (note how this writer describes ELT baldly as an 'industry'), would surely be regarded as somewhere between risible and scandalous. As we noted above, the possession of a specialist lexis is what defines a discipline: this textbook *explicitly disavows* it and assures the would-be language teacher that they will not have to deal with anything academic. The only terms used will be, we are told, 'simplistic' ones [*sic*], in 'simple everyday English'. As in the previous example, 'scholars and academics' are referred to with a substantial dollop of disdain, implicitly caricatured as elitists or head-in-the-clouds theorists, lacking practicality or even useful insights. Truly, anyone can do it, this teaching English.

This is, to repeat, a firmly established and powerfully influential discourse – one which holds that to be a successful TESOL teacher, no specialist knowledge about language is needed, only an ability to speak the English language, plus some methodology-related 'skills' and some personal 'qualities', most of which are in no way specific to the field. As Breen (2018: 20) remarks, brutally but accurately, on the way the teaching of English (albeit for academic purposes) is seen in universities: 'Perhaps it is even the word *English* that conjures up images of classroom ball-games such as those described in CELTA course textbooks and literature.' Ouch. It is little wonder that EFL teaching is often regarded as such a dubious career path to choose, surrounded as it is by 'stereotypes and stigma' (Breen 2018: 6), or that, as we shall see in later chapters, properly skilled teachers often feel so disempowered and disrespected, quite apart from being underpaid compared to other professionals (Stanley 2016). One of our British MA students, who had worked in two very different countries, told us how in one aspect at least these two teaching contexts were frustratingly alike:

> In both South Korea and the UAE, the school leaders were either from that country and/or culture and often what they wanted me to do instructionally

was problematic for me as an educator, mainly because I had more academic qualifications in ELT than they did (often they had no education qualifications), so my knowledge base about ELT instruction was greater. As a result, I disagreed with how they wanted me to teach certain things – rather than provide authentic language learning opportunities, they just wanted me to teach and drill vocabulary.

But of course, given the ubiquitous and relentless global discourse which holds that anyone who can speak English can teach English, it is perfectly natural that 'school leaders' with no qualifications in the field would feel able to overrule an MA-qualified professional like this one, with years of teaching experience, teacher training qualifications and a track record of classroom-based research. If even people who wish to train as TESOL teachers may be assured that their training need not involve any specialist knowledge, difficult terms, theory or suchlike woolly-headedness, why should laypeople assume any different? An added difficulty, of course, is that one of the rather important groups of laypeople involved in this endeavour are the students themselves, and they will have an opinion, too. A blog aimed at native-speaking 'travel and teach' EFL teachers notes, sarcastically:

Two things you also get taught on the TEFL course and early on in your career are:

1 Never tell students you only did a four-week course. They might not understand just how thorough that training is and wonder why they're paying so much for you to be there.
2 Never admit how long you've been teaching if it's only a few weeks/months. They might not understand just how thorough your recent training was and wonder why they're paying so much for you to be there.

Why the secrecy? Could it be because within ELT everyone knows students won't like it, won't put up with it, Lord forbid, won't pay for it?[6]

The CertTESOL, CELTA or CELTA-type course that the blogger is referring to is, to be fair, a pretty intensive affair ('highly concentrated and demanding' according to Dewey 2015: 181), and few people find it easy. At a typical four weeks long, though, such a training course can only be regarded as skimming the surface of the discipline of language teaching. And it really can only be seen as *training* – a word which, as Edge (2003, cited in Breen 2018: 31) mischievously notes, 'collocates just as happily with dogs and seals as with teachers' – rather than the more substantial and nuanced something suggested by 'teacher education' or 'teacher professional development'.

However, worse even than sketchy training, or training which is largely unmoored from the discipline of language study, is no training at all. The voluntary teaching undertaken by well-meaning Westerners in developing countries is therefore often a 'complete shambles' (Bunce 2016: 6), while advertisements for native speaker teachers sometimes contain a disarming, not to say alarming, frankness about the whole affair.

> All applications are welcome and all resumes are read. We are interested in helping people start a new and successful life in China, in whatever capacity we can. NO EXPERIENCE NECESSARY, NO DEGREE REQUIRED!!! We do not have much requirement about the teachers. As long as you are a native level English speaker and like teaching kids, its ok [. . .] We do not care your past life or experience, we will develop your potential. Qualifications: People who are outgoing and love kids.[7]

Now, we are obviously not suggesting that that all English teachers are untrained, or that none of them have any special expertise. Nor do we think that all teachers should have a degree in linguistics: that would hardly be desirable, even if it were to be achievable, and the disciplinary concerns and objectives even of applied linguistics are in any case not quite the same as those of ELT. But we do think that what links the bemused Chinese lecturer with the 'anyone can do it' school manager, the language-averse EAP teacher, the applied linguistics-phobic teacher trainer and the textbook writer who promises 'simplistic' terms, and what links all of them in turn with the entirely untrained amateurs, is their missing the point of what the central topic of language teaching actually *is*. Even supposedly radical recastings of TESOL and TESOL training often tend to skate over questions of language in favour of an emphasis on such issues as, say, the discourses of power (Kumaravadivelu 2012), or feminist and postcolonial conceptions of time and space (Appleby 2010). We do not suggest that these matters are unimportant. We do, though, think that they can only seriously be addressed in language teaching settings through a proper understanding of language and sociolinguistics. Indeed, writer/researchers like these quite clearly draw on, and build on, their own substantial knowledge of language and linguistics to develop this kind of thinking. And in any case, the potential of such theoretical work to influence thought and behaviour is blunted unless it is embedded firmly within a context where the primary concern and field of expertise of the language teacher is acknowledged to be *language*, and where language teachers therefore own their professional identity and disciplinary space.

Admittedly and demonstrably, some teachers succeed quite well anyway, even without any real knowledge of how language works. Well over half a century ago, M. A. K. Halliday and his colleagues recognized this in the introduction to a seminal book on linguistics and language teaching. They then qualified that recognition with a point which still stands: 'We certainly do not overlook . . . how much a gifted teacher may achieve even without a very adequate basis of reference. Our contention is simply that with a better framework he [*sic*] can almost certainly achieve even more' (Halliday et al. 1964: x). However, as we shall begin to argue in the next chapter, the changing nature of English in the world is making the available 'window' for such teachers to succeed, or even just to manage as they have managed in the past, progressively smaller. We contend in this book that an understanding of language itself, at the very least an 'adequate basis of reference', is becoming indispensable for the pursuit of English language teaching in the global settings of the twenty-first century, and that the language-shaped hole in much teacher training, initial teacher education and teacher professional development therefore needs to be filled.

1.3 What kind of language knowledge do teachers need, and why?

Language specialists have long found themselves frustrated by the widespread indifference and incomprehension that surrounds the discipline of linguistics, even among many of those who work in language education on a daily basis. As we have noted elsewhere (English and Marr 2015), the struggle to achieve due prominence for 'linguistics' (we will explain how we are using this term in a short while) in school curricula, and in language teaching in general, goes back decades. Halliday et al. (1964) claimed to see a new focus on language as early as the 1940s, and on linguistics itself from 1955, but a generation on, little had changed. Depressingly, Carter and his working group (1982) and Stern (1983) were effectively starting again from scratch. That early-1980s relaunch, too, in the end made very limited headway, as is evidenced by the fact that twenty years later the case had to be stated all over again (see e.g. Trappes-Lomax and Ferguson 2002). In the United States, Fillmore and Snow (2000), in a far-reaching report for the US Department of Education, outlined a possible language curriculum for *all* pre-service teachers (not just language teachers), at *all* levels, which included not only a basic training in descriptive linguistics, but such things as sociolinguistic issues, language and cultural diversity, child language development and the language of academic discourse. This inspiring and exciting vision of a language-aware education system, too, quickly faded from view. It is to be hoped that the current generation of language-in-education proponents (e.g. Giovanelli and Clayton 2016, Ellis and McCarthy 2011) have substantial reserves of patience and perseverance.

Happily, there are at least a few positive indicators on the horizon. In the area of TESOL research, the past decade or so has seen an enormous expansion of activity in the field of English as a Lingua Franca (ELF) studies. The term itself is somewhat problematic, and arguably does not do the field justice (we look at it in detail in Chapter 3). The work done by ELF scholars and researchers has, though, been of the first importance in reorienting attention in TESOL, at least in the academic sphere, towards the language itself. Dewey (2012: 143) points out that historically, 'language teacher education in the UK has been primarily concerned with approaches and methods, with relatively little attention given to the subject matter "English"'. This is absolutely right, and the wind of change blowing from the ELF quarter has hence been very welcome. But it can still go further: what about the subject matter 'language'? We outline in Chapters 6 and 7 some of the specific areas where we think that knowledge about language is of direct benefit to language teachers. For the moment, though, it will perhaps suffice to note – and of course Dewey (2012, 2015) does implicitly acknowledge this – that it is not possible to come to a rounded understanding of *English* without a firm grasp of the essentials of *language*. Why is the kind of professional linguistics development laid out for example in Giovanelli and Clayton (2016), including the classroom applications of phonetics and phonology, pragmatics, stylistics, corpus linguistics, language attitudes and so on, still not thought indispensable for language teachers of all kinds? How does anyone imagine that teachers can effectively teach English – or any language – without a grasp of how the mechanics of pronunciation work, why speakers have non-native and regional accents, how slang relates to dialect and register, how speech sounds relate to the orthography of the language, how and to what extent the spoken and written grammars differ, whether non-standard forms should be considered 'correct' or not, how the tense-aspect system works, and so on, and on?

One partial answer to this question is that the discipline of English teaching is stuck in something of a vicious circle, particularly as 'English' is used as a label for at least two quite different things. As the title of this book suggests, we are primarily interested in TESOL rather than mainstream school teaching of English in Anglophone countries; but the question of language expertise, or lack of it, applies across the board. In UK secondary schools at least, decisions about what elements of language should be taught tend to be taken by literature specialists, who are not only often entirely ignorant of linguistics but sometimes actually dismissive of it. They might regard literature study as being more prestigious and of greater academic value, and be reluctant to cede the name 'English' to the study of language (Goddard 2016). One teacher at a secondary school in the south of England, an enthusiastic teacher of English Language A Level and keen observer of language, wrote to us:

> We have found some resistance to the teaching of English Language A Level since we started offering it a couple of years ago. Not resistance from the students – take-up numbers by students are similar, if not better than those signing up to do Literature – but more from colleagues and, indirectly, parents. Where does this come from? I can lay the blame wholly on lack of awareness. And it starts at the top. Many teachers don't really know what English Language A Level is. Just the other night, during a Recruitment Evening, the Head of my school asked me to talk to a student and her mother about English Literature; I was happy to do so, as I also teach it – but his final comment as he made his way out of the library, 'I know it's for the enemy, but . . . ' sums up senior management's attitude to the subject. The Head is an Oxford English Literature graduate.

The fact that this very same problem was identified by Halliday et al. (1964: 184) more than half a century ago indicates the excruciatingly slow pace of change in this area. In fact, research into how teachers of school subjects view themselves suggests that, for instance, science teachers strongly identify with science as a subject itself (Helms 1998: 812) while, as Giovanelli (2015) shows in his study of sixth form teachers who had been asked to teach on the newly developed English Language A Level course, 'participants' reasons for wanting to become an English teacher were very much related to wanting to be a teacher of literature' (2015: 421). It was literature that they had both a passion for and expertise in, not language at all. The result was, and still is, that large numbers of secondary English teachers are unable to deal with the technical aspects of an entire tranche of their own academic specialism, 'English'. Our secondary teacher continued,

> At a recent INSET [i.e. a training day] an examining board employee, and a teacher herself, was keen to move away from English Language GCSE issues

and onto the delivery of the English Literature GCSE because she felt 'more confident' with English Literature.

This sounds very similar to the secondary school English teacher reported by Myhill (2016) who confessed that while she was comfortable explaining *caesura* and *enjambement* to her students, she would not like to try to explain what a complex clause [*sic*] is (let alone, we imagine, what a phoneme is, or whether Standard English is an accent, a dialect or something else altogether).

While there is of course some overlap, and some movement between the two professions, teachers engaged in TESOL (especially overseas) and teachers who teach English to (mostly) native speakers in mainstream school classrooms tend to find little obvious common ground. They often come from different academic backgrounds and think of themselves as being engaged, broadly speaking, in rather dissimilar pursuits. This is fair enough. Where they surely *should* find common ground, though, is in having a serious interest in the matter of language.

How far should this commitment to language knowledge extend? As far as TESOL teachers are concerned, it seems to us as to many others (see e.g. Joseph and Ramani 2003) that it should surely be mandatory to have some experience of successful language learning, for reasons so obvious that they scarcely need explaining here. Ellis (2016: 602–3) lays them out convincingly. Would we not expect a language teacher to have some understanding of what it is like to learn a foreign language as an adult, in the way that a piano teacher must have already learned to play the piano and has some understanding of what it takes? Of course, the perception of native-speaker TESOL teachers as invariably monolingual is unfair to many teachers and exaggerates the case (Ellis 2016). But where an English teacher actually *is* monolingual, the implications are serious. Let us be clear – it means that they are unable or unwilling to do what they are asking their students to do. It means that they lack the ability to juxtapose one language with another; they lack the necessary language awareness to understand things from their students' point of view. But in the TESOL field there is virtually never an expectation or demand from employers that the teacher should be able to speak another language well, or that they should at least have had recent(ish) experience of learning one. When you stop to think about it, that is rather extraordinary.

The question of what constitutes language awareness or language expertise does not concern only native speaker English teachers, be they monolingual or polyglot. How we 'do' language learning and teaching is a complex and sometimes even conflicted issue globally, and the specifics vary not only according to language but according to national/cultural attitudes and beliefs about language and education. So the French dictation or *dictée*, for example, continues its stately march down the centuries, impervious to changing linguistic and pedagogical fashions, even into the internet age. The website www.lalanguefrancaise.com cheerfully offers you thirty *dictées* to improve your French ('*pour améliorer votre français*').[8] Thus, the idea of 'French' is elided with the idea of French *writing*, and 'learning French' identified with learning to master complex grammatical structures and the 'deep' or 'opaque' orthography of the language, in which the pronunciation of words corresponds only in part to their spelling. Seen from the traditional perspective of the French education system and French cultural mores, this makes perfect sense: mastery of complex grammar is a sign of educatedness (indeed, it is perhaps *the* principal sign of educatedness). The iconic status of the *dictée* simply reflects this educational-cultural-linguistic emphasis. Little wonder then that so many French teachers and students can tend (in our experience, at least) to be somewhat resistant to the insights of descriptive linguistics, and especially to the insistence of linguists that standard French, like any other standard language, is in essence no more than a socially privileged dialect.

Chinese education, too, relies heavily on dictation, as well as repetition and rote learning; here, though, the emphasis is on developing the skill of memorization rather than that of decoding complex grammar. The mark of educatedness lies in the number of written characters that you are able to recognize, and then reproduce – and of course the orthography of Chinese is almost entirely opaque, in the sense that while there are patterns and recurring root forms or 'radicals', every character has to be learned separately. In short, every linguistic culture has its different emphases, its foibles, its own concerns, and these will be reflected in the way they set about the business of language learning and teaching. English has its own set of concerns, of course, and much of this book is devoted to examining them.

1.4 About this book

Most books aimed at prospective TESOL teachers, or practising teachers who are undertaking an MA course or something similar, tend to dwell heavily on specific pedagogical areas such as assessment, classroom management or methodology. Where they are concerned with language itself, the books are often of the 'How To Teach Vocabulary' type, or are descriptive grammars, or are devoted to broad sociolinguistic issues such as 'native-speakerism' or the role of English as an international language. As will have become clear by now, we set out here to write a slightly different kind of book – one which touches on all these issues and more, but which places *understanding of language* at the heart of the language teaching enterprise. We suggest that the need to understand how language works is more acute for the case of English than it is for any other language in the world today. This is for two reasons. One, the role of English as the international lingua franca, which has enormous linguistic and pedagogical implications; and two, the related role of English as a marker, carrier and perhaps producer of 'cultural capital', which has social implications. This is why TESOL needs to be rethought and recast, with language awareness placed front and centre, and a dual focus on transcultural communication and the role of English in societies.

Before we give a brief overview of the content of individual chapters, we should point out that certain core themes recur throughout the book. For example, we take the need for sociolinguistics knowledge to be a given: it is a fundamental theme which runs throughout the book, and underlies everything we argue for. Detailed discussions of issues specific to sociolinguistics, though, can be found particularly in Chapters 2, 3, 4 and 8, while questions of language description and language analysis are to be found particularly in Chapters 6, 7 and 9. Inevitably, readers will find a bit of everything in most chapters.

1.4.1 Overview

We begin in Chapter 2 by addressing a thorny issue head-on: is English different? We suggest that the language's role as the international lingua franca does indeed make it different in certain key respects from other 'big' world languages. Perhaps more importantly, we argue that this lingua franca role presents both difficulties and opportunities for English teachers, which can realistically only be met if teachers position themselves as disciplinary linguists. We supply some sociolinguistic context in Chapter 3, which looks at lingua francas from a historical perspective and discusses the development of ELF as a distinct field of study, and some of the problems inherent in it. Chapter 4 deals with some of the unique challenges which surround English teaching in the twenty-first century: in particular, the way English is often ideologized as a 'must have' commodity for both individuals and societies, and the slowness with which the worldwide practice of TESOL has begun to respond to the changed and changing role of the language and what learners and other stakeholders want from it. Chapter 5 reappraises the role and identity of the modern ELT professional in the light of this discussion. In the pair of chapters at the heart of the book, 6 and 7, we lay out the type and range of linguistics knowledge that we think is necessary if teachers are to successfully navigate this shifting scene, while in Chapter 8 we turn to the matter of what the learner brings to the classroom in the shape of their existing linguistic knowledge and cultural capital, why it should be welcomed and what can be done with it. Chapter 9 outlines an actual classroom approach based in linguistic ethnography for developing teacher and student awareness of language by noticing and analysing the communicative behaviour that surrounds us all, and presents examples of how the resulting materials might be used. Chapter 10 concludes the book by arguing that English teaching has unique characteristics and challenges, and that the challenges are best met by teachers positioning themselves as language specialists.

In writing this book, we wanted to encourage teachers to question some of the received wisdoms about language and methodology and to trust their own experiences of what works well, with whom and under what circumstances. This, we hope, will challenge some of the commonly held ideologies about language education, including the tired old diktat of 'target language-only' classrooms – where never a word from another language must be heard! We also wish to encourage teachers to look beyond and supplement the models of English use that they are presented with in their regular teaching materials, and by highlighting the importance of linguistic choice in shaping meaning (e.g. through modality, register or genre) to show how an awareness of this can develop transcultural pragmatic competence. We hope, above all, to encourage more teachers to work on and develop their language awareness, and we particularly hope that they will feel emboldened to claim and own their identity as professional 'workers with language'.

We do not wish to try to reinvent the wheel. The UK Committee for Linguistics in Education (CLiE), the Association for Language Awareness (ALA), the English and Media Centre in London and others are doing sterling work in the area of encouraging language and linguistics awareness among teachers, and the development of the ELF field, as we noted above, is encouraging a renewed focus on language and languaging behaviour. But our experience of working with hundreds of international teachers, in the UK and overseas, suggests strongly that the impact of all this on the broad field of international TESOL is still to be properly felt. We therefore think that another push from our side is timely, as we look back on decades-long careers working in this and related areas.

1.4.2 A note about terminology

When we use the word linguistics, as in our previous book (English and Marr 2015), we throw our net wide. This is crucial, as will become apparent in due course, for it is by adopting a wide-ranging view of what the field encompasses, we feel, that teachers will find it of most practical use to them. Like Giovanelli and Clayton (2016), then, we make no distinction in this context between linguistics and applied linguistics, and like them, we use the term linguistics quite intentionally 'to refer to all aspects of the field covering language as a system, the study of its users, and as an underlying set of principles of thinking about communication and the construction of meaning' (2016: 4). This is admirably well put, and reflects our own thinking exactly. We should also note that we regard, for example, transcultural communicative practices and the study of multimodal texts (Li 2018, Kress 2010) as being an integral and indispensable element of our conception of linguistics.

1.4.3 Who we are writing for

When we were originally invited to write a book for English language teachers, it was conceived of as a short pocket book containing some core reading for newly qualified native speakers heading off to work in far-flung parts of the world. However, as we started thinking through our ideas, we quickly realized that this was not the book we wanted to write, nor the book we felt teachers needed. Our experience has been in working with teachers from most parts of the world and certainly has not been limited to native speakers or those from the core English-speaking countries. Much of the content of this book has developed as a response to the many discussions we have had with these teachers on Master's and professional development courses in the UK and elsewhere. They work across the educational spectrum, all over the world, from mainstream schools and universities, both state and private, to private language schools and institutes, and you will hear some of their voices here and there throughout. This book, then, is written for English teachers and teachers in training wherever they might be, and whatever languages they speak. It is also for those involved in the delivery of English language teacher education and professional development, including

B.Ed. and MA programmes in English, TESOL and Applied Linguistics and even short initial training courses such as the CertTESOL and CELTA. What brings this rather disparate group together is their professional connection with language, and it is this which is the focus of the book.

1.5 Conclusion: English and the challenge facing TESOL

Our contention, put very shortly, is threefold. We think that

- the 'language awareness' agenda is a vital one for ELT, and should continue to be extended from linguistic description to linguistics very broadly understood, including a social linguistics of pragmatics and social context;
- this is a necessary response to the changed sociolinguistic landscape, in which English must be conceptualized primarily as an international lingua franca and vehicle of intercultural communication, rather than primarily as the 'property' of native speakers; and
- it is immaterial whether or not English teachers are native speakers of English: they should claim and own the discipline of language study, and position themselves as critical language experts within their institutions.

Without this kind of rethinking, TESOL will be ill-fitted to face the challenge of the twenty-first century – a challenge which demands what Canagarajah (2014: 767) calls a 'new paradigm' in which, for instance, pragmatics will be seen as being as significant as grammar (or even more so!) in accounting for a speaker's language competence. Understanding how language works, and how English works in the world, is set to become a core area of the ELT teacher's skill set. Apart from anything else, given the narratives and aspirations attached to English, English teachers face bigger (and more unrealistic) expectations than teachers of many other subjects. If they are not to be uncritical consumers of top-down government language policy (Hult 2014, Shohamy 2006), and to find themselves buffeted by the shifting and inconstant winds of institutional decisions made by people with little or no knowledge of language matters, then the clear way forward is to become specialists in these matters themselves, and in that way have their voices heard. We hope this book will help in some small way.

Suggested readings

Giovanelli, M. and Clayton, D. (eds) (2016), *Knowing About Language:*
    Linguistics and the Secondary English Classroom. Abingdon: Routledge.
While the title indicates what this book's primary focus is, it actually has
relevance far beyond the context of the secondary school. A wide selection of
chapters from well-chosen contributors makes it abundantly clear that there
are vital applications from linguistics in all kinds of language teaching and
learning environments, at all levels.

Andrews, S. (2007), *Teacher Language Awareness*. Cambridge: Cambridge
    University Press.
With a strong emphasis on grammar, this book argues that language awareness
is fundamentally a matter of professionalism, and that language teachers must
therefore accept 'the challenge of being language-aware'.

2

Is English Different? The Numbers and the Narratives

There is little point in trying to treat English as 'just another language' (Ostler 2010: 8).

2.1 Introduction

This chapter provides the context for questions to be addressed in subsequent chapters – questions such as why people learn English; what they expect; what it actually means to teach English; who it's for, what it's for and what it can and cannot do. English, to a much greater extent than other 'big' languages, has come to be associated with ideas such as development and modernity, in addition providing a means for disseminating or promulgating these ideas, ideologized and hard to define though they may be. Furthermore, it has become in some sense a product for consumption, widely marketed as bringing benefits and advantages to those who learn it. It can even be argued that in certain contexts, an individual's proficiency in English may serve as a proxy for desirable non-linguistic features such as educatedness, high social status or (again) modernity. While numerous discussions over more than two decades have served to challenge the 'common sense' approach to the position of English in the world – English as a neutral and beneficent tool for progress – (see e.g. Pennycook 1998, Phillipson 2009a, Canagarajah and Ben Said 2011), this approach is still shared by many teachers, learners and policymakers today. This chapter explores these issues from a sociolinguistic perspective. We suggest that while in some ways English behaves much like any other major world language, its exceptional role as a global lingua franca means that in some sociocultural ways, it really *is* different – or that at the very least, the fact that so many people strongly feel it to be so, means that it is not treated in the same way as other languages.

2.2 The allure of English

Ideologies of linguistic superiority have existed for a very long time (Phillipson 2003: 47–50), and linguists therefore tend to be sceptical when claims are made for a particular language to be considered somehow 'special' or 'different'. And of course, English is not special in any linguistic sense. Despite the assertions routinely made in newspaper columns and popular language publications such as Bill Bryson's *The Mother Tongue* (1990), it is not radically more flexible than most other languages, nor does it have a vastly greater number of words in common use. To suggest that one aspect or another of its grammar makes it particularly easy to learn or suitable for widespread use is, in linguistic terms, entirely without merit – though that does not stop people from doing it. 'Unlike many other languages dominant in Europe and other parts of the world, English is gender free,' avers the website of one UK-based language school. 'There is no masculine or feminine!'[1] While this is undeniably true, it is neither here nor there. The popular discourse of 'English is special', as Pennycook shows in a measured debunking of the whole idea (1998: 143–6), has its roots less in scientific linguistic fact than in British colonial-era beliefs about the demonstrable superiority of certain cultures to others. This is not to say that English speakers are uniquely solipsistic: pretty much all language communities cherish their own myths and ideologies of 'specialness' (see English and Marr 2015: 89–92). Muslims very often think of Classical Arabic as being somehow holier or closer to God than other languages. French speakers are encouraged to prize the supposed clarity of French: '*Ce qui n'est pas clair n'est pas français; ce qui n'est pas clair est encore anglais, italien, grec ou latin*', according to the eighteenth-century aristocrat Antoine de Rivarol. Everywhere in the world, speakers of minority languages in diglossic speech communities tend to report that in their home language, as opposed to the language of the dominant majority, the sounds of words are easier and nicer, mothers' lullabies are softer and jokes are funnier. For linguists, it is axiomatic that these are culturally bound judgements: to say that a language is special is not really a linguistic judgement at all, but a social one.

And yet, there *is* something special about English. Consider the following figures, from the languages department of a medium-sized university, in a

Table 2.1 Numbers of students by language, summer semester 2016

Scheduled number of classes per foreign language

German	3
French	12
Italian	8
Chinese	3
Portuguese	10
English	116

medium-sized city in South America. At the beginning of each semester, all students have to choose a language option in addition to their main subject of study. The department then works out how many classes will be formed at each level, for each language on offer (each class holding about sixteen to twenty students). The results for one typical semester are shown in Table 2.1. These are totals across all levels of proficiency, from Level 1 (beginner) to Level 5 (advanced). The biggest total of classes at any single level in this semester was English 1, which had twenty-two groups of students (a total of about four hundred students). So just the beginner's English level had something like two-thirds of the total number of students of *all* the other languages at *all* levels, put together. Put crudely, English was nearly ten times as popular as the language with the second highest demand, French.

To take an even more striking example, Wei and Su (2012: 11) report that, according to a Chinese government census, of all the people in Mainland China who had ever studied a foreign language, as many as 93.8 per cent (a total of more than 390 million people) had studied English, 7.1 per cent had studied Russian and 2.5 per cent Japanese – and some of these, as is obvious from the figures, must also have studied English. Scarcely 0.3 per cent reported studying any other language. Interestingly, the same authors go on to note that only about 7 per cent of mainland Chinese used English often, and only about 5 per cent could use it very proficiently. What are we to infer from this? For one thing, surely, that English is just something you do, either at school or college – or increasingly, online – whether well or badly, and whether you are actually going to use it or not. More than 90 per cent of young Europeans study English at school and it is taught increasingly at a very young age (Linn 2016: 2). In Vietnam, the figure is 98 per cent at secondary level and 90 per cent at tertiary (Vu and Burns 2014). For very many people, in very many parts of the world, to learn English is simply a default position.

This is why, for all that the British Council might assert coyly that 'language acquisition around the world is increasingly being seen as a skill for personal as well as national development' (British Council 2016), everyone knows *which* language is in fact being referred to. To a large extent, this is also why native English speakers are often characterized as being poor linguists and reluctant to learn other languages. Now, to be honest, that's actually often true – as any secondary school language teacher in the UK or USA will tell you! But this is not so much because they are arrogant, stupid or lazy: it is more because *the default option is not available to them.* Learning another language to a passable standard, especially in a classroom setting, is a difficult and time-consuming business: if you do it, you want to be sure that your investment will pay off. So which foreign language is likely to be of the greatest benefit to you? For an English speaker, there is very often no clear answer. French has traditionally been the first choice, probably for reasons more to do with its historical role as the language of diplomacy and the bearer of a prestigious literary culture than with any immediate communicative advantage. There is some aspirational, middle-class interest in Chinese now, as indeed there was in Japanese a generation ago, presumably linked to the growing economic power of China. In the UK, Arabic is a popular option for religiously-minded Muslims, but hardly for the bulk of the population. In the United States, Spanish is an obvious option, but it suffers from relatively low prestige in that country. German is obviously okay, but only if you think you're going to need to speak to people who are native German speakers – it has very little reach beyond that particular speech community. In short, if you're an English speaker, the question of 'which language?' is quite tricky. For pretty much everyone else in the world, though, the answer is glaringly obvious, because English is 'not only an international language, but *the* international language' (Seidlhofer 2011: 2; emphasis in the original).

The effective identification of English with the very idea of 'international' goes well beyond the familiar 'X-language + English' approach to street signage and other official communications, common wherever in the world it is expected that people other than locals need to be informed. Consider, for example, newspapers in Thailand. The Thai word for newspaper is หนังสือพิมพ์ – *nangsuphim.* If you want one of the local newspapers written in English, though – the *Nation*, or the *Bangkok Post* – you don't ask for an 'English newspaper'. Rather, you fall back on *farang*, the all-purpose Thai word for foreign or foreigner, especially one of European descent, and ask for a *nangsuphim farang*, or 'foreigners' newspaper'. You will not thereby find yourself being offered a copy of *Bild* or *La Gazzetta dello Sport* (let alone a Vietnamese or Chinese title!), even if that is what you wanted. Thais speak English to most foreigners. Most foreigners speak English to Thais. So a newspaper in English is simply a foreign or foreigners' newspaper – the equation is simple.

2.3 Threat or promise? 'Linguistic imperialism' and the case against English

In its reach and visibility, then, in the impact it has on ordinary lives across continents, rather than in its structure, lexis or supposed expressiveness, English is different. To get the measure of this difference, it might be instructive to examine the discourse employed by those with a vested interest in global ELT, such as the British Council. The British Council, though, as we saw above, actually tends to err towards a rather un-triumphalist, if ever-so-slightly complacent tone. More revealing, perhaps, to look at the words of the harshest critics of English, those commentators associated with the 'linguistic imperialism' (or LI) school (see Phillipson 1992, revisited in Phillipson 2009a). A number of critical scholars have followed the lead of Phillipson in taking up the Gramscian concept of 'hegemony' to explore and explain the role of English in the world, and particularly the native speaker-based agencies and institutions through which ELT is promoted. Their unforgiving view of how English operates has proved durable: quite recent examples include Kumaravadivelu (2016), who qualifies the hegemony of English as 'colonial', and Bunce et al. (2016), who refer to English as 'the Hydra'. Phillipson himself has repeatedly described English as a '*lingua frankensteinia*' (2009b; 2014: 17). The idea of LI seems to suggest that English represents such a threat to other languages and cultures that it needs to be repelled as a matter of urgency, if we are not to end up with, for example, an 'English-only Europe' (Phillipson 2003). And English is regarded as being not just threatening, but *uniquely* threatening. While conceding that other languages might display imperialistic tendencies, or might have done so in the past, Canagarajah and Ben Said (2011: 389) nevertheless insist that 'there is a good case to be made that LI by English is different in degree and kind'. Bunce et al. (2016), meanwhile, claim that 'the expansion in the use and learning of English is unique in the history of imperial languages' and that the learning of English leads to an 'uncritical hostility to, and a devaluing of, other languages' (2016: 3). Edge (2003: 703) likens English language teachers to 'imperial troopers' who move into a territory after it has been pacified. It is hard to think of any other language being routinely referred to in such heightened terms. In fact, it is precisely this discourse, one of distrust of and resistance to the spread of English, which makes the point most forcefully that English *really is different*.

The conception of English as predatory and threatening is, though, far from self-evidently true or unproblematic. Indeed, there are at least two countervailing views to this one. First, and most obviously, for a large proportion of the actors employed in the delivery of ELT – publishing companies, national education ministries, schools and universities, private language schools, teachers and learners of all kinds – the 'problem' of English is either an invisible problem or is not perceived to be a problem at all. What is sometimes called the 'common sense' view of English holds that English is natural, neutral, beneficial and available to all (see Pennycook 1998). This view has been challenged for some decades now, by the LI school, as noted above, and indeed by many others, but it has proved remarkably resilient: it is a view that continues to be held by a great many people. Certainly, and perhaps predictably given the financial stakes involved, producers of coursebooks tend to blithely ignore what some concerned academics see as the debatable and controversial aspects of English (Linn 2016). As with the issue of reliance on native speaker norms (which we discuss in Chapters 4 and 5), this is an area where the conversation which is carried on among some academic linguists seems often to be at odds with, or to be barely registered by, most members of what might broadly be termed the practitioner community. We should note, of course, that scholars of the LI persuasion would certainly argue that this supposed lack of interest in ideology is in fact a heavily ideologized view in itself. But to be clear: as a general rule, and despite the fears of Rajagopalan (1999: 200) that this hostile discourse was creating needless guilt complexes among teachers, the staffrooms of ELT operations around the world are not abuzz with worried conversations about linguistic imperialism.

It is not the case, either, that all or even most scholars, many of whom have some reservations about the hegemony of English, therefore accept the argument that English is an imperialistic or colonizing force. It has been a controversial claim from the very beginning. One eminent applied linguist, in a withering review of Phillipson's original, fierce polemic (Phillipson 1992), wondered aloud whether the whole thing was supposed to be a spoof, before concluding glumly that 'I fear that the book is not meant to be a spoof. It is too serious for that, quite humourless in its intent' (Davies 1996: 485). Even some who were broadly sympathetic to the author's message, like one multinational reading group at Purdue University in the United States led by Margie Berns, found his tone 'condescending and patronizing' (Berns 2003: 39) and – rather splendidly – 'felt colonized . . . by his authorial imperialism' (2003: 43). Certainly, as Jenkins (2006a: 169) remarks, a good many readers of the book were probably 'provoked by its rhetorical style' as much as they were stirred by its content.

Going further, critics such as Brutt-Griffler (2002) have argued that the spread of English in many contexts might be regarded as the result of speakers' struggle *against* imperialism rather than as an act of imperialism in itself, and that speakers are always agents, not simply hapless victims of circumstance – a point also made forcefully by Kamwangamalu (2016) with regard to African parents actively choosing to have their children educated in English, even though that education may be in other respects substandard. It is noteworthy that in some North African countries (most recently Morocco), conservative Arabist/Islamists have proposed that French be replaced by English in school and university curricula (Lefevre 2015). In this particular case it is the French language that is regarded as elitist, hegemonic and colonizing, as well as being evidently the most serious threat to Arabic language and culture. English is here seen as presenting much less of a clear and present danger, being unconnected to the secular elites who comprise the major resistance to Islamist ambitions. This is plainly a result of the history of French colonialism in the region, and resistance to it, and it follows the official shift from French to English as the principal second or foreign language in other former French African colonies such as Rwanda (where schools moved to English as medium of instruction in 2008), Gabon (2012) and Senegal (2013).[2] English may very well feel like a neutral, even an empowering code, if those who colonized you spoke French. The same principle applies in eastern Europe and in some of the ex-Soviet republics: it is perfectly obvious that most young Poles, say, or Latvians or Hungarians, do not view learning English in the same way as they or their parents view learning Russian. English does not feel to them like an imposition.

There is also the question of how distance in time, or attitudes to the ideological associations of a language, may affect one's perspectives. In a university seminar we once listened to a group of Spanish-speaking academics and researchers who were strongly in favour of revolutionary Cuba vociferously attacking the 'imperialism' and 'colonialism' of English. They were unironically oblivious to the history of Spanish linguistic imperialism in the Americas, and the extermination of indigenous languages on the island of Cuba. Indeed, they refused to talk about it. On another occasion, a British-Pakistani student of ours who was a highly committed Muslim and keen student of Arabic decried passionately, in a class discussion, the colonial imposition of English on Egypt. Reminded by a fellow student that Arabic had itself been imposed on Coptic-speaking Egypt a thousand or so years earlier, he was indignant. That, his argument went, was the 'right' – that is Muslim and Arabic – kind of linguistic imperialism, and had brought great blessings and benefits. Cultural context is everything.

Viewing all this from the perspective of current developments in sociolinguistics, it is hard to avoid the feeling that the LI approach, while it has raised important and necessary questions about how English functions in the global social order, is something of a blunt instrument. It has also probably had its day, at least in its strongest form. A number of commentators have argued for a more nuanced view of how English interacts with other languages in multilingual environments, highlighting the polycentricity of English, its characteristics of intense mutability, mobility and flux, and its huge variety of creative, localized manifestations (see e.g. García 2011; Blommaert 2010, 2014; Blommaert and Rampton 2011; Pennycook 2010). This approach is of a piece with the turn towards the study of language as social practice, and especially *multilingual* social practice, in the field of ELF studies (Jenkins 2015), and with the rapidly developing theorization of the area configured loosely under headings such as translanguaging (Li 2018, García and Li 2014), polylingual languaging (Jørgensen and Møller 2014) or metrolingualism (Otsuji and Pennycook 2010), with its strong emphasis on speakers' dynamic multilingual practice. In the light of such approaches, where the borders between supposedly discrete languages show themselves in practice to be porous, moveable, finally perhaps even illusory, and where speakers perform and claim identity through the creative use of English alongside other local languages in multilingual environments, it is much more difficult to sustain the idea of a monolithic and imperialistic English, which is simply imposed on its luckless subjects.

We will have a good deal more to say later about these new approaches to English, and indeed to language in general, later in this book. For now, though, it is enough to note that while there are differences of scholarly opinion as to whether the spread of English is to be welcomed or not, what is *not* at issue is that this is a quite extraordinary phenomenon – hence, of course, the urge to explain and debate it, as well as to deplore and resist it. Seidlhofer (2011: 3) puts the case starkly:

> The global spread of English is unprecedented and unparalleled, and comparisons that are often made between the role of English in today's world and the role of Latin, French, Arabic, and other lingua francas in earlier times simply do not hold. No other language called 'world language' has ever had both the global expansion and the penetration of social strata and domains of use that English now has. This fact may sometimes irk speakers of other 'big' languages, such as those of French [. . .], but even they cannot but reluctantly acknowledge it.

'Unprecedented and unparalleled'. English is not, then, simply *primus inter pares* among the big languages of the world, contemporarily and historically: it has gone beyond the traditional role of an elite lingua franca (which we discuss in detail in Chapter 3). In the process, English has gathered powerful narratives and associations, which further set it apart from other languages on the global stage, and carry serious implications for the role of the teacher of the language. It is to these narratives that we now turn.

2.4 The narratives of English

We noted in Section 2.2 that the learning of English, for many people in many parts of the world, has become a default position – something that you just do, without necessarily reflecting at great length on it. Where the rationale for English learning is explicitly made, though, the same themes tend to appear again and again. Most powerfully, English is represented as bringing tangible benefits and advantages to those who learn it, along with the rather less tangible advantage of symbolic or cultural capital (discussed in Section 2.5). If we conceptualize languages as 'commodities that command an exchange value' (Tan and Rubdy 2008: 2), then English is perceived as having a uniquely high instrumental value, which is why parents often desire it so intensely for their children, even where, as in southeast Asia for example, some scholars and educationalists might prefer investment in the teaching of indigenous languages (Tan and Rubdy 2008, Hadisantosa 2010). This metaphor of currencies of exchange, the equation of English with commodities, is typical, and the discourse recurs in a very similar form wherever in the world you happen to look. In Peru, for example, Niño-Murcia (2003: 1) notes that 'a nearly universal ideology . . . manifests itself in the belief that "hard currency" cultural capital in the form of English competence is needed for technological advancement, employment opportunities, national progress and international travel'. Note the way that the symbolic, abstract notion of language as 'cultural capital' (Bourdieu 1991) has all but given way here to a concretized, monetized ('hard currency') version of itself. It has a very twenty-first-century feel about it. And indeed, in an inspired turn of phrase, one of Niño-Murcia's interviewees tells her that 'English is like the dollar.' We may take this characeristically Latin American allusion to mean that English is not only desirable but reliable, usable at once and everywhere, guaranteed to keep its value, the standard against which other languages are judged.

Now, in being regarded as having high instrumental value, English is still not that different to any other big language used as a regional lingua franca where there exists a substantial underlay of local languages. To take a very few examples, Russian in the ex-Soviet republics of Central Asia, French in large parts of north and west Africa, Hindi in large parts of India, Spanish in the Andean region, Putonghua in mainland China, would all be regarded as carrying significant economic advantage for speakers of the local languages who choose (or are given the opportunity) to learn them. It could even very well be argued that there would be a significant economic disadvantage attached to *not* learning the regional or national lingua franca. All these languages, in short, might be regarded as hegemonic in their own region. However, English, unlike any of the other big languages, plays the role of hegemon *worldwide*, and it plays this role in addition to – above and beyond – the regional lingua francas, so that in any one of the above contexts, the acquisition of English as well as the regionally hegemonic language would be considered a very desirable goal. In India, for example, while it would unquestionably be helpful for an individual to acquire Hindi as a national lingua franca (more in the centre and north of the country than in the south, admittedly), English as a commodity is often seen as equally valuable, if not more so. And its value does not derive only from its role as an international means of communication: the impact of Indian films like *Hindi Medium* (2017) and *English Vinglish* (2012) relies on their audience's buying into the idea of English being personally transformative and empowering for an Indian in India itself.

At this global level, English has come to be associated with economic advancement, technology and social and geographical mobility; even with such desirable abstractions as 'development' and 'modernity'. These ideological concepts tend not only to be associated with English, but to be disseminated, or promulgated, through English (which as Coleman 2011 remarks, is at the same time often conceptualized as an impartial or neutral language). Even concepts like 'freedom' or 'democracy' can fall into this category, which might help explain why the Chinese government tends to row back periodically in its enthusiasm for mass English language learning, stressing instead the importance of Chinese language and culture (Fang 2016, and see Guo and Beckett 2007, Geng and Yuan 2015). Perhaps the key concept associated with English is the amorphous idea of 'globalization'. Countries which have taken a decision to view globalization as *explicitly requiring* the mass teaching of English to their populations range right across the continents, from Colombia (British Council 2015), to Ukraine (Smotrova 2009), to South Korea (Cho 2015). In South Korea, indeed, 'English fever' is a nationally recognized phenomenon (Park 2009), as middle-class families compete to 'secure English as global linguistic capital for their children's competitiveness and belongingness in the global market' (Song 2016: 637). For these governments and these aspirational sectors of society, globalization appears to *demand* English, as a means to 'increase human capital' (Wedell 2011: 270). We say more about this in Chapter 4.

It is at the individual level, though, that the most intriguing narratives of English are played out. Here, proficiency in English sometimes appears to represent rather more than just that. In fact, it seems to have come to serve in some contexts as a proxy for a bundle of other, highly desirable but non-linguistic personal attributes. Depending on where in the world, these might include educatedness, creativity, high social status, or just 'modernness', however that might be defined. In some highly unequal societies, it might be a key way in which you differentiate yourself from your poorer, more rural compatriots (see e.g. Baker 2012 for Thailand). It is here too, naturally enough, that the question of learners' identities, or desired identities, comes into play. The concept of 'investment' (Norton 2000 – note the use of a monetary metaphor again!) is a helpful one in exploring how the various associations of English interact with learners' identities in their desire to learn the language. In a class in New Delhi, for example, Bhattacharya et al. (2011) noticed 'a powerful link being forged between English and class etiquette. Students consider English "a manner-full language" and link it to "discipline" and being "civilised" . . . Students indicated the deep investment they are making in the acquisition of English, their strong desire to speak it and the aspirations the language encodes for them' (2011: 481). In Pakistan, meanwhile, students of English regarded their investment in English as being in effect an investment in their identity as 'educated people', the sort of people who would have access to symbolic – and in due course real – capital (Norton and Kamal 2003). Rather than having a desire to speak English as such, we might suggest, learners like these essentially want to *become the kind of person who speaks English*. With its emphasis on identity and aspiration, this represents a subtle but vital twist on the more instrumental motivations which are sometimes understood to drive English language learning.

Now, it is self-evidently the case that English might index any number of other desirable characteristics – from a sense of belonging for Mexican migrants to the United States (Ullman 2010) to an unconflicted sexual identity for gay Korean men in Seoul (King 2008). It has associations with a glamorous international elite (see e.g. Dashti 2015 for the case of Kuwait); learners might consider it 'sexy' and 'hip' (Johnson 2009), or want to 'sound cool' (as reported by one of our Latin American ex-students). In societies which limit women's opportunities, learning English might have a particular allure. A Bangladeshi teacher who teaches at a university in Saudi Arabia wrote to us:

> *Usually girls do better here because they stay at home and do assignments and study. The boys never want to complete assignment or study at home. Even they (boys) are reluctant to take part in classroom activities. On the other hand, girls are more active and want to participate and compete with their classmates. For the girls learning English is kind of empowerment.*

But for many, the essential narrative of English is the one which ties the language to the international economic order, and thus in turn ties the teaching of English to 'the emergence of a dynamic subject that aligns with the enterprising self of neoliberalism' (Flores 2013: 514). English represents individualism, ambition and aspiration in a way that no other language in the world can, and coursebook publishers, with their talk of 'aspirational content' and their representations of glamorous workplaces, know it better than most (Garton and Graves 2014, and see Block et al. 2012, Gray 2010a on how English and neoliberal economic and political ideas have become entwined). Cambridge University Press's recent (2016) contribution is actually called *Empower*. We look in more detail at learners' expectations of English a bit later on, but we should note immediately that the promised benefits of learning English are not as clear and unambiguous as is often assumed, by aspirational learners, ambitious parents and national governments alike (see Coleman 2010, Bunce 2016). Indeed, we will suggest that to some extent at least, learners might be falling for a sleight of hand – what might be called the English 'trick'. More of this in Chapter 4.

In the academic literature which has accumulated around these topics, a key reference point is invariably Bourdieu's (1991) elaboration of the notion of language as cultural capital. Actually, Bourdieu was chiefly concerned with standard French, and it was this that he referred to as the *langue légitime*, imposed by the state by means of the centrally controlled French education system. It has, though, been asserted time and again that the theory applies at a global level to English (for instance, by Joseph and Ramani 2003: 188 – 'English is undoubtedly cultural capital.') This can seem an impossibly abstract proposition. Where, exactly, is this cultural capital? What does it consist of, and how can we recognize it? But it is important to realize that this really is not – or not always – simply an abstract proposition or a theoretical formulation. Here and there in the discourse which surrounds global ELT we can glimpse the actual, tangible outworking of the claim that English represents increased cultural capital. To show how this works in practice, let's take the example of ELT advertising campaigns in Latin America.

2.5 It's all about the maid: Status, class and linguistic shaming in ELT advertising

If we were to accept the proposition that English does represent cultural capital – let's say in the sense that it indexes a number of other desirable, non-linguistic, status-enhancing attributes, as we suggested above – then we would expect also to be able to find the negative corollary of this. We would expect to find that *not* having proficiency in English is apt to be felt by oneself or perceived by others as an embarrassing deficiency, which lowers an individual's status and threatens their social class position. Unsurprisingly, it is those who make a living out of teaching English to the middle and upper classes – or aspirants to the middle and upper classes – who have been the quickest to note that this is, indeed, precisely the case. They have further noted that there are profits to be made in highlighting this sociolinguistic sensitivity, and even, of course, encouraging it.

In a series of advertisements for the online provider Open English, which air repeatedly on cable TV in Spanish-speaking Latin America, amusing scenarios are set up in which a hapless character known as Wachu is shamed in front of others by his poor English. In one, for example, a spaghetti Western is being made. But the tense build-up to a shoot-out ('Get out of town, cowboy', drawls a black-clad baddie) is ruined when the cowboy's response is such a mangled and heavily Spanish-accented 'Co-man mamey' ('Come and make me') that his adversaries, instead of drawing their six-shooters, end up laughing so hard that they practically have to hold each other up, while our hero sweats with miserable embarrassment and the director looks on in exasperation.[3] Significantly, the other actors are represented not as English speakers but as fellow Spanish speakers: to reinforce the point, one even shouts, '*¡Qué mal inglés!*' ('What bad English!'). The fear being played on here, then, is that of being shown up in front of your peers. If your English is poor, your friends and colleagues will laugh at you for being clumsy and bumbling, for lacking sophistication and worldliness, for being stuck in a Spanish-speaking provincialism. All these shame-and-embarrassment Open English television ads feature poor old Wachu making a fool of himself in different English-requiring situations, and the ads have become something of a comic genre in themselves. They are very well made, and genuinely funny. Younger, middle-class Latin Americans, especially, tend to be familiar with them and like them – and needless to say, no one wants to recognize in themselves the Wachu character.

An advertisement for another online English-teaching company, EF Englishtown, takes a different approach, though it is perhaps only slightly subtler.[4] A smartly dressed businessman enters an open-plan office. Immediately one of the office workers leaps out of his chair, terror on his face, shouting (in Portuguese or Spanish according to where the ad is being shown), 'The gringo's here!' Comic chaos rapidly ensues as people hide in cupboards and behind pot plants, pretend to be talking on the phone, try to disguise themselves by festooning themselves with Post-it notes and so on, in order to avoid having to speak English to the visitor. He finally approaches one calm, efficient-looking young woman and asks in English where he might find Mr Silva's room. She responds unhesitatingly, 'Oh, I'll take you there.' For good measure, she then extends her hand to the now-smiling visitor with a confident 'Hi, I'm Clara', as her co-workers look on sheepishly. Intriguingly, the visitor, for all that he is referred to as 'the gringo', is not, to judge from his accent, a native speaker of English. Is this an oversight, or was it thought no one would notice, or is this in fact a knowing, deliberate nod to the global lingua franca role of English? He could, after all, very easily be Swedish, or French or South African – he's still a gringo in most South American terms.

It is perhaps worth making explicit what associations and connotations are being drawn on here. The office setting is of great importance, of course (see Gray 2010b). If English is, as Jakubiak (2016: 198) argues, often 'framed as the primary tool through which individual people enter the transnational marketplace, a spatial imaginary of increased work and financial opportunities', then the modern open-plan office, with its desks and phones, sticky notes and pot plants, is an immediately identifiable, tangible reification of that 'spatial imaginary'. The lobby of an international city centre hotel or an airline business class lounge would have served equally well. Clearly, these office workers are in their own country – Brazil, in the Portuguese version, we are given to understand. But the office is revealed as an integral part of the 'transnational marketplace' at the instant that 'the gringo', the English user (who might or might not be a native speaker), crosses over the threshold. Only one of the office's staff proves herself competent to rise to the challenge thus posed. What the ad is suggesting, then, is that you must stop hiding, *literally* hiding, from the social-linguistic reality. English is potentially everywhere, including in what you had hoped was your own comfortably Portuguese-speaking space: this is English as the unsettling, insistent *Et in Arcadia Ego*. You cannot sustain your claim to membership of the white-collar classes if you do not have ownership of this vital asset. Rather, you will inevitably find yourself muted, then humiliated in your own workplace by one of your more globally aware colleagues.

The most suggestive and illustrative of all this genre of TV English advertising, though, is another EF Englishtown offering, in which the social class-indexing aspect of competence in English is foregrounded in a brutally effective, though still ostensibly comic manner.[5] The whole thing takes barely twenty seconds, and it's something of an advertising masterclass. It goes like this.

It is morning, and a young man comes downstairs for breakfast. His parents are already sitting at the table, which is set with bowls of bread, cereal and fresh fruit. He, like them, is white and they are all fairish of hair – in fact, they could as well be Canadians or Germans as Latin Americans. He is dressed in an ironed, smart-casual shirt and is carrying a backpack. Perhaps he is off to his university class? All the signals that the target viewer is intended to pick up indicate that this is a prosperous, urban, middle- or upper-class household. With the stage thus efficiently and quickly set, the sociolinguistic psychodrama begins. Our young man calls out his cheerful 'Buenos días' – and his mother greets him in American-accented English, 'Good morning sweetie. What do you want for breakfast?' Astonished, he turns to his father and asks '¿Qué le pasa a mamá?' – 'What's wrong with mom?', to which his father replies in English, 'Nothing'. Sitting down at the table, the young man, in Spanish, agitatedly demands explanations – What is going on? Why is everyone speaking English? Why have my parents turned into gringos? And then the last straw: the family's maid, dressed in a uniform, as is the custom in this social milieu, smilingly leans over him with a coffee jug and asks in English, 'Coffee?' The young man howls 'Noo-o-o-o' in horror, and the scene cuts to him sitting up in bed, screaming: it has all been a nightmare, and one which has him immediately reaching for his laptop to sign up for online English classes. We get a fleeting, almost subliminal glimpse of a surfboard and a guitar leaning against his bedroom wall – the implication is that he has been enjoying himself too much up until now to pay attention to this serious matter. But why, exactly, should the nightmare cause him to buy an English course? Why the desperation, the sudden realization that he needs to start working on his English *right now*, without delay, even while he's still sitting in bed? To the audience at whom this advertisement is aimed, the answer is obvious: it's all about the maid.

To understand this kind of advertisement fully, we need to understand some of the assumptions upon which it rests, which in turn means understanding the social and sociolinguistic patterns of the society that it springs from. Latin America has long been identified as one of the most unequal regions in the world (Hoffman and Centeno 2003), in which the middle class is chronically prone to erosion and economic instability, where access to decent-quality schooling is a key class distinguisher, and where decent-quality English teaching is often available only through expensive private education (Niño-Murcia 2003, de Mejía 2005). The resultant anxiety among the middle classes about their own class position is often refracted through the prism of language. Historically, in Hispanic Latin America, the divide has typically been between those who speak Spanish and those who speak indigenous first languages (Nahuatl, Aymara, Mapuche, the Mayan languages and so on), and speak Spanish either poorly, or with an identifiably rural, low-prestige accent, or not at all. In the dominant discourse of these societies – one which is often internalized by the speakers themselves – such people have been popularly characterized as backward, ill-educated and unsophisticated, socially and geographically immobile (see Marr 2011 for a discussion of this for Quechua in Peru). This remains largely the case today, despite decades of academic and activist lobbying for a revaluing of indigenous languages and a turn to intercultural, bilingual education policies (Cortina 2014, de Mejía 2005).

In recent years, as the presence and influence of globalized English has spread into hitherto-resistant Latin America (see e.g. Mora et al. 2018), the discourse associated with English-as-opposed-to-Spanish has come to mirror very markedly that of Spanish-as-opposed-to-indigenous-languages. That is to say, in the minds of the urban middle classes, it is now English that is associated with modernity, sophistication, aspiration and social status. This is what is being hinted at here, and the hint is unlikely to be lost on the young, middle-class, urban watchers of cable TV. If you can't speak English, people will think of *you* socially in the same way that you think of your maid (who is very likely to be a migrant from a rural area, and may well speak accented and poorly schooled Spanish). It's supposed to be brutal, and it is: the young man's scream is his awareness of this suddenly hitting home. Worse even than this, the strong suggestion is that the maid is even now learning English and getting ahead ('Coffee?'), while he has been frittering away valuable time (remember the surfboard and the guitar!) There is an overwhelming social imperative to learn English, and the young man now needs to act immediately if his class status is not to be compromised and his inherited social capital fatally eroded. Advertisements like this tell the tale of how English has come to operate in global contexts as a marker of class status and social identity: of how it represents, in short, cultural capital.

2.6 The roots of English exceptionalism? Consequences of being *the* global language

There are several other strands in the narratives of English which suggest that it is something of an outlier among the world's big languages. While there are certainly prestige varieties and authoritative voices in English (you might think of the *Chicago Manual of Style*, the *Oxford English Dictionary* or *Merriam-Webster*, BBC English and so on), the language lacks a recognized, official academy established to formulate and police norms. English speakers neither have, nor do they appear to feel the need for, the equivalent of bodies such as China's State Language Work Committee, the *Académie française*, the *Pontificia Academia Latinitatis* (which regulates Church Latin from its office in the Vatican), or the *Türk Dil Kurumu*, the Turkish Language Institution founded at the behest of Atatürk in 1932. By the same token, English is highly pluricentric in nature (Kirkpatrick 2009). A core of written standard English might be said to exist; but it is hard to define precisely, and is not easily identified with any one country, region or group of people. It is in any case more accurate to think of English as having multiple codified standards, varying according to country or region of the world (Hickey 2012). At the same time, no real spoken standard exists. The accents and dialects of English vary enormously, and although there are a number of recognized national varieties, and varieties with more and less prestige (see Schwyter's 2016 interesting account of the development of what came to be known as BBC English), it is not often seriously argued that there is a single 'real' or 'proper' spoken English which is in the ownership of a particular national or regional speech community.

Strikingly, this seems to apply to at least some extent to English as a Second Language (ESL) contexts as well as to those of what Kachru (1985) famously labelled the 'inner circle'. It has been argued that not just American, Irish or Canadian speakers, but Nigerians, Indians and Singaporeans, for example, now often think of English as 'their' language (Tupas and Rubdy 2015). Even some English as a Foreign Language (EFL) speakers (see our discussion of the ASEAN countries in Chapter 8), are beginning to appropriate English for themselves, at least in the sense of viewing a command of the language as a universal basic skill, unattached to a particular culture or historical homeland (Cogo and Jenkins 2010, Kirkpatrick 2009); though as we will note later on, this is an uneven process. Tupas and Rubdy (2015: 1) are insistent: 'There is no one English, but many Englishes. No one has exclusive rights to the language; anyone who speaks it has the right to own it.' Now, of course this is an ideologized assertion rather than a statement of objective fact (just as its opposite would be), but it contains a truth which resonates with many users of English, especially NNSs in postcolonial contexts (see Canagarajah 2013). Part of the abstract of a talk which we attended, given at a conference on ELT in southern India in 2012, reads as follows:

> English is no longer the white man's language [. . .] Today, when a nonnative speaks in English, he hardly ever remembers it as a foreign tongue. The users of the English language today are viewed as makers of meaning rather than learners of the language.

Now, the claim that 'English is no longer the white man's language' is not, admittedly, a particularly nuanced or subtle one – but it makes the point effectively enough.

English, then, is notably pluricentric, has no obvious owner or undisputed authority, and tends to have a high degree of inbuilt tolerance of variation. This in itself is more than enough to complicate the business of teaching the language. But while it is important, this is not at the heart of what makes English different, and what makes teaching English unlike teaching any other language on earth. Lots of languages, as we have already noted, are used as a lingua franca, and there are lots of big languages that are used as a lingua franca by a great many people (de Swaan 2001). But English is different because its *primary* role is that of the international lingua franca. We began this chapter with numbers – and it is the numbers again, here, that tell us that something unprecedented is happening. In the early 1990s, it was estimated that *at least 80 per cent* of interactions involving English as a second or foreign language did not involve a native speaker, and the figure is likely now to be a good deal higher (Seidlhofer 2011). Of all the communicative events which take place in English in any given hour, on any given day, only a minority involve a native speaker of the language. This is why, in the final analysis, the question of whether or not native speakers feel they have ownership of the language is, to quote Widdowson, 'irrelevant' (1994: 385). English is already the property of all, and of none. The large truth which is (perhaps) beginning to impinge on the worldwide practice of ELT is that teaching English necessarily means teaching, to a greater or lesser degree, and whether the teacher is fully aware of it or not, lingua franca English (a term which we look at in more detail in the next chapter).[6] The far-reaching implications of this will occupy us, in various ways, throughout the course of this book. But let's finish this chapter by taking a preliminary look at some of the ways in which the characteristics of English which have been discussed might impact upon teachers' initial education and training, continuing professional development and classroom practice.

2.7 Conclusion: Teaching the exceptional language

It is important to be clear about what we are saying here. We are not suggesting that English is exceptional in any linguistic way; nor that it is more fitted than any other language to be the international lingua franca. As will become apparent in the next chapter, which deals with the phenomenon of lingua francas in general, what we are suggesting is that English has essentially the same social features as any other big, desirable, important language, only much more so. Spanish, to be sure, has more native speakers than English, but to refer to it as 'global', as Mar-Molinero and Paffey (2015) do, is a stretch too far. More than 90 per cent of Spanish speakers live in the Americas, and its role as an international lingua franca is, in the great scheme of things, negligible. Much the same applies to the situation of the official language of China, known there as Putonghua, the 'common language'. It functions as a common language for the Chinese in China, yes – but not for many other people, and not in many other places. The differentness of English lies in the sheer number and geographical spread of its non-native users (perhaps three to every one native speaker, according to Crystal 2003), making it 'the most widespread means of international and intercultural communication that the world has ever seen' (Seidlhofer 2011: ix).

So how do we respond to the 'differentness' of English? How might TESOL practice be different if we decided to take fully on board the reality of how English functions? How should teachers engage with the layers of narrative and competing discourses which surround the 'exceptional' language? How might a contemporary, globally and linguistically aware approach to training ELT teachers look? We pursue these questions in the following chapters of this book. For now, though, let us lay down a few markers, very briefly, for what is to come. Here are some propositions:

1 *TESOL practice needs to be linguistically and sociolinguistically informed*

That the primary role of English is that of an international lingua franca is a 'well-rehearsed fact' (Jenkins 2006b: 32). However, there is still very limited awareness at classroom level, especially in EFL contexts, of the sociolinguistic realities of worldwide English use (Sifakis 2014). The fact that most learners of English are as likely to find themselves using the language to other NNSs as to NSs (and statistically, much more likely) should be having a transformative effect on learning and teaching.

2 *Native speaker linguistic and cultural models cannot automatically be considered normative*

NS norms of 'standardness' should certainly inform teaching, but to teach NS models as though they were the only correct or appropriate type of English is no longer feasible. Students need informed and guided exposure to NNS and non-standard Englishes as well as the more traditional kind. The international character of English also means that the development of transcultural awareness, rather than the teaching of NS cultural models, must be a priority.

3 *Recognition of the primacy of English (for now) must be accompanied by respect for other languages*

We accept that we live in 'a world currently dominated by the necessity of English' (Davies 2017: 186), and we believe that good quality English language teaching should be as widely available as possible. However, we also believe that respect for and interest in other languages should form part of the ELT classroom environment, and that students' own languages should be regarded as a resource, not a hindrance to learning. We attach central importance to this aspect of the language classroom, and it is a recurring theme throughout the book. We discuss the question of the learner's linguistic knowledge and cultural capital in some detail in Chapter 8.

4 *Teachers of English bear a special responsibility*

Twenty-first-century narratives of English have an impact on the relationship between teacher and students, especially in mainstream education. Where governments regard English as a cornerstone of national development, media and websites shout that 'ENGLISH and SUCCESS have become synonyms!'[7] and command of English operates as a proxy for modernity and mobility, teachers bear a particular burden of responsibility. A skilled and sensitive teacher will help guide learners towards an understanding of what English can do, and what it cannot.

5 *Language is first and foremost a social phenomenon*

We regard using language, and teaching and learning, and teaching and learning language, as primarily *social* undertakings. This means that ELT has to be much more than a mixture of words and phrases, grammatical structures, methodologies and activities, and teacher training must go far beyond this, too. Openness to the language-using world of social interaction which surrounds us must be the starting point of every lesson.

All of these propositions lead to one final, overarching proposition, and one that we have already suggested in Chapter 1: that *modern ELT demands the centrality of language and language knowledge.* Specific disciplinary knowledge has often been dismissed as irrelevant, even elitist, as we saw in the last chapter. However, to claim that only knowledge of English and pedagogy are needed in order to teach English is to make a category error: language teachers should know about *language*, and ELT training and practice need to be rooted in linguistic and sociolinguistic awareness. You could probably get away with teaching other languages in that way, just about, and for the time being. But not English, and not now. In that sense, English really is different.

Tasks/Discussion

For teachers: In your institution, or in others that you have worked or studied in, how does English sit in the curriculum with respect to (a) other languages and (b) other subjects? Is it regarded as a true academic discipline, like history or maths, or as a 'skills' subject? How is it regarded by students? To what extent do they see it as an academic subject, and how do they view it in comparison to other languages that they speak or learn?

For teachers and students: Discuss how ELT providers (e.g. online learning platforms, language schools, and including English-medium educational establishments) advertise themselves where you live. What assumptions, narratives, prejudices, fears, aspirations do they draw on? Who features in the ads, and how realistic and persuasive are they?

Suggested readings

Kirkpatrick, A. (ed.) (2010) *The Routledge Handbook of World Englishes.* Abingdon: Routledge.
A compendious handbook which gives some sense of the sheer scope and scale of English worldwide. A very broad selection of native and non-native speaking contributors show how English is used across the world, using a mixture of theory and discussion of current issues, perspectives and approaches. There is also a helpful historical overview.

Low, E. L. and Pakir, A. (eds) (2017), *World Englishes: Rethinking Paradigms.* Abingdon: Routledge.
An impressively varied collection, edited by two eminent Singapore-based academics, this title offers solid and challenging discussions on topics ranging from post-colonialism through contact varieties to corpus linguistics and language testing, always from a highly international perspective.

3

What Kind of Language Do We Teach? Lingua Francas and Lingua Franca English

3.1 Introduction

In this chapter, we set out to place the growth and spread of English in the specific sociolinguistic context of lingua francas (LFs) worldwide, in preparation for the following chapters which deal with the learners and teachers of today's globalized English. We think that English *is* different, as we argued in the previous chapter – but only in certain ways, and to a certain extent. English has a global reach and allure greater than that of any other language, but it still belongs unequivocally to the group of 'big' modern languages which de Swaan (2001: 5–6), calls the 'supercentral' languages, along with Arabic, Chinese, French, Russian and Spanish, and perhaps one or two others. In many ways it functions like these languages, too, though on a vastly larger scale. Naturally, it also shares many characteristics with the other languages used as LFs in different parts of the world, historically and in the present day: Kiswahili in east Africa, Hausa in west Africa, Urdu in Pakistan, Ottoman Turkish, ancient and medieval Latin, Bahasa Indonesia, Phoenecian, Nahuatl, Greek, to name a very few. The fact that it is English which plays a pre-eminent role in the world today, and not one of the other languages, is no more than a product of historical chance: we can say quite categorically that English does not have any 'special qualities or characteristics which recommend it for that role' (Darquennes 2016: 28).

To provide a sociolinguistic framing, then, for our later discussions, we devote the first part of this chapter to the concept of 'lingua franca' itself, looking at some examples of historical LFs, how and why they develop and spread, and to what extent they are accepted, resisted, welcomed or simply worked with in the societies in which they operate. We will then move on to consider the increasingly salient conceptual model of English as a Lingua Franca (hereafter ELF). We should point out at once that ELF, in the sense in which the term is meant by specialists working in that very particular sub-discipline of applied linguistics (see e.g. Jenkins 2007, 2015; Seidlhofer 2006, 2011; Cogo and Dewey 2012) is not the principal concern of this book. And yet we are of course concerned with English, and with the learning and teaching of English as the global lingua franca. As will become clear, we very much welcome the renewed focus on language, and on language as social practice, that ELF research has stimulated within the world of ELT, and we think that an informed awareness of this area can be hugely useful, even transformative, for the global teaching profession (see Sifakis 2014). We will suggest, though, that perhaps some of the controversy that the notion generates, and some of the lack of interest or even outright hostility to it among many teachers, actually stems from understandable confusion around the meaning and connotations of the term 'lingua franca' itself. Let's start there.

3.2 The problem with 'lingua franca'

It always feels a bit formulaic to begin with definitions and discussions about terminology, but here there is no way round it, so we make no apology. *Lingua franca* is a problematic term. The main difficulty, as we about to see, lies in the fact that the meaning of the term has shifted over time, for reasons that are not altogether clear. Whatever the reasons may be, though, it is now the case that several different definitions of lingua franca exist concurrently, some very precise, some rather fuzzy, with the result that it is not always apparent what any individual writer or speaker means by the term or what connotations they attach to it, unless they take the time to spell it out. Let us emphasize once again that this is more than the standard academic argument about terminology. Unavoidably, the confusion which surrounds the term lingua franca goes to the very heart of the debates about ownership, power and agency that surround the field of TESOL studies: is it possible to speak of the 'ownership' of a language? Do native speakers 'own' English? Is the relationship between NS and NNS speakers in LF contexts an equal one? In order to understand the role of English as a global lingua franca, and why this role is controversial and conflicted in a way that medieval Latin, for instance, never was, it is worth trying to unpack the terminology. And for it to make sense, we have to start with some historical perspective.

Languages of wider communication (LWCs) have been around for millennia. Some of the earlier ones we know about are Akkadian, used across Mesopotamia and beyond until the Greek-speaking Alexander the Great's conquest of the region; Aramaic, which was spread by traders from its Middle Eastern heartland as far afield as China; and Kw'enlun, a form of Malay spoken in the Indonesian archipelago around the beginning of the Christian era (Ostler 2005). The original name Lingua Franca, though (language of the Franks, or western foreigners), was that given to an Italian-based LWC used in the eastern and southern Mediterranean from medieval times right up as far as the nineteenth century (see e.g. Darquennes 2016; Knapp and Meierkord 2002). Also known as *Sabir*, from its word for 'to know', it was a colourful melange not only of Italian and French dialects, but also Arabic, Greek, Berber, Turkish and other languages, spoken by a presumably equally colourful cast of crusaders, slave traders, sailors and pirates, along with merchants and even diplomats (EC 2011). It was widely known of across Europe, cropping up for example in Swift's *Gulliver's Travels* (1726) and Molière's *Le Bourgeois Gentilhomme* (1671). What is most interesting about it from our point of view, though, is that it had a simplified morphology (verbs were not inflected, and adjectives did not agree with nouns), and was limited in terms of both function and domain. That is to say, it was clearly actually a pidgin, albeit a fairly stabilized one. It was no one's native tongue, and it died a natural death once its communicative functions had been superseded in the Mediterranean region by fast-expanding French. Indeed, its final demise has been connected to the French conquest in 1830 of Algiers, which had been a stronghold, and was the final redoubt, of Lingua Franca-using pirates (Brosch 2015: 73).

When, later, the term lingua franca was first widened to cover link languages other than this particular one, it was with this original sense of pidgin. A lingua franca was understood as being a reduced, simplified, mixed code which belonged to no single speech community and had no native speakers. This is still the definition, or one of the definitions, given by a number of sources today. Some have added to it the category of artificial languages like Esperanto and Volapük, which equally lack native speakers and cannot be said to belong to any particular regional or ethnic community. However, as time has gone by, that definition has been widened not once, but twice – a process carefully and patiently traced by Brosch (2015). It's worth following this. First, the definition of lingua franca expanded to include a natural language (i.e. not a pidgin or an artificial code, but an ethnic/national language like, say, Arabic or Portuguese or Tamil) when this is being used as a link language between speakers of two different languages, but is not the mother tongue of either of them. So that might include, for example, an Igbo-speaking Nigerian and a Hausa-speaking Nigerian using English to communicate, or a Moroccan speaking English to a Dane. It would include Tim, a native English speaker, having a conversation in Spanish with a Swiss person, as happened the last time he was on a plane bound for South America. Next – and this is the tricky bit – the term was widened by some linguists to embrace any language used between speakers who do not share the same mother tongue, *even when it is the native language of one of them*. This means us speaking our own native English with the Nigerian, Swiss, Moroccan or Dane, for all of whom it is a second or foreign language. It is this extension of meaning that has been particularly associated with the field of ELF studies (see Kimura 2017: 268).

The outcome of all this widening of definitions, predictably, is a situation in which usage is 'partly inconsistent and can be misleading' (Brosch 2015: 71). This is putting it mildly. As will become apparent if we look at just a few of the definitions of the term, there exists in fact a chaotic jumble of usage. The Oxford English Dictionary, for instance, gives as one of its definitions of lingua franca that it is a 'mixed jargon', but allows several other definitions. Jenkins (2007: 1) insists that LFs are *always* mixed – that hybridity is a fundamental characteristic of such codes. Samarin (1972) does not hold this to be the case at all. Dakhlia (2008) allows two meanings: a 'normal' or natural, ethnic/national language used as a contact language, or a mixed, pidginized code with a temporary life span. Samarin (1987: 371), meanwhile, stipulates that a LF is only such when it is used between speakers 'for whom it is a second language'. House (1999) concurs. The translators of the European Commission (EC 2011) dismiss this, however, and allow the term LF even when native speakers are involved. Seidlhofer (2011) and Jenkins (2006a) similarly allow NSs, but note that in ELF contexts, they are in a minority. UNESCO's definition, back in 1953, adroitly sidestepped the question of NSs altogether: 'A language which is used habitually by people whose mother tongues are different in order to facilitate communication between them' (cited in Samarin 1972: 661).

It is, to be honest, a wearisome business to try and find one's way through all these terms, and there are very many more partly overlapping definitions and contesting voices than the ones we have reproduced here. Given this fundamental disagreement about how the core term lingua franca itself is to be understood, it is perhaps inevitable that confusion and misunderstanding continue to dog the debate around ELF. Having established this historical background, and planted these terminological and conceptual warning signs, we will return to the knotty issue of ELF in Section 3.4. But for the moment, let's consider how lingua francas operate, and what implications this holds for the teacher and the learner of English.

3.3 'By bible, trade and flag': How lingua francas spread, and what they're for

Lingua francas – however we end up defining them – do not all develop and spread in the same way. They might appear with an invading army, like Arabic in north Africa; they might grow out of a trading language, like Kiswahili in east Africa; they might be spread as a vehicle of religious proselytization, like Nahuatl in colonial Mexico, or because of their cultural prestige, like Greek in the Roman empire and far beyond. Most, one might intuitively feel, become established through a mixture of these mechanisms, and others: Ostler's (2010) trio of 'conquest', 'commerce' and 'conversion' is of course essentially the same as Davies's (1996: 3) spread 'by bible, trade and flag'. We can also consider the adoption of a LF primarily in bottom-up terms, or primarily top-down. So we might draw a distinction between LFs that have arisen unintentionally, or organically, like Aramaic and Persian, and those that have been established intentionally, through a process of explicit language planning, such as Akkadian in ancient Mesopotamia, or English in independent Singapore (Ostler 2005).

The latter tends to necessitate the involvement of a determined, not to say authoritarian, state actor. This is something we encountered during visits in the early 2000s to Uzbekistan, which at the time was considering shifting what had been a school curriculum largely taught in Russian to a curriculum largely taught in English, bypassing the new national language, Uzbek, in the process. When we asked why the Ministry of Education would wish to engage in such a massive undertaking, we were confidently assured that it would ensure Uzbekistan's modernization and position in the global order – a fairly common rationale for the promotion of English, as noted in the last chapter. No serious thought seemed to have been given to the implications of such a move and the economic, social, educational and cultural difficulties that would be likely to ensue. Thankfully, the project was never carried through. Nevertheless, the Uzbek case was not quite so devoid of logic as it might at first seem. Uzbekistan was engaged in the process of emerging from the Soviet Union and seeking to establish its own national identity. All schooling had previously been through Russian and hence all the teaching materials and libraries were filled with Russian language books. The curriculum itself was Russian. Uzbek had largely been used in spoken interactions and is anyway not the sole local language – Tajik (a variety of Persian, as opposed to Uzbek, which is Turkic) is widely spoken in the east of the country. Few or no educational materials were available in Uzbek, nor were there libraries filled with Uzbek publications. It therefore seemed, to the powers that then were, a pragmatic idea simply to 'skip' a language and choose English, in which there was a wealth of materials and a wealth of books to fill their university libraries. Surely, so the thinking went, it would make sense for all our children to become fluent users of English so that English would be the lingua franca of intellectual life, replacing Russian.

Away from authoritarian planning, though, a LF is generally first of all a language of *convenience*. It serves an obvious purpose, and hence people do not generally need to be physically forced to learn or use it. Certainly power, in its crudest sense, is often a factor in language spread; but while this may mean imposition by force, just as often it does not – or not directly. It is actually rather difficult to distinguish between the (ostensibly beneficent) spread of a LF in the purest sense of a link or 'vehicular' language used by non-native speakers to each other and the (ostensibly oppressive) imposition of a language by its native speakers on others. This takes us immediately, and most unhelpfully, back to the tortuous terminological issues that we attempted to outline in the preceding section. If the distinction is difficult to sustain, it is perhaps because in the end, the *outcome* tends to be much the same. It is next to impossible, for example, to disentangle Islamization from Arabization in the Middle East of the seventh century: religion, politics, military conquest and the dissemination of Arabic language and culture all marched hand in hand. Added to this, the heyday of the Arab warlords was a short one, while the process of language spread and social and religious acculturation was highly protracted (Berkey 2003). There is little doubt that Alexander spread Greek, with his conquests, by the sword – but the role of Greek as a vastly widespread LF continued long, long after Greek military and political power had departed the scene, and Athens was no more than a provincial town of the Roman Empire. Indeed, it was still the administrative language of the Byzantine empire when the Ottoman Turks took Constantinople, fully a thousand years later (see e.g. EC 2011, Darquennes 2016). Portuguese, in similar fashion, continued to be widely used as a language of commerce and administration in Asia for ten generations or so after Portugal had ceased to be a serious power in the region (Ostler 2005: 503). And Latin, of course, remained the LF of European scholars, scientists and clergy not only for many hundreds of years after the fall of the Roman Empire, but for many hundreds of years after it last had any native speakers.

Military and political power might help establish a LF, then, but are not necessarily needed to maintain it. As García (2011: 401) reminds us, it has long been apparent that the study of language spread is not really concerned with language as such; we noted in Chapter 2 and in Section 3.1 that there is nothing *linguistic* about English that particularly fits it to be the global lingua franca. Rather, language spread is to do with the language behaviour of speakers, and more precisely, with how different languages are perceived, valued and used. It invariably implies a widespread awareness among speakers that in order to communicate beyond the local, to integrate, to trade, to gain social and economic benefits, perhaps simply to be included, people need to learn the language (García 2011: 398). The process might be helped along if the language in question carries the prestige of being the language of a high-status or powerful group (see Darquennes 2016), but the correlation is not a regular or predictable one. Kiswahili, for example, was initially spread by trade, and then by colonial administration, but these days its legitimacy appears to be derived as much from its associations with a notional pan-African identity as with the power of any one societal group. And in any case, powerful groups, along with their languages, are by their very nature as likely to be regarded with suspicion and resentment as with admiration (Ostler 2010). Indeed, quite often it is precisely because a language is *not* the language of one particular, powerful group of speakers that it comes to be regarded as an acceptable LF. Hence the adoption of Bahasa Indonesia, for example, and not the language of the numerically dominant Javanese population, in newly independent Indonesia (Kirkpatrick 2010), and hence the adoption of English as an official or co-official language in post-British-colonial countries like India, Nigeria and Malaysia.

A genuine link language has this defining feature: that just as it is adopted when speakers perceive it to be useful, so it can fall out of use when no longer wanted or needed, or when the group which imposed it no longer wields power. History holds quite a few of these sociolinguistic ghosts. Ottoman Turkish no longer unites the Balkans with Anatolia, north Africa and the Middle East. Tupi or Tupinambá, the *língua geral* (common language) of early colonial Brazil, is now virtually extinct, though it has left an indelible mark on the vocabulary of Brazilian Portuguese (Jensen 1999). Latin left little permanent trace in the speech of the ordinary people of Roman Britannia (Baugh and Cable 1993),[1] while the once unchallenged place of Russian, the state lingua franca of the USSR, is now bitterly contested in ex-Soviet states such as Latvia and Estonia (Cheskin 2015), as well as in Central Asia, as we saw with the Uzbek example above. It should not be forgotten, therefore, that speakers always have *agency* (see Brutt-Griffler 2002), even if this is at times constrained or hard to discern. By the same token, speakers do not simply swallow languages whole, as it were. Language is always changed as it finds new speakers, so that 'Indian English', for instance, is not simply English transplanted to Indian soil, but a local code adapted to local needs, rooted in its own distinct cultural and linguistic context (Pennycook 2010).

There has always been the potential for resistance to language spread. We pointed out above that where a lingua franca, as a language of convenience, has obvious utility, speakers will tend as a general rule to adopt it. However, this does not mean that the process is always a smooth or uncontested one, nor that attitudes to LFs, especially where they are perceived as being imposed, are necessarily always positive. At independence from British rule, Indian and Pakistani elites imposed what to very many people were unfamiliar language varieties in the shape of Hindi and Urdu, leading to sustained resistance which, especially in the case of India, continues to have the potential to cause serious social unrest. A recent newspaper article on this topic warned the Indian prime minister that by 'quietly expanding the role of Hindi in government' he was 'playing with fire'.[2] Perhaps less obviously, the now (largely) uncontested position of French as the official language of France is in fact the result of centuries of struggle. French, or Île-de-France *francien*, was imposed as a national language by François I in 1539 in what is known as the edict of Villers-Cotterêts. The edict ordered that most official documents must not henceforth be written in (lingua franca) Latin, but only '*en langaige maternel françois et non aultrement*' – thus excluding languages like Occitan, Picard and Breton, and privileging those people who had had the good sense to be born near the centre of political power (see Soleil 2004). The aim may ostensibly have been to establish clarity and avoid confusion; but the new state lingua franca, unlike dead Latin, was the mother tongue of a powerful group. Violent confrontation ensued – how could it not? The power dimension of this kind of move is invariably obvious to everyone concerned, on whichever side.

So how can populations be reconciled to a LF which comes, as it were, with baggage? One time-honoured way of ensuring adherence to a new regime has been to co-opt the elite, or future elite. Thus for example, the Inca ruling caste, while content to allow newly conquered peoples to maintain their own languages at the regional level, had the sons of local chiefs schooled in the imperial capital of Cusco (in the south of modern Peru), where they would become fully competent users of the administrative lingua franca, Quechua, before returning home to act as governors of 'their' lands (Mar-Molinero 2000: 58). In Roman Britannia, the emperor Agricola, according to Tacitus, 'provided a liberal education for the sons of the chiefs', sowing a cult of admiration among the colonized elite for the Latin language and other Roman ways (the toga, the bath, the banquet). 'All this in their ignorance, they called civilization', the Roman historian remarks, 'when it was but a part of their servitude' (Tacitus, *Agricola* XXI). Tacitus's words still have the capacity to sting today, and co-opted elites are rarely among the most popular people in their own country, but as Mullen (2016) argues, the picture in occupied Britain, at least, was probably rather more nuanced than this famous observation suggests. Her research indicates that, despite what earlier generations of commentators assumed, Latinization was not necessarily accompanied by wholesale Romanization – and nor, by the same token, was the persistence of Celtic languages necessarily indicative of a rejection of Roman culture. Mullen concludes in a very contemporary way that Roman Britons used language to negotiate 'multilayered identities' (2016: 574), probably involving a great deal more creative, dynamic, innovative and locally flavoured use of British Latin than has hitherto been thought.

In general terms, then, where LFs come into play, it is perhaps helpful to think less in terms of simple adoption or imposition of an existing code, and more in terms of language being adapted, appropriated and reworked in order to fit new communicative needs and discursive practices, leading in the end to a 'dynamic bilingualism' (García 2011: 400). This approach, informed by the theoretical insights of translanguaging (García 2009) of course fits very much with the contemporary concerns of ELF research, as has already been noted (Seidlhofer 2011). How it sits with the actual teaching of English, however, is rather more problematic. The awareness that most English language use in the world is actually lingua franca English use is something which has the potential radically to transform classroom practice – but *only if teachers are prepared*. In ESL contexts especially, students might well use English creatively and dynamically, and not necessarily with reference to

NS norms: this is part of the deal. Resentment of English, too, even among those who strongly wish to learn it or are actively engaged in learning it, is not something outlandish or illogical – it is a naturally occurring feature in widespread LFs. Teachers simply need to understand and be able to respond to it. As we have already suggested, and as we shall continue to argue in subsequent chapters, today's ELT professionals need to be specialists in *language*, and this necessarily includes having some understanding of the sociolinguistics of LFs and language spread. How can you teach the world's lingua franca effectively if you don't understand how lingua francas work?

3.4 Ownership and equality: The ELF debate and the terminology trap

What lessons might we draw from this background discussion which might help illuminate the debate about ELF? As we have already said, we do not want to be sidetracked into a long discussion of what ELF is or what it isn't. However, some observations on this debate do seem to be called for. The fundamental lack of any common understanding of what is meant by the term lingua franca, it seems to us, automatically leads to a debate about the place of the native speaker. It is for this reason that issues of power, ownership and authority come into play. If it is accepted that ELF is at base a kind of English, albeit perhaps one that consists of a diverse range of characteristic features, tendencies and communicative strategies rather than a narrowly described lexis, grammar and phonology in the traditional sense (Thompson 2017, Jenkins 2015), then an exchange between an ELF-user and a NS of English is an exchange in which one person is obliged to speak the language of the other. This naturally involves at least the possibility of an element of inequality, something which is arguably not present in most laypeople's conception of a 'lingua franca' exchange. As Phillipson (2003: 40) insists, reasonably enough, 'communication between native speakers of English and those for whom English is a foreign or second language is asymmetrical, often to the disadvantage of the latter. This communicative inequality is obscured when English is referred to as a "lingua franca", a concept that appears to assume communicative equality for all'.

Against this, Jenkins (2007: 2) argues that ELF is not, in fact, a variety of English (despite the name) but a 'foreign language of communication' which happens often to resemble UK or US English, but which is heavily influenced by the speakers' other language(s) – and is therefore, as we noted in Section 3.2, a hybrid. Cogo (2012: 103–4) suggests that ELF is a 'natural language', that students can choose to speak if they wish to, as an alternative to trying to sound like a native speaker. To go further, if ELF is conceptualized explicitly as first and foremost a resource whose speakers draw on a 'mutually recognized set of attitudes, forms, and conventions that ensure successful communication', then 'all users of [ELF] have native competence of [ELF], just as they have native competence in certain other languages and cultures' (Canagarajah 2007: 925). So you could, by this measure, be not terribly proficient in 'English', but still be considered a 'native' user of ELF.[3] Indeed, you might very well be more skilled in this variety, or rather in the use of this communicative resource, than an English NS. It has regularly been argued (e.g. Jenkins 2017, Seidlhofer 2010: 364) that NSs of English are likely to find themselves at a disadvantage in intercultural encounters – and that therefore if there is inequality or disadvantage in the exchange, it could actually, counter-intuitively, be the NS who suffers it.

In either case, the suggestion is that in ELF contexts the NNS of English is able to deal on fair or even rather favourable terms with the NS of English. The slippage of meaning that has taken place around the idea of lingua franca, the muddled and probably unfinished semantic shifting that we attempted to describe in Section 3.2, makes it possible to include native speakers within the definition *and* to claim a level playing field for all (or indeed, to claim an advantage for the NNS!). In the end, this elasticity of meaning unfortunately leaves the way clear for people to claim the frankly improbable, as when the European Commission's Translation Unit defines ELF as 'a *neutral* language or jargon of which *nobody can claim ownership*, but [which is] also . . . the *mother tongue of one of the parties* in the exchange' (EC 2011; our emphases). A neutral language that is actually the mother tongue of one of the speakers in an exchange? That doesn't sound quite right. And by the way: if the mother tongue speaker of English is not allowed to claim any ownership of or special relationship with the language – well, has anyone told them? According to Wright (2009), the answer is probably no. Native speakers 'may not have understood the new rules of engagement, or even grasped that there are such new rules' (2009: 105). Or, of course, it might just be that these 'new rules' do not in fact exist, or that they are not really rules at all. As we shall see in Chapter 4, scholarly discourses around ELF and the role of the NS are often 'stuck at the meta level' (Jenkins 2006a: 172), 'unnoticed or unacknowledged' (Paradowski 2013: 312) – in other words, they are light years away from the perceptions and assumptions of most ordinary teachers and learners of English, or native English speakers themselves.

Let us try to be absolutely precise with our terms. In the case of a pidgin or hybrid LF, everyone is pretty much on an equal footing: there is obviously no risk of a NS turning up to upset the power balance. But this cannot be the case with an 'ethnic' or natural language, unless of course the language in question (like Latin in medieval Europe) no longer has any native speakers. Brosch (2015: 77) sums it up thus:

> By definition the speakers of a pidgin have all learned it with a more or less similar amount of effort and can communicate roughly on the same level, while with an ethnic language a native speaker, who made no conscious effort to acquire the language to a very high degree, will in most cases easily outperform an L2-speaker.

In true ELF contexts, where communicative events take place only and exclusively among NNSs, perhaps one really can break free of 'native-speakerism' (Holliday 2006), the baggage of culture, the tyranny of imposed NS norms and the inevitability of superior NS proficiency in most, if not all communicative areas. It might occur, for example, in Association of Southeast Asian Nations (ASEAN) contexts, where Thais need to talk to Filipinos, or Singaporeans to Indonesians, about their shared and particular issues, as well as in the Asian region more broadly (Kirkpatrick 2010, 2011). We discuss this further in Chapter 8. At the Far Eastern Federal University in Vladivostok, Russian learners study the styles of English characteristically used by Japanese, Korean and Chinese speakers (Kirkpatrick 2009), while Korean airline pilots preparing to fly a new route to, say, Hanoi, will familiarize themselves with the kind of English used by Vietnamese air traffic controllers (Kim and Elder 2009). But once there is a native speaker involved, ELF is liable to revert to just being *English*, with all its baggage of standards and norms. This is often the case at least as much, we would suggest, for the NNS involved in the exchange as for the NS. One person has to speak the native language of the other, and the resulting power imbalance is likely to be felt, no matter how fervently it is denied or how scrupulously ignored.

What this implies is that ELF can really only be a neutral language if it is considered in much the same light as a pidgin: not really English at all, but a hybrid, protean, shifting code with few strict norms and no native speakers (see e.g. Tan et al. 2006). The proponents of ELF insist that it is not, of course, a pidgin or a reduced, simplified code (Dewey 2012: 151,

Seidlhofer 2011, Cogo 2012); in any case contemporary ELF research has taken a 'processual turn' (Sewell 2013: 4), and now lays as much emphasis on the communicative *behaviour* of speakers as on the particular *forms* of language they choose (Thompson 2017, Jenkins 2015). That is all well and good. But it is the unstable, unagreed-upon, ever-widening and often misleading definition of the term lingua franca that confuses the issue.

Now, as Kirkpatrick (2011) notes, it is the supposedly 'neutral' aspect of ELF that sets warning lights flashing among scholars of the linguistic imperialism school (which we talked about in Chapter 2) – and not only them. ELF is conceptualized, fuzzily, as being a true lingua franca, which belongs to everybody equally and in relation to which NSs of English hold no linguistic capital and have no vested interest. 'When a native speaker is involved in ELF communication, his/her assumed privileges are no more', states McNamara, firmly (2012: 201). This 'English' can therefore be positioned as being as neutral as the original Lingua Franca of the Mediterranean was. For some observers, this proves triumphantly the fact that English has finally broken free of the traditional NS elites of what Kachru (1985) famously labelled the 'Inner Circle'. For others, though (e.g. Phillipson 2008), it suggests that those who ultimately benefit most from English are now enabled to entrench their power even further. The uneven nature of the global linguistic exchange is disguised behind a convenient fiction of equal participation, equal proficiency, equal power relations and equal ownership – all through the use of an ill-defined but agreeable-sounding term. In this reading, the use of the term lingua franca is, in essence, a trap for the unwary.

For Brosch (2015: 77), the idea of ELF as unowned and culture-free is simply 'wishful thinking'. And despite the warnings given by some (Vikør 2004, for instance) that the notion of a neutral tongue should not be romanticized or taken as evidence of a desire for equality, there does seem to be something about the notion of lingua franca that encourages wishful thinking – an earnest desire to make the uneven playing field at least *look* even. The European Commission's Translation Unit (EC 2011), discussing the role of English as the current lingua franca of Europe, projects the idea of a benignly neutral language back to the time of the original Lingua Franca which we discussed in Section 3.2, with results that verge on the Pollyannaish. That language, they suggest, 'was a good reflection of the social mobility of those days, which entailed complex contacts, both hostile and peaceful but always between equals, with the *lingua franca* as a "third space", a sort of "buffer" space' (2011: 22). Now, we presume that their intention is to contrast the supposed rough equality of the medieval Mediterranean with the structured inequality of later French and British colonial rule; and we presume that they are referring principally to linguistic equality, rather than any other kind. But still – it takes some effort to conceive of encounters involving pirates, crusaders, mercenaries, slave traders and the like in terms of 'social mobility', let alone of 'contacts . . . always between equals'.

3.5 Progress and obstacles to progress in thinking about lingua franca English

Arguments about NS 'ownership' and privilege naturally lose their force when the LF variety in question, as we noted in Section 3.3, is clearly and demonstrably no one's native variety. Take the example of Greek. The dialect of Greek which arose from contact between speakers of several already-existing dialects, and which was used as a contact or link dialect between them throughout the Hellenistic and Roman periods, was known as Koine Greek (κοινὴ διάλεκτος, that is *koine dialektos* or the 'common dialect'). The term *koine* is still used as a technical term in sociolinguistics to describe this kind of overarching or unifying variety of a language, which is often levelled and simplified, is more or less stable, and might be standardized. Crucially, its use is *not* generally seen to confer advantage on any particular group of speakers. Imperial Aramaic, for example, the administrative language of the Persian Empire at its peak, was firmly distinguished from local varieties of Aramaic (EC 2011). The so-called *Lengua General* of colonial Peru, similarly, was a koine variety of the Incas' administrative language Quechua, referred to above, which showed some influence in its morphology from the language of the Spanish conquistadors and settlers, but grew mainly out of the contact between speakers of different regional varieties of Quechua brought together in the newly formed urban centres (Itier 2011).

It is just about possible to imagine a kind of modern koine English, a levelled, unified variety, influenced by native and non-native usage, and used as a link language by native and non-native alike. There have even been calls for such a code, such as Kirkpatrick's rousing (and definitely challenging!) declaration, 'It is time . . . for applied linguists to provide a description of lingua franca English, for by so doing they can liberate the millions upon millions of people currently teaching and learning English from inappropriate linguistic and cultural models' (2006: 81). But the contemporary project of

ELF, as we noted above, does not appear to be heading in that direction. Indeed, even the early focus on attempting to identify at the least an ELF 'core', if not a full linguistic description (Seidlhofer 2001, Jenkins 2006b), has given way to a focus on ELF predominantly as communicative practice (Seidlhofer 2011, Jenkins 2015, Sewell 2013). And in any case, while English has a fairly clearly defined standard written form, but huge flexibility with regard to spoken form and no overarching central authority (as we saw in Chapter 2), it is not at all obvious that there exists either the will or the means to establish such a koine variety – or even that there is a gap in the market. English will continue to be used as a global LF for the immediate future, for all that Ostler (2010) claims to foresee its end, and envisages it declining gradually to become once more the property only of its NSs. But its historical link with its native speakers for the moment at least endures, even where the native speaker is not physically present, in the continued reliance on NS models found, in very large parts of the world, in English language teaching and learning. For ELT programmes to succeed, insists Davies (2017: 186), 'what is essential is a described and assessable model for the curriculum, for the textbook, for the examination – a need which support for English as a lingua franca . . . has not come to terms with'. It is difficult to argue with this. Some progress is being made towards establishing assessable models of ELF, but it is a slow and uneven path (Newbold 2017, Blair 2017, McNamara 2012).

To sum up, it is certainly the case that, as we saw in the previous chapter, English is highly pluricentric and difficult to 'own'. But this does not mean that it is everywhere and always a genuine lingua franca in the sense in which many people understand that term: a neutral, third code, owned by no one involved in any given encounter. At root, therefore, it seems that part of the reason for the controversy – not to say confusion – which often besets the field of ELF lies in the slipperiness of the terminology itself. Defenders and proponents of ELF theory may make repeated efforts to clarify the situation, as they see it. Some have accused sceptics of misunderstanding, misrepresentation or even lacking academic rigour (Ishikawa 2015 is an example) – which is regrettable, to be honest. They may deplore teachers' stubborn refusal to shift away from the traditional dependence on NS norms, despite all the sociolinguistic evidence that they should (Jenkins 2006a, Sifakis 2014). But expository clarification and impassioned argument will not make the problem go away. We should repeat the point of our discussion of terminology at the beginning of this chapter: different people understand different things by the term lingua franca, mean different things when they use it, and set it about with different connotations and associations. This must go some way to explaining why the idea of ELF, despite its prominent presence in the academic arena, has had such limited traction among ELT practitioners and learners and indeed, has 'so far had little if any substantive impact on current teacher beliefs' (Dewey 2012: 145). It is difficult to reason clearly, let alone explain to others, about an English that might not actually be English, used as a lingua franca which is not actually most people's idea of a lingua franca.

There is one further aspect to the ELF debate that we should comment upon, as it is particularly germane to the broader topic of this book. NNESTs, arguably even more than NESTs, often feel real discomfort in acknowledging 'non-standard' or non-codified Englishes (see Blair 2017), especially in the face of resistance or outright rejection by learners, learners' sponsors, head teachers and other stakeholders. ELF can be quite a hard sell, even to those who are likely eventually, we can say with some conviction, to end up using just such a kind of English themselves. Partly this is down to the heavy investment (in all senses) in the idealized construct of 'English' which is necessary in order to qualify as an English teacher in most parts of the world (see Chapter 8). But it is also because of the divide which marks academic linguistics from the working assumptions of most classroom teachers, to whom a 'post-normative' (Dewey 2012) approach to language might not sound very appealing.

It may be self-evident to professional linguists that standard language X is at best an abstraction, a product of social forces, hedged around with ideology, subject to shift and flux, inherently possessing no more grammatical correctness, permanence or integrity than any other dialect or variety of language X. But for many teachers, in many parts of the world, such thinking can come as radically new, shocking, undermining and destabilizing. At one teachers' conference in southern India at which we were the keynote speakers, Tim gave a talk on the subject of standard languages and language change, pointing out that languages were not fixed in stone, and that if they were, we would regard the people of São Paulo and Lisbon, for example, as speakers of bad Latin rather than good Portuguese. He tried to ignore, as the talk went on, the growing rumbles and mutterings of disagreement rising ominously from the room. Finally feeling that he had made his argument at sufficient length, he finished, with a possibly ill-advised flourish, 'Standards are slippery!' At that point, a fellow keynote speaker, an Indian academic who was sitting next to us, could not contain himself any longer. He leapt to his feet, seized the microphone from Tim's hand and, turning to face the audience, shouted,

'No! Standards are not slippery – *speakers* are slippery! They must learn to speak correctly!' In the ensuing uproar, it was uncomfortably clear who was in the minority. As Blair (2017: 350) laconically notes, 'there are many language change deniers'.

This does not mean that we are stuck forever with the traditional, NS-centred norms and standards. It does not mean that the insights offered by ELF research have no place in the classroom: as we will argue in Chapters 8 and 9, they certainly do, if properly contextualized within a larger communicative framework. But it must be recognized that a great deal of professional and intellectual confidence is needed for teachers to adopt this approach, especially in the face of widespread cultural/linguistic conservatism and institutional scepticism or hostility. This confidence can *only* come from a firm grasp of the discipline of language study, including sociolinguistic awareness and a thorough understanding of how (especially oral) interaction really works. As Sewell (2013) rightly insists, teachers need to be aware of norms, but should treat them critically, while developing in their learners a critical awareness of language variation. Put simply, teachers need to be critical linguists.

3.6 Conclusion

Perhaps one of the most important effects that the ELF debate has had is to remind us that *all* language use is at root a matter of negotiation, accommodation and social practice. The idea of norms being adapted and practice developed anew in each new cultural or interactional context (Canagarajah 2007, Pennycook 2010) is a helpful one. However, it surely applies as much to NS usage as it does to NNS usage, and in that sense the distinction between a reified or idealized 'native speaker English' and another equally idealized 'ELF' is a false one (see Sewell 2013). As we argued in Chapter 1, a knowledge of standard English and the mechanics of methodology might qualify you in many places as a teacher (or perhaps a 'language instructor'), but really, they hardly begin to suffice for the challenge of global English teaching in the twenty-first century, where the use of the language is characterized primarily by diversity, fluidity, creativity, change and flux. *This* is the reality that accompanies the teaching of the world's lingua franca, rather than adherence to a fixed model, whether native or not. The future of ELT will lie with linguistically aware teachers, by which we mean teachers who are not only highly competent pedagogues but critical linguists who will be able to put new ways of thinking about language to transformative use in their classrooms.

In the next chapter, we look at what it is that learners expect to learn when they enter the classroom, what learners and other stakeholders in the business of ELT hope or expect to get from it, and whether they are likely, finally, to be disappointed.

Tasks/Discussion

For teachers: What models of English are your students most familiar with? Why? Who decides on these models, and on what grounds? Do students ever ask you questions about the different kinds of English they encounter, and how these relate to the kind of English that you are teaching them? How do you deal with these questions?

For teachers and students: Think about who you communicate with in English, where and when. (If you do not use English much, think about who you expect or think you might use it with in the future). Are these people native speakers of English, or non-natives? Does it feel different to speak or write to non-native speakers? How? What effect might communicating with other non-native speakers have on the way you speak or write?

Suggested readings

Ostler, N. (2010), *The Last Lingua Franca: English Until the Return of Babel.* New York: Walker.
Highly detailed, written by a historian and linguist with a grasp of world languages through history, this book avoids cliché and Anglocentrism to put English in its proper context as the latest (and perhaps last) 'world language'.

Prodromou, L. (2008), *English as a Lingua Franca.* London: Bloomsbury.
The disciplinary area of ELF studies has moved on substantially in the time since this was written, but the book retains a good deal of its impact and relevance. What sets it apart from most of the work in this area is that it is written in an unapologetically personal style, from a bilingual's perspective, illustrating how lingua franca English actually feels in use.

4

What Do Learners Expect to Learn? Beliefs, Prospects and Realities

> We must accept that identifiable standards and models are familiar and useful for both teachers and learners, and that language use and learning goals are variable and contextual. It is part of the job of teacher education to square this circle, by developing a critical language awareness in prospective and experienced teachers (Blair 2017: 349).

4.1 Introduction

In this chapter we look at the expectations that surround English language learning. What kind of English do students want, or think they need? What about other stakeholders? We suggest that there is a mismatch between what is often taught in classrooms around the world, and how English actually functions – as a global lingua franca, as discussed in the previous chapter. We look at how learners are in danger of being disappointed (the English 'trick'), and how expectations can be met or managed. Finally, we argue that teachers need to take on the responsibility of educating learners, institutional managers and other stakeholders about the realities of global English today, and that this demands real linguistic and sociolinguistic awareness. We begin, though, by considering a rather curious phenomenon. There have been, as we pointed out in the previous chapter, decades of academic discussion about lingua franca English, World Englishes and the redundancy of the native speaker model ('The native speaker is dead!' proclaimed Paikeday, back in 1985). And yet, for the most part, the global practice of TESOL carries on quite unruffled, with NS models of English at its heart. What is it that drives the attachment to NS models and NS-derived notions of standardness?

4.2 What kind of English? Standards, 'native-speakerism' and language attitudes

The fact that there is any debate over whether or not we should teach only and always Standard English, with pronunciation modelled on prestige NS norms, actually tends to come as a surprise to most teachers and trainee teachers (Suzuki 2011, Seidlhofer 2001). Often, even those teachers who are familiar with the debate show little enthusiasm for the idea of teaching a 'denativized' English, and do not foreground it in their classrooms (Young and Walsh 2010, Sifakis 2014) – and remember our little anecdote in the previous chapter about the angry Indian professor! No wonder, then, that the existence of such a debate is news to *learners* – assuming they ever get to hear about it. It is strongly to be suspected that, in EFL contexts at least, for most learners of English, the notion of teaching a standard is unremarkable and uncontroversial, while that of teaching some kind of lingua franca English (however defined) requires a good deal of thought and explanation, for the reasons that we outlined in the previous chapter. To be sure, lots of learners are fairly relaxed about not sounding native-like, especially if they have been exposed to a range of different accents (Subtirelu 2013), but an unexamined preference for both a native-speaking teacher and a standard language model is still the default position for many. This should not surprise us too much. Certainly, as we acknowledged at the start of this book, the field of ELF has developed theoretically a great deal in recent years. It was probably never intended, in any case, that ELF should be described, codified and taught as a body of knowledge in the traditional manner (see Jenkins 2015, Seidlhofer 2006: 45–8), and the early emphasis on the description of a pronunciation 'core' has gradually given way, informed partly by the theoretical insights of translanguaging, to a highly nuanced account of NNS-NNS strategies for communication and the way in which they are at once both fluid and systematic (Cogo and Dewey 2012: 2–5, Jenkins 2015). But the central problem for ELT still stands. If you are going to have structured English language teaching, in most cases leading to high-stakes examinations – in many places, you cannot graduate from high school or university if you have not 'passed English' – then it has to be based on something concrete. And whether we like it or not, for many teachers, learners and other stakeholders, this will not be an open-ended framework built around concepts such as 'intelligibility' and 'communicative effectiveness', but an acknowledged standard form of the language, a 'described and assessable model' (Davies 2017: 186), which for the time being at least is inevitably associated with NSs.

In some ways, of course, this is problematic. As we saw in Chapter 2, there are really a number of standard Englishes – and there is no one standard that applies to spoken, rather than written English. Also, as Seidlhofer (2006: 46) reminds us, the idea of languages being discrete, monolithic, bounded units is a 'convenient fiction'. And yet: it is a convenient fiction which has real cultural presence and real purchase on the minds of speakers, not least as a space where identity is invested. This applies of course to native speakers (ask a French speaker, say, or a Greek or a Bengali, if they think there is or should be such a thing as a standard form of their language!), but it applies to learners, too. And as we also suggested in Chapter 2, learners of English are apt to invest the language with distinctive narratives – of aspiration, social mobility, prosperity, modernity and a range of other things, some quite tangible, some less so (Norton 2000, 2010). We consider the whole concept of the 'native speaker' at some length in the following chapter. But let us at least establish at this point where the discussion comes from.

For some people, it is one of the enduring mysteries of the field of TESOL that, decades after the 'tyranny of native-speakerism' (Swan et al. 2015: 1) first came under sustained attack, and years after the battle against it was substantially won in university seminar rooms and the pages of academic books and journals, in the unforgiving, real world of language teaching, attachment to it seems as strong as ever (Cook 2016, Gray and Morton 2018: 74–5). By 'native-speakerism' is meant an ideological attachment to the NS model of correctness, an implicit acceptance of the proposition that native speakers have some sort of ownership over the language, a special claim to it or a privileged relationship with it (Holliday 2006, Swan et al. 2015). Davies (2013: 26) points out that the model of the 'native speaker' (a C2 equivalent in the Common European Framework of Reference for Languages) is in fact an *idealized* model, and not all native speakers will have this kind of language competence: highly competent NNSs will be able to outperform many of them in certain areas. But in practice, native-speakerism is an ideology which means that native speakers can be employed as teachers, or promoted to positions of power and responsibility, or looked to as models of correctness, solely because of their place of birth, and regardless of their actual competence, knowledge or skill with language – a theme we pick up in Chapter 5. While this is good news for footloose young westerners, as we remarked in Chapter 1, it is something which rightly frustrates and infuriates trained and skilled non-native English-speaking teachers (NNESTs) all over the world.

There are some who suspect conspiracy. Kumaravadivelu (2016) relates that as a graduate student in the United States, he was warned by a fellow Indian academic that a shadowy 'they' would never allow him, as a non-native speaker, to establish himself in the field of ELT methods and materials. (He seems not to have asked who 'they' were – perhaps he thought it obvious.) He goes on to explain that he has often felt since that his 'life as a nonnative professional was being managed and manipulated by subtly invisible, and seemingly invincible, forces . . . In many different ways, I continued, and still continue, to encounter the power of the forces undermining my professional aims and activities' (2016: 68). This is strong stuff, and rather alarming. But does it represent reality? There are, after all, numerous NNS professors of TESOL and Applied Linguistics in university departments in the UK, US, Australia and beyond. In fact, it is really hardly necessary to summon up the image of a mysterious cabal of native speakers who somehow influence attitudes and opinions about the ownership of language, for the language attitudes are already out there. The practice of ELT is driven on the whole by what its stakeholders want and value (and are willing to pay for). By 'stakeholders' we mean not only the learners themselves – schoolchildren, university students, the customers of private language schools and online learning platforms – but all those other people and institutions with an interest in the results of language teaching. These would include the schoolchildren's parents, school management teams, municipal school boards, regional chambers of commerce, employers and employers' associations, national governments and ministries of education, among others. For good or ill, by the very nature of things most of these people are unlikely to be informed of or particularly interested in the debates which animate contemporary applied linguistics. This is why, as Blair (2017) notes, 'pedagogic principles and practice are still largely unaffected by academic discourses on language change, intercultural awareness and lingua franca use' (2017: 347; and see Jenkins 2006a, Dewey 2012, 2015). Language attitudes do not tend to depend on the narratives established by academics, whether these academics are broadly favourable to a NS-centred model of English teaching, or broadly critical of it. These attitudes already exist in societies, and they are formed in specific cultural contexts.

Japanese culture, for example, has traditionally held very particular views about the Japanese language, with a strong emphasis on biological race and the deep, even mystical link between language and nation (Lee 2012, Befu 2001). The explicit privileging of a particular race and nation in this way may well make some uncomfortable, but the fact remains that many Japanese people would find the idea of a non-Japanese teaching their language rather strange. 'Native-speakerism' is simply not, for most Japanese, a controversial issue. The assumption that language is best learned from a native speaker is then quite easily transferred from Japanese language to language in general, with the result that a 'socially ingrained ideology of native English persists, and pedagogical beliefs that English should be learnt from a [native speaker of English] remain strong' (Galloway 2014: 3; and see also e.g. Galloway and Rose 2013, McKenzie 2008). To downplay or ignore the existence of this ideology is to miss a fundamental element of the context within which English is learned and taught in places like Japan. Jenkins (2006a: 172), for example, bemoans the fact that parents in Japan and Korea insist on NS teachers for children's immersion summer camps (known as 'English villages'). Fair enough: but she makes *no mention at all* of societal language attitudes in these countries, leaving the reader to infer, presumably, that this is yet another example of neocolonial 'native-speakerism' of the kind suspected by Kumaravadivelu. It is an odd omission – almost as if the Japanese and Korean parents did not have agency in this matter, did not have their own decided and firmly held views about language and language teaching derived from their own cultures and societies.

In China, to take another East Asian example, the ELF model has gained virtually no traction. NS-centred teaching and models of language are strongly preferred, and British or American accents are accounted the most desirable, even though students have difficulty recognizing them (Fang 2016, Wang 2015). Indeed, one British teacher who had taught mixed-nationality classes in the UK told us that a native-like accent was a key goal for her Chinese students: '*Many of my students have wanted to "speak better English", so their learning goals have tended to be vague. However, many Chinese students I have taught are very concerned with accent and "sounding British" as a measure of success.'* Another teacher who had taught in China remarked that many students '*requested to be in classes taught by British teachers as this was viewed as the more desirable accent to pick up'.* This might seem odd, even suspicious if one is of a conspiratorial frame of mind. Where did they get such decided opinions from? But it is not, in the end, because of the machinations of the British Council or a cartel of British coursebook publishers that the students think like this. Their attitude is perfectly explicable by reference to the dominant discourse about language within China, where the 'best' model of Chinese is held to correspond to the pronunciation of Beijing, and received notions of correctness, purity, provenance and authenticity in language have historically had a strong cultural grip (Marr 2005). One Chinese MA TESOL student in London recalled that before she left China, 'I thought English in London would be very lovely, because it is the home of the English language . . . it is the real English' (2005: 5). Her shock upon arriving in London and encountering the *really* real English of the capital, in all its native and non-native varieties and shades, was palpable.

For all that some academic linguists might sense a native speaker plot, and others feel that learners have simply internalized a sense of their own unworthiness from monolingual-dominated societies, a good many students, and not only East Asian ones, really do idealize NS norms and expect to be taught them (Swan 2017, Subtirelu 2013, Davies 2013). As Cook (2016: 187) puts it, regretfully, the native speaker is 'still the ghost in the machine'. Whether the learner is actually well served by a NS-centric paradigm of ELT is, of course, another question altogether. We turn to it in Chapter 5.

4.3 Managing learner beliefs and expectations

The teachers we spoke to in the preparation of this book reported, as one might expect, a huge range of motivations and expectations around their students' learning of English. They ranged from the instrumental (a Greek teacher's students want '*to get a good job, to learn academic skills, to travel, to pass exams*') to the pragmatic ('*they have to*', said a teacher in Saudi Arabia: '*they are driven by obligation*') and the fanciful ('*they want to be famous international soccer players or singers*' said a Colombian). We want now to look at two aspects of TESOL where teachers need to be able to guide the expectations of their learners and of other stakeholders (especially, once more, parents and school and college managers) and will need to draw on knowledge *about language*, as well as knowledge *of the language* in order to be able to do so. We look first at the question of how the teaching of English has, in large part, failed to keep pace with the shifting reality of global English use. We then move on to consider to what extent the insistent discourse that English brings guaranteed benefits can be justified.

4.3.1 The 'mismatch': English in the world and English as a subject of study

In Chapter 2 we suggested that, to at least some extent, English is different from other 'big' languages, whether historical or contemporary. Different not in any structural or aesthetic sense, but in its polycentricity, the breadth of its global reach, and the compelling power of its narratives and associations. The feature which really sets twenty-first-century English apart from the other languages, though, is its unchallenged role as the global lingua franca – with all that this implies for how it is spoken and written. And here, the observer of global ELT can hardly fail to be struck by the 'mismatch' (Seidlhofer 2011: 9, Galloway and Rose 2017: 3) between the way in which the role of English in the world has developed and the way in which it is still usually taught and learned.

Some students have a pretty clear idea that they are likely (statistically, at least) to be using the language to at least some extent in a lingua franca context (see e.g. Kirkpatrick 2012), and language-aware teachers will incorporate reflection on this into their teaching. One Colombian teacher we work with reported: '*Many of my students want to sound like a native speaker, until some reflect on the fact that the contact they may have with native speakers is by far less, compared with the chances of speaking English with non-native English speakers.*' However, a great many others have still not reset their expectations about who they are likely to be communicating with, and in what kind of English (Galloway and Rose 2013; Pinner 2016). And for this, inescapably, teachers as a whole (as well as the people who train them) have to take some of the responsibility. As we discuss in more detail in Chapter 8, many teachers are heavily invested in a traditional view of language, and a correspondingly conservative view of English. Moreover, if they are either unexposed to or frankly uninterested in academic debates about language, they may have barely registered the way that the use of English has become predominantly lingua franca use (Suzuki 2011). And so, as Barbara Seidlhofer remarked at the start of the millennium, 'the daily practices of most of the millions of teachers of English worldwide seem to remain untouched by this development . . . and most classroom language teaching per se has changed remarkably little considering how the discourse *about* it has' (Seidlhofer 2001: 133–4; emphasis in original).

In our experience of global ELT, for all the theoretical progress in the intervening couple of decades, this observation remains substantially accurate. And here, perhaps, is where we see most clearly the chasm that exists between the opinions of academic linguists on the matter of language and the opinions not only of the average layperson, but of the average English teacher, wherever in the world they may be. Deep-rooted attitudes to language are hard to shift, as is detailed for example by Pedrazzini (2015), whose teachers on an MA course in Milan tended to fall straight back on their preferred US and UK models, even after they had completed a set of tasks and discussions designed to raise awareness of lingua franca English. One of Dewey's (2012) MA student informants, having gone through a similar series of awareness-raising exercises, in her feedback apologetically described the teaching of a non-NS-centred model of English as a 'nice idea but a bit pie-in-the-sky', thoughtfully adding 'sorry' and a sad-face emoji (2012: 153). While some of Dewey's other informants were more positive than this one, it is hard to resist the impression of many teachers, and many students, feeling indifference or offering quiet resistance to the very idea of a denativized English.

Now of course, some students will indeed be communicating primarily with NSs of English, and may even be intending to go and work or study in an English-speaking country, about which they will have certain assumptions and expectations (see e.g. Turner 2011). And naturally, as we noted above, learners have their own individual and societal ideas about language, and therefore about what they expect to learn in the language classroom. If many students prefer to learn with reference to a supposedly fixed, standard variety of English, along with prestige NS models of discourse and pronunciation, then this is simply one more part of the teaching context, a psychological-cum-sociolinguistic aspect of the pedagogic challenge which teachers should be equipped to engage with. But while it is entirely understandable, given societal ideas about language, that a learner should express a desire to speak 'American' or 'British' English in a native-like way, the research suggests that for many, if not most learners, this is an unrealistic goal (Derwing 2010, Munro and Derwing 2011), and may even be based upon a misunderstanding of what native-likeness *is* and where it resides (see Chapters 5 and 8 for more on these issues). In this situation, it must be the teacher who assumes the responsibility of acquainting learners and other stakeholders with the sociolinguistic reality. Who else, after all, will impart this crucial information? As we suggest later, this means that teachers need to do meta-level linguistic work, such as reassuring students that a non-native accent, as long as it is intelligible, is no handicap (Cook 2016, and see Chapters 6 and 9).

We should perhaps note at this point that the responsibility of 'being intelligible' or 'making oneself understood' does not (or ought not to) fall entirely on the learner. The native speaker who is a genuinely sympathetic interlocutor or simply has a genuine desire for communication will make efforts to understand, accommodate and make allowances, search for meaning, may even recast or reformulate to check what they think was said (Hann 2010: 182). Native speakers can be taught, or trained to be more sympathetic interlocutors and better communicators across linguistic lines (see e.g. Subtirelu and Lindemann 2016), but actually of course, this kind of collaborative activity does not just take place across language: it is an intralingual phenomenon too. There generally has to be some accommodation, good will and effort involved when a Mancunian speaks to a Minnesotan, say, or a New Zealander to a St Lucian. And of course, it happens within countries. And in highly multilingual contexts, as ELF researchers have repeatedly pointed out, NNS-NNS interaction is characterized not only by creative use of English, but by a whole range of *comprehension* techniques. The Polish customer and the Bangladeshi shopkeeper in London will make an effort to understand one other, just as the London-born patient and the Nigerian doctor will.

Teachers can help with all of this. They need to develop students' confidence by exposing them to non-native and non-standard Englishes (alongside Standard English, of course!) and pointing to differing contexts, participants and communicative strategies. In short, teachers need to educate students about language: this is a language classroom, just as it is an English classroom, because it is a classroom where *language* is taught. And in order for this to happen, knowledge about language must be built into all teacher training, at all levels, from the very start. As Dewey (2012, 2015) and Pedrazzini (2015) conclude from their own experiences, a single module or a one-off series of awareness-raising activities on an MA course (what Suzuki 2011: 151 calls 'single-shot instruction') is too little, too late and too unsystematic to really change teachers' minds.

Learners will have legitimately different expectations of what they are going to learn and why. Inevitably these depend on the context in which they are learning the language and the intentions and motivations they have (beyond the need to pass an exam, which is of course a more than reasonable goal in itself). There is a world of difference between, say, a Vietnamese scientist studying in preparation for a PhD in Australia, an Italian teenager going to work as an au pair in the United States, and a Kenyan primary student preparing to move into an English-medium secondary school in her home country. Some will have a need of great grammatical accuracy and access to formal or academic registers, others much less so (Swan 2017). Teachers must therefore discuss with learners what they will talk and write about, to whom, where, when and for what purposes. Now, to some extent, of course, this approach resembles the familiar notion of Needs Analysis, common in ESP and beyond since the 1960s and which now tends to be conceptualized as a multifaceted philosophy of teaching, involving students as democratic participants, rather than just an information-gathering technique (Far 2008, Hyland 2006: 73–80). But actually it is not quite the same thing. We conceive of the language-aware, language-focused ELT classroom as a place where such things as situations, modes, practices, participants and communicative needs and resources are discussed on a permanent, ongoing basis, as an integral part of every class, within a context of explicit reference to issues of sociolinguistics, pragmatics and educational culture.

Hence, for example, it has been noted that Chinese students' experience of language education, which we might better describe as the ideology derived from language education in China, prevents many of them from valuing lingua franca English as a communicative tool, even when they admit it works. That is to say, even a successful communicative event may not be thought of as successful if the language used did not correspond to grammatically 'correct' standard English (Wang 2015), perhaps even spoken with a particular prestige accent, as we saw earlier. Here we see how the relentless emphasis on NS models and norms that still forms the centrepiece of most ELT practice, in most of the world, in China meshes with home-grown language attitudes to produce a distorting effect on how students think about communication in English. This mindset is unlikely to be helpful to students when they eventually come to attempt real-world communication in English. How can students move beyond it, if not through explicit discussion, debate and analytical tasks, set up by a language-aware teacher who has a firm grasp of the issues? In Chapter 9 we will show how this kind of teaching can work in practice.

The 'mismatch' is real. Our aim is not to provoke, and we do not wish to suggest that teachers who teach in a 'traditional' manner are failing their students. We do, though, think that the need to move away from a NS-centred, standard-only conception of ELT towards a diverse, global, linguistically informed and language-aware approach, is now becoming urgent. As Lock (1996) rightly insists, learners invest a good deal of time and effort in learning a second language in a classroom setting: they are entitled to expect that what they are taught should actually equip them with the ability to communicate effectively in that language. They therefore need a description of the language that doesn't focus solely on what is grammatically 'correct' or 'standard' in terms of structure and form, but goes beyond this to show some of the range of communicative resources that are available and how these might be used in various social interactions (Lock 1996: 1–3).

And there is another, equally good reason why learners should also be invited to reflect upon how English really works. All language teaching presents the language concerned, to at least some extent, as an idealized construct: if this were not the case, the task of teaching would become an impossible one. But English, as we have already argued, is something of a special case. In Chapters 2 and 3, we discussed the particular status of English as a global language and the particular characteristics of lingua francas. We noted above all that the reality of English use in the world is that it very often does not involve native speakers of the language. Indeed, it might involve speakers from almost any linguistic, cultural or educational background, from anywhere on earth, with almost any level of proficiency. Given this context, it scarcely needs emphasizing that things like negotiation of meaning, adapting to one's interlocutor, developing flexibility, learning to tolerate difference – in short, transcultural communication skills – along with some sociolinguistic awareness and an understanding of how language and culture interact, are not optional extras but a central pillar of learning how to communicate in English. Of course, these are useful attributes for learners of any language, but for learners of English in the twenty-first century, they are indispensable. If the mismatch between how English is used and how it is taught is ever to be corrected, humble 'English teachers' need to shift their focus and begin to think of themselves as language and communication experts, who have vital information to share with their students. It is information which goes far beyond how to conjugate the present perfect tense, or how to write a formal letter.

And there is a further thing.

4.3.2 The 'trick': What English delivers and what it promises to deliver

If you had been able to take an inventory of the linguistic attainment of Europeans of, say, the eighteenth or nineteenth centuries, it is a fairly safe bet that the results would have shown a strong correlation between wealth, status and power, and a decent grasp of Latin. We would not for a moment, though, suppose that our Prussian Junker, British lord, or Spanish grandee occupied their elevated social position *because* of their command of Latin.

Rather, it was of course the case that for the members of this stratum of society, wherever in Europe they happened to be educated, their expensive, elite education would include a thorough grounding in Latin. Command of Latin was an indicator of social status: it was not the cause of it (Grin 2003: 47). In the same fashion, it might be argued, the claim that English offers unique opportunities for individuals to improve their lot by connecting globally through English (what Jakubiak 2016 calls 'the discourse of English for globalization') blurs cause and effect, holding as it does that 'facility in English *causes* rather than *indexes* particular subject positions and access to resources' (2016: 199; emphasis in original). It's not so much that English makes you part of a prosperous, internationally connected elite; rather, it's that if you're that kind of person already, you're more likely to have had access to English.

And we can go a little further than this, of course. The implicit or explicit claim that English, any more than Latin in previous generations, automatically brings social and economic benefits merely serves to obscure the fact that moneyed elites tend to hold on to their power through embedded sociopolitical structures: their gates do not swing open to anyone who happens to learn a certain language. It has been claimed that English as medium of instruction (EMI) schools in developing countries lead to social division and unequal allocation of resources, even to a kind of 'language apartheid' (Shamim 2011: 305, and see e.g. Bunce et al. 2016, Coleman 2011). Of course, linguists, perhaps naturally, given the inevitable solipsism which accompanies much academic specialization, tend to fasten on the question of language. But there is good evidence to suggest that in societies that are already highly unequal, a privileged language may merely mark, or index, the privileged sector of the population. Reading, for example, Shamim's (2011) account of English and EMI in Pakistan, one cannot fail to be struck by how the divide in the school system does little more than mirror the divide in the society as a whole. English schools are private, Urdu schools public. English schools are well funded, Urdu schools struggle for resources. English schools get the best trained teachers, Urdu schools make do with the rest. The author argues passionately, and very reasonably, for improved English language education in public schools. But does anyone seriously think that if everyone in Pakistan were to become bilingual tomorrow, the two-tier school system would cease to exist? As Davies (1996: 494) insists, it is surely the case that language 'is indicative . . . not causal of social divisiveness'. Proficiency in English, then, seems often to correlate with the amount of resources that an individual already has access to, rather than being the deciding factor that enables the individual to increase that amount – and this tends to hold true as much for underprivileged non-English speakers in developing countries as it does for migrants settling in countries like the United States (Niño-Murcia 2003, Warriner 2007). English language skills alone, absent other benefits such as specialized job training, advanced education or a supportive social network, are unlikely to change a person's social status or life chances.

A further aspect of the 'trick' is suggested by the way in which the teaching of Chinese is now being represented as a potential provider of cultural capital for disadvantaged children in UK schools (Chen 2017). If English in itself is as replete with advantage and promise as is often claimed (and as we discussed in Chapter 2), then surely these English-speaking children should have abundant cultural capital already? But of course, they do not. While high social status in the UK has historically been associated with the British model of Standard English-with-RP (in common parlance, 'BBC English'), little of the same status adheres to the Multicultural London English (Cheshire et al. 2011) spoken by many young, working-class Londoners, or to the everyday speech of, say, Sheffield or Swansea. And for non-natives who learn to 'speak English', it might not be the right kind of English, as was the case for Blommaert's (2010: 96–97) interviewees in a poor part of Cape Town, uneasily half-aware that the variety of English they were being taught at school was not that of the South African elite.

But there is no evidence, either, to show that changing one's own way of speaking to approximate to a higher prestige variety will assure upward social mobility. During a now all-but-forgotten controversy from the 1980s and 90s, a polemical educationist, John Honey, urged that all children in British schools be taught not only how to write Standard English but how to speak it with an RP accent, given the supposed superiority of these modes of expression (Honey 1989, 1997). He received substantial support from some sectors of the press and public opinion. Others argued, though, that all else being equal, simple command of a prestige spoken variety (cf. the *langue légitime* of Bourdieu 1991) will not materially alter a child's life chances. This is for the straightforward reason that there is little evidence that it was primarily their speech that was holding them back in the first place, as opposed to, for example, poverty, poor education, entrenched inequality, class or racial prejudice or any of a host of other social factors (see Trudgill's withering 1998 review of Honey's 1997 book *Language is Power: The Story of Standard English and its Enemies*). Cultural capital does not flow directly or inevitably from the language or variety you happen to grow up speaking, or for that matter from one that you learn in later life. Despite the promise of the discourse of 'English for self-improvement', just as a poor Londoner does not become a rich Londoner by acquiring Standard English and an RP accent (or, for that matter, by learning Chinese), a poor Thai does not automatically become a rich Thai by learning English.

4.3.3 The 'trick' and national-level expectations for English language learning

At the level of government language policy, the equivalent discourse, that of 'English for national prosperity' or 'English for development' also carries more than a hint of linguistic determinism, lazy assumption or just wishful thinking. As we noted in Chapter 2, the narratives that unfold around global English seem to exert an irresistible pull for national governments. The very name of the Asian phenomenon of 'English fever' (see e.g. Park 2009 for Korea) suggests the heated, intemperate way in which English has been positioned as an urgent national priority. In China, 'English fever' grew to such a peak that the government – itself very substantially responsible for encouraging it – seems finally to have taken fright, moving to downgrade the role of English in the all-important *gaokao* examinations, and invoking Chinese cultural nationalism to try to temper students' enthusiasm for all things English-related (Wang and Li 2014). But while there is suspicion of English because of the possibility that it may bring ideological contamination with it, there seems to be no doubt at all regarding its economic benefits: the Chinese government's ambivalence stems from a desire to maintain political control, not from scepticism about the need for English.

This lack of scepticism is by no means restricted to East Asia. Governments worldwide often simply assume the existence of the economic benefits and invest heavily in ELT while seeming hardly to consider that building expensive English competence might not actually be the wisest use of resources (Coleman 2010, Nunan 2003). It is not really to be expected that providers of ELT will draw attention to the flawed assumptions, even supposing they recognize them. According to a British Council website: 'Governments are implementing English language policies grounded partly in an economic rationale, propelled by a focus on building the proficiency of the population in part to boost a country's competitiveness in a globally integrated marketplace'.[1] Tantalizingly, this is an assertion which is both highly specific and hopelessly vague. Investment in English is driven by an economic rationale. Proficiency in English will boost competitiveness.

But how, exactly? And how much will this be worth, in hard currency? In short, is it actually possible to prove that English is beneficial and to quantify this supposedly guaranteed benefit?

According to many commentators, it is not. To begin with, as Grin (2003) shows, it is *very* difficult to assess the economic benefits of languages, even in the most specific of circumstances (such as the salary differential accruing to a particular individual who speaks language X, and has been recruited for a particular X-requiring job). The exact nature of the link between English proficiency and income is in fact so difficult to pin down empirically that some have come to the conclusion that the 'belief that English competence is always linked to economic benefit is clearly a myth' (Kubota and Okuda 2016: 79). Even if it is accepted that English competence will produce a benefit, that does not mean that it should always and everywhere be considered a priority. Governments in poor (or just highly unequal) societies might be tempted to allocate scarce resources to English that would better be spent on boosting literacy in the mother tongue. For the very poor, meanwhile, struggling to survive, the spread of English is at best 'a sideshow' (Bruthiaux 2002: 290). In addition, it is self-evidently the case that where the quality of teaching is so poor that virtually nothing is learnt, which is all too often the outcome in state schools in developing countries (Nunan 2003 for the Asia-Pacific region, Kamwangamalu 2016 for Africa, and see e.g. Bruthiaux 2002, Wedell 2011), the supposed benefits of English are *entirely absent*.

This leads us to a last point which is so obvious as to be banal. A lot of people – including, it would seem, a lot of the people who make decisions in ministries of education worldwide – simply do not understand, or do not remember, how difficult and time-consuming the classroom learning of a language to any real level of competence actually is. How many British adults, for example, speak passable French, despite nearly all of them having spent some years studying it, with what by any global standards are extremely well-equipped classrooms, excellent materials and highly qualified teachers? Of course, there might be questions of motivation, of inappropriate assessment regimes, a lack of reinforcement outside the classroom and plenty of other problematic issues. But the brute fact remains that, as one Peruvian teacher remarked wearily to us about the unreal expectations of her students and their parents, '*if they want to get a good job using English, they should study and practise more than two hours per week*'.

It is not enough, either, to assume that an ever earlier start – English taught from the age of six or seven, as is the case in large parts of Eastern Europe and East Asia – will lead to greater success. As we have shown elsewhere (English and Marr 2015: 224–6), the link between age and ease of learning a language is vastly more complex, and more conditional on context and environment, than is generally believed by the public (see e.g. Singleton and Ryan 2004). To claim that children will simply 'pick up' a new language effortlessly if they are exposed to it, is a grotesque oversimplification. Language education planners who are surprised at the poor results obtained by a regime of two or three hours of English a week really should educate themselves about the realities of language learning. But unfortunately, as we have learned over the years from working with hundreds of English teachers from almost every corner of the globe, decisions being made about language teaching by people who know nothing about language is pretty much par for the course. There will be plenty of professional empathy with the teacher in Saudi Arabia who told us: '*The politics in the institution where I work says that they send students to my class with X level of English and that I have to give them back with B1 level of English, no matter how.*'

4.4 The expectations of others: English learning as display

In considering what it is that people expect or wish to get from English language learning and teaching, it is important to take into account the views of other stakeholders, as outlined above, besides the learners themselves. This is particularly so, naturally, when the learners in question are schoolchildren, who have relatively little agency of their own, particularly in the early years. '*My primary students,*' commented one American teacher in the Arabian Gulf to us, '*since they are only aged about seven to nine, only care about pleasing their parents or not upsetting them.*' This is perfectly natural. However, the whole notion of involved stakeholders can lead to tensions and even perverse outcomes in the learning process. As we saw in Chapter 2, a potentially important aspect of attitudes to language learning is the notion of 'investment' in a desired identity (Norton 2000, 2010), a notion which might equally be conceptualized as buying into a valued and valuable commodity (Niño-Murcia 2003). Consider now the following statement, from an MA TESOL student and teacher in an elite bilingual school for girls in South America, regarding the school's language policy as laid down by its academic committee:

The academic committee expects both teachers and students, to use only English. Students that are capable of talking with their teacher using Spanish and mixing it with English or students that answer in Spanish to an English question are not communicative enough for committee's expectations. Though this is not a random decision, because of an ideal English perception: parents are highly involved in this requirement since there are complaints about their daughters' performance because they do not read signs on the street, do not talk in English when they ask them to do it; usually in front of other adults. But, it is usual that students communicate with their cousins from the United States or sing songs in English, and when they travel abroad help their parents with communication. So, it is not a matter of ability, but about how parents believe their daughters have to communicate in English even when is not necessary.

The school, at the same time, interested in fulfilling parents' expectations, demands to 'show' English all the time. As a result, the communicative activities that are influenced by content and should occur naturally inside the classroom become a futile exercise that exhibits students talking in English, without any specific learning purpose but to assure parents that their kids can speak English . . . The school should have a strategy that encourages parents' communicative awareness for comprehending that their kids are going to use English for a specific purpose, at the right moment, and with an audience according to their necessities.

The words the teacher chooses – *show, exhibits* – are rather striking, and it is perhaps worth spending a little time in trying to understand what is happening here. It appears to be the case that a number of parents, having made a considerable financial investment in private bilingual education, are disappointed when their daughters are reluctant to give an English 'performance' on cue in front of other adults, whether this be reading a sign out loud or something more substantial, like reciting a poem. (Anyone who has witnessed the grisly spectacle of a child being obliged to recite a saccharine, rote-learned poem in English, with accompanying rote-learned gestures and facial expressions, to an audience of cooing relatives, will understand both how this cultural trope operates and why the children might wish to resist it.) The girls are, note, perfectly able to use English *in communicative contexts where it is naturally required* – speaking to relatives visiting from the United States, interpreting for their parents abroad or singing along to English songs – but this is not good enough for the parents, who complain to the school. The academic committee of the school (how many linguists on that committee?) responds by stipulating that English be used at all times, by staff and students alike, even where it is unnecessary and even inappropriate to the context. Code-switching (or, we might say, naturally occurring translingual behaviour in a bilingual environment) is simply prohibited. Oddly, this is labelled a 'communicative' approach, but as the teacher rightly insists, it is in fact a 'futile exercise' which has nothing to do with genuine communicativeness (and see our discussions in Chapters 5 and 7 of how the whole concept of communicativeness is routinely misunderstood).

How are we to interpret all this? We might suggest that the most strongly desired outcome of bilingual education for these 'highly involved', aspirational parents is not instrumental communicative competence, but the ability to produce on demand a 'show' or display of English, a demonstration of the kind of cultural capital associated with English and expensive private schools that we explored in Chapter 2 ('It's all about the maid'). Appropriacy to context is ignored. So, we should point out, is the girls' natural right to negotiate their identity through language choice (López and Bartlett 2014: 344). But the stakeholders' expectations are supposedly fulfilled, and it is they who are footing the bill. The teacher is surely right to note that what is really needed here is 'a strategy that encourages . . . communicative awareness' on the part of the parents and, we would argue, the pupils themselves, and above all the (presumably linguist-lacking) school academic committee and management team. Who is going to provide such a strategy? Only a linguistically aware teacher, a disciplinary professional with the intellectual confidence that comes from a real engagement with the field of language study. And even then it will be far from easy, given how little real language awareness tends to exist among non-specialists – we are forced to include in this category a great many language teachers with no background in the study of language – and how much public discourse around language is framed by myths, misconceptions and misunderstandings (Bauer and Trudgill 1998, English and Marr 2015: 208–28). Inescapably, given the unique role that English plays in the world, and the uniquely high hopes and expectations that are invested in it, part of the English teacher's job is to be an explainer about how the language really works at the societal level. As we have seen, learner expectations and reality are often at odds with each other.

4.5 Conclusion

The relationship between English on the one hand and social mobility, progress and access to resources on the other, is far from being a predictable or obvious one. This leads to a certain tension and ambiguity in the critical literature surrounding the place of English in the world. And indeed, the role of ELT in development 'is a confusing issue for many TESOL professionals', according to Bruthiaux (2002: 275). The idea that English offers mobility and modernity is routinely treated sceptically or downplayed, as in this extract from the publicity for an MA course in TESOL: 'English is associated with modernisation in some parts of the world. In developing countries it can be seen as key to social mobility, *even if that is more discourse than reality*' (emphasis added).[2] However, just as often (and sometimes even by the same people), the potential for English to confer these benefits is accepted, but it is inequality of access to it which is deplored: 'While English opens the door of privilege and access for *some*, often the *few*, the way many countries organise education systems means that the English door is closed for the *many*.' (Bunce et al. 2016: 1; emphasis in original; see also Tupas and Rubdy 2015, who talk of 'Unequal Englishes').

This is an odd and difficult aspect of the discourse around the place of English in the world: it is both desired and feared, its apparent power simultaneously deplored and denied. The uneasiness of many commentators with regard to the whole question of what English *does* in the world is summed up in what has been called the 'access paradox':

> English teachers, who take issues of language, power and identity seriously, confront the following irresolvable contradiction. If you provide more people with access to the dominant variety of the dominant language, you contribute to perpetuating and increasing its dominance. If, on the other hand, you deny students access, you perpetuate their marginalisation in a society that continues to recognise this language as a mark of distinction. (Janks 2004: 33)

Where you have an 'irresolvable contradiction', then an untenable or at least uncomfortable position cannot be far behind. And there are plenty of them around, from 'we have to challenge the hegemony of English, while at the same time granting people their right to access this capital' (Joseph and Ramani 2006: 189) to the – frankly bizarre – simultaneous claims that English is a 'bully, juggernaut, nemesis, malchemy (negative alchemy) . . . unnerving border crosser, criminal and intruder' but that there is 'nothing intrinsically evil' about it and that everyone should have the opportunity to learn it (Bunce et al. 2016: 1–2). Perhaps the solution to all this lies beneath what is suggested by the odd punctuation in Janks's first sentence. Was that comma after *teachers* perhaps misplaced? 'English teachers, who take issues of language, power and identity seriously. . .' Well, demonstrably, some do not. And most, we may be sure, do not worry about or dwell on these issues while they are preparing a warm-up activity, marking a vocab test or teaching the third conditional. We would have written: 'English teachers who take issues of language, power and identity seriously . . .' – and this is probably what she meant.

Let's see if we can formulate a way through this tricky terrain. In 2001 Seidlhofer claimed that the 'whole orientation of TEFL . . . seems to have fundamentally shifted: from correctness to appropriateness, from parochial domesticity and exclusive native speaker norms to global inclusiveness and egalitarian licence to speak in ways that meet diverse local needs' (2001: 135). But this was not actually the case in 2001, and it is still not the case today. The orientation may have shifted at the level of academic discourse, but on the ground, as it were, change has been slow in coming and is now long overdue. We therefore agree that the traditional approach which relies on the NS/Standard English model alone is no longer fit for purpose. However, if it is to be finally toppled, it should not be on purely ideological grounds or (as Kumaravadivelu might argue) because it conceals a neocolonial conspiracy, but because it misleads learners. It especially misleads those very many learners who have an unexamined attachment to notions of standardness and correctness in language, derived from their own cultural, sociolinguistic and educational contexts. Users of English in the twenty-first century are highly likely to come across a great deal of variety in English – variety of accents and dialects, of non-native and lingua franca usage, of non-standard and regional forms of expression, of communicative practices and so on. They need to be prepared to deal with this, at the very least in the sense of having enough language awareness to not *expect* standardness and native-likeness as a matter of course. Indeed, learners who are allowed to proceed throughout their language learning career with their notions about NS ownership unchallenged are likely to suffer a grave disappointment, to say the least, when they finally encounter real English use and discover the 'mismatch'.

The English classroom, then, should be a place where learners are exposed to, and encouraged to talk and think about, a whole range of Englishes. If teachers are to rise to this particular challenge they need to be equipped with the necessary technical and theoretical tools. And for this to happen, teachers (and the people who train them, and employ them, and design the curricula and materials they use) must come to an acknowledgement that, for a language teacher, knowledge about language is not an optional extra, and still less an airy theoretical indulgence. It is a fundamental part of their discipline. For non-native teachers and academics, meanwhile, it is not enough to rail against the perceived power of the native speaker in the world of TESOL: in fact, that is a *distraction* from the real problem, which is a lack of language awareness among stakeholders, native and non-native alike, compounded by the same lack of awareness among teachers. Few non-native teachers will ever become native-like – and why on earth should they? But by positioning themselves as language experts, they both empower themselves and begin to move the debate beyond tired old NS/NNS tropes. Part of this expertise, too, lies in being able to guide student and other stakeholder expectations about what English actually does, and what is achievable in a classroom setting, in a given context. As Joseph and Ramani (2006: 189) regretfully note, sometimes a lack of resources and other inbuilt limitations may mean that the experience of learning English merely succeeds in instilling in students an awareness of the status and importance of the language, without actually giving them any great competence in it – a cruel trick.

Knowledge about language, then – linguistics knowledge, in other words – should be a core element of the English teacher's professional identity. But what, exactly, does this identity consist of? Does it differ, particularly, depending on whether or not you are a native speaker of English? How do or how should language teachers think about their work and their profession? This is the subject of our next chapter.

Tasks/discussion

For teachers: How do you deal with the expectations laid on you by your institution, as well as the expectations of students, parents, managers and other stakeholders? Do you feel these expectations are different from those experienced by teachers of other subjects? How do you deal with the 'mismatch' – the fact that the way English is often taught does not prepare students to function with 'real' global English? To what extent do you think students are aware of this?

For teachers and students: Millions of people all over the world are learning English at this moment. Think about why *you* are learning English. What do you expect or hope to gain from it? If it was not you but someone else who decided you should learn English (e.g. parents, relatives, a school, your government), why do you think this decision was taken? What other language or languages might have been a possible alternative to English?

Suggested readings

Álvarez, J. A., Amanti, C., and Mackinney, E. (eds) (2016), *Critical Views on Teaching and Learning English Around the Globe: Qualitative Research Approaches*. Charlotte, North Carolina: Information Age Publishing.
Goes beyond purely the numbers of global English learners to take a critical look at teaching and learning around the world, in 'core' countries and elsewhere. Each chapter is based on original qualitative research and plenty of room is given to the voices of teachers and learners themselves.

Blommaert, J. (2010), The *Sociolinguistics of Globalization*. Cambridge: Cambridge University Press.
This book explores the ways in which languages are used in global interactions. English obviously plays a large part in it as a result of its special status as the global lingua franca, but the discussion emphasizes the way speakers' linguistic repertoires often encompass multiple varieties and registers. There is little stress here on language as form, and much on the fluidity and flux inherent in contemporary language use, as people move and interact more widely than ever before.

5

What Does It Mean to Be an English Language Teacher? Identity and Expertise

Those of us who teach this language have an awesome responsibility (Janks 2004: 40).

5.1 Introduction

In the previous chapters, we have mainly discussed issues concerning the current role of English in the world and the attributes that have accrued to it, whether justified or not, during its relatively rapid rise from being just another language to undeniably being *the* language of global communication. A consequence of this, as we have seen, is the commodification of the language itself, promoted by governments as a means to economic development and marketed by commercial outlets as a desirable marker of internationalism, modernity and social prestige. Against such a backdrop, it is no wonder that English language teachers find themselves in a particular predicament, different to that in which other subject teachers might find themselves, whether they realize it or not. This predicament has many different strands not just in relation to the commodification of English, but to the often competing and unrealistic aspirations of the different stakeholders, as we saw in Chapter 4, not to mention the fluidity inherent in how the language itself is actually used, and where and what for and by whom. English language teachers have to negotiate all these different factors, as well as the pressure that those political and commercial interests that have attached themselves to the language place upon them. Pressure not just to get students through exams, but to prepare them for world citizenship, to entertain them and keep them happy, to help them get a job, a promotion, a new life, no matter how unrealistic these aspirations may be. It is no wonder that Hilary Janks, cited at the start of this chapter, commented on the 'awesome responsibility' of the English language teacher.

In this chapter, then, we explore this 'awesome responsibility' by focussing specifically on the teacher. In particular, we look at the teacher from the perspective of identity and agency, paying specific attention to questions around native-speakerism (Holliday 2006: 385), expertise, institutional status and disciplinary knowledge. We encourage teachers to reflect on how they are positioned and, just as importantly, how they position themselves in their own teaching contexts and how these attitudes both reflect and promote teachers' sense of professionalism. Our aim, here as throughout the book, is to show teachers that only by upping their game with regard to their knowledge of their actual subject – the study of language – can they develop the confidence and authority to navigate the challenging environments in which they work. We start off by tackling the topic that we touched upon in the context of learners' beliefs and preferences at the beginning of the previous chapter, one which causes great consternation among language professionals worldwide: the thorny question of the native and the non-native teacher.

5.2 Native or non-native should not be the question!

> '*I think the idea of being an English teacher that is not a native speaker remains in my mind as something not positive, although I know for a fact that this should not be a limitation.*'
>
> (Experienced, MA graduate, non-native speaker teacher)

If we view the English speaking world from the perspective of what has been referred to as the 'core' community of English language speakers (Kachru 1985) it might seem that ELT, as in teaching English language to 'foreigners', is the province of the native speaker. After all, it is they who know the language best, so the thinking goes, and hence it is they who will be able to provide not only the best model for students to emulate but also the most accurate and authentic language. In fact, despite the ease with which NSs use their language, their fluency and range, this is by no means a guarantee that they actually know much *about* the language, or indeed, about language per se, a point made by Leung (2005: 130):

> The problem lies in the tendency to assume that there is an almost hard-wired relationship between the status of being a native speaker of a language and a complete knowledge of and about that language . . . and that all native speakers share the same knowledge.

This is not to say that native speaking teachers are necessarily worse than non-natives; any of them can be good or bad teachers for a variety of reasons regardless of their linguistic heritage. However, to believe, as many still do, that a native speaker can teach the language simply by dint of being a native speaker is to miss the point about the fundamental importance of disciplinary and professional knowledge. It would be like saying that because we can use our bodies freely, we must surely know all about physiology or anatomy, which is obviously arrant nonsense. Unfortunately, though, due to a general lack of awareness and understanding among non-specialists, institutions, students and their parents and some teachers themselves, the demand for the NS persists.

There are many problematic issues that arise as a result of native-speakerism, not least of which is that it leads to non-native speaker teachers receiving less favourable terms and conditions even despite having high level qualifications and years of classroom experience. The Moroccan teacher who spoke to us as we were preparing this book, a former student of ours who has a teacher training qualification as well as a PhD in Applied Linguistics, commented on what he called '*the discriminatory attitude that exists . . . to favour passport and citizenship over competence, experience and academic qualifications*'. A Polish graduate from our masters programme made the rather depressing point that, '*as a non-native teacher, I think we are still left un-preferred by learners. Thus, non-native teachers are paid less*'. Such experiences, as we have found over many years of working with ELT professionals, are sadly not uncommon (and see Mugford and Rubio-Mitchel 2018 for Mexico). Equally problematic, at least for the profession itself, is that the prevalence of unqualified native speaker teachers employed throughout the world undermines the status of ELT itself. In fact, the perception, particularly in the 'inner circle' (Kachru 1985) countries, that it is a short-term job which young and mobile native speakers can use to travel the world (as we noted in Chapter 1), or 'a fall-back option for failed authors, actors, and amateur musicians' (Breen 2018: 5), undermines the professionalism of those teachers, native and non-native alike, who invest great effort in developing their skills and knowledge for a profession that they have chosen and are committed to. The thinking which lies behind the 'if you can speak it you can teach it' approach does great damage to the self-esteem of hard-working language specialists.

This much is uncontroversial, at least among those who move in ELT circles. But there is a much deeper point here than one about unfairness, societal language attitudes or lazy prejudice. A central issue with regard to native-speakerism is that it misses the point about what 'native' English, or 'native' any language come to that, actually is, and who its speakers actually are. It ignores the linguistic and sociolinguistic realities of the many English speech communities (Hymes 1977; Labov 1972) in which people share the language but may use, or choose to use, particular varieties or dialects which identify them as a member of a given community. So while there are clearly native speakers of English (as there are native speakers of other languages), there isn't a universal model of native speakers' use of language (Leung 2005: 130). There isn't even a universal model of who native speakers actually are, either. The prevailing assumption in global ELT, rather vaguely held, is that they are standard British or American English speakers, probably white, with RP or 'General American' pronunciation. If there is a 'type' which corresponds to the linguistic notion of the idealized native speaker (Davies 2013) then this is surely it.

Of course, this is far from the truth in almost every aspect. Not all NSs are white, not all speak standardly, though many could if they chose to, and the vast majority do not have so-called RP or General American accents. This can often surprise those who visit 'native-speaking' countries, and whose image of the native has been largely formed by the EFL coursebooks they have been brought up on. The true linguistic and cultural diversity of many parts of the English-speaking world is often glossed over in coursebooks, while communicative activity tends to be tightly circumscribed in terms of register, and only very limited amounts of non-standard (let alone non-native) usage are encountered (Garton and Graves 2014; we discuss the importance of exposing students to a range of varieties and registers in Chapter 8). Unfortunately, such skewed views of the linguistic reality can have a real impact on teachers' professional lives, as the teachers' comments above indicate. In her discussion of the native/non-native issue, Aneja (2016) explores in some detail, for example, the notion of the racial idealization of the native speaker. Two of her interviewees (one Indian, one African-American) commented on students' disinclination to have non-white ESL teachers, despite the fact that they are native speakers. In the eyes of some employers and students, 'Indians were not real native speakers' (Aneja 2016: 558). This illustrates how notions of nativeness are linked in many people's minds not only to language ('real' English) but to ethnicity too ('real' natives must be white, mustn't they?').

However, it is not just that not all NESTs always speak standardly or conform to a cultural or racial type. The overwhelming majority of English language teachers in the world today are NNESTs from non-inner circle countries, and as we saw in Chapter 2, most incidences of communication in English in the world, at any given moment on any given day, will not involve a native speaker. The NS/NNS dichotomy is therefore to a large extent irrelevant. In fact, as we argue later, a focus on pedagogical expertise and disciplinary knowledge (alongside language proficiency, of course) would provide a fairer and considerably more reliable gauge of teacher quality than a mere reliance on, as the teacher cited above said, 'passport and citizenship'.

5.3 Native speaker: A redundant concept?

Not only is 'native' not a useful criterion to assess language skills, it also carries with it all kinds of problematic notions about how we classify speakers/people and languages. Who can claim the label 'native' and who cannot, who counts as a 'native-speaker' and who is excluded from that identity is a constant site of struggle and can have significant consequences for people's lives. This is particularly true for a language as (politically) powerful as English.

The above comment, from an applied linguistics online discussion group, encapsulates some of the points we have already made and prefigures the argument that we now move on to. As our former student's comment suggests, a fundamental problem with the concept of the native speaker is its association with perceived nationhood – a point also made by Aneja (2016). However, in times when the movement of peoples around the world is so fluid and on such a large scale (see Blommaert 2010) the normative notion of the native speaker, in highly diverse societies at least, is beginning to lose its grip. In the UK, for instance, the majority of the population will have been brought up monolingually, speaking the language of the wider community in all domains – at home, at school, in the street and so on – though of course there will be variation of accent, dialect and register within this broad picture. That is not to say that speakers in this group are themselves necessarily monolingual, though, as they may have learned other languages either at school or in the home. We ourselves, for instance, are native speakers of English, and identify as such, but we are not monolingual because we have learned other languages and have lived and worked in countries where those languages are spoken. Additionally, within these so-called monolingual societies, many families inhabit two linguistic cultures with one language typically used in the home while the language of the wider community used in almost all other contexts. In such cases, family members may consider themselves to have *two* native languages. The children who live opposite Fiona in London, for instance, use Bengali with their mother but for all other purposes, including between themselves, they use English. In this case English is their primary language in the sense that it is the one they use most freely and most of the time. Whether they themselves would consider English their *native* language or not, though is a moot point. It has more to do with the meaning of native itself than the meaning of fluency and domains of use; it is more obviously a social, cultural or even political question than a strictly linguistic one. This is the problem with the term 'native' and its connotations of nationhood, culture and ethnicity.

This terminological problem is most stark in the context of those postcolonial or 'outer circle' countries where the linguistic legacy of English prevails either as the official language (e.g. Tanzania, South Sudan, Malta) or an official (or 'scheduled' in India) language alongside other languages (e.g. Pakistan, Malaysia). In such contexts, there is the additional question of whether you identify your English as a variety of a kind of 'core' standard English (associated with the UK or USA?), as a variety of a regional group of Englishes (West African? Caribbean? South Asian?) or as a standard variety in its own right. In very many of these countries, English sits alongside the other languages spoken by the population, and those who use English, typically the more urban and educated, may consider it to be one of their native languages on the grounds that they have grown up using it in all domains alongside their other language or languages. This was noted by Wilson (2016), whose study on language proficiency and notions of ownership revealed that his 'outer circle' participants 'all laid claim to English through being educated in English; having English as part of their personal and national identity; their personal feelings of proficiency in English; and a claiming of English as a language in which they confidently operate.' (2016: 360). Nativeness is, then, to some extent a matter of personal feeling. This is not, of course, an issue for those who were not brought up speaking English, but rather speaking another language or languages in all domains – Japanese in Japan, German in Austria, French and Arabic in Algeria. In this context, English is a foreign language, even if it is a very familiar and extensively used one. A Polish person brought up in Poland would consider Polish to be their native language, no matter how well they spoke English and even if they were living in the UK today. For any children they might have, though, born and brought up in the UK, the situation would be different. For them, English would not be a foreign language. But whether they would consider it a native language would depend on attitude towards culture, ethnicity and nation, as with the London Bangladeshi family referred to above.

So is nativeness even a helpful concept? In relation to language teaching, the concept is and should be redundant, as it is not who you *are* that is of relevance to the profession, but what you know and what you do. That is not to say that language proficiency and fluency do not count – of course they do. But to hold 'nativeness' as the gold standard is an inevitably flawed criterion precisely because what a native speaker knows or says and how they know or say it is too random and varied to be able ever to be quantified. As Blommaert (2010: 103) points out, 'No one knows *all* of a language. That counts for our so-called mother tongues and, of course, also for the other "languages" we acquire in our life time. Native speakers are not perfect speakers.' Being a native speaker does not mean you are an *expert* in the language or that you have the knowledge and professional skills to teach the language – as this comment from a British informant of ours pointed out:

> *I am a native English speaker so I am very confident in my knowledge but I sometimes need to remind myself of grammatical rules as although they come naturally I need to make sure I can articulate WHY the language I'm teaching works in the way it does.*

Regrettably, though of course to some extent understandably, given the societal attitudes to NS models which we discussed in the previous chapter, this kind of thinking has still not been taken on board by employers worldwide. This is why professional organizations such as the British Association for Applied Linguistics (BAAL) insist that 'native speaker' requirements for teaching posts should simply be abolished, as the following from an email circulated through the BAAL mail list confirms in no uncertain terms:

> Could I remind you of the BAALmail guidelines at https://baal.org.uk/ baalmail/, and ask members to read them before posting to BAALmail? In

particular, please note that BAAL does not support the posting of job vacancy announcements that call for 'native' language speakers, as this demonstrates discrimination on the basis of a personal attribute (Email received 2nd November 2017)

Perhaps, in any case, nativeness is not really about language at all but more about cultural and social attributes such as emotional attachment, ease, familiarity and shared points of reference – and maybe even a kind of 'embodied' sense: 'X language is part of *me*'. So for 'non-native speakers' who have their own 'native language' feelings, English or whatever other language, fits within a different paradigm – something unrelated to nativeness but very much connected to context and purpose. Blommaert's (e.g. 2010, 2016) concept of repertoires is helpful in identifying proficiency, in that it considers what registers (e.g. formal, casual, academic, technical) and varieties (e.g. regional, cultural, ethnic) as well as languages (e.g. Italian, Kiswahili, Urdu) a speaker might have in their personal repertoire and in what contexts they might use them. For example, a NNEST in a non-English speaking country may use English only in the classroom with her students, and the other languages of her repertoire in all other domains as appropriate. However, if she were teaching in an English-speaking country, she would have to use English in most public domains, including the classroom, and her other language(s) only in the more private social domains with her fellow language nationals. At the end of the chapter we ask you to explore this for yourself.

It really should be beyond debate by now that it is knowledge and professional expertise that make a language teacher effective, not whether they were born into a given language or claim it as their birthright. Rampton pointed this out decades ago, arguing that, while natives might be able to model standard forms and 'real' English pronunciation, the linguistic knowledge of the non-native teachers was likely to equal if not exceed that of the natives (Rampton 1990). And 'real' pronunciation is just that – real, and not necessarily some kind of standard or prestige model, although of course pronunciation can be viewed from a social perspective too when considering issues such as regional dialect, social class or group (such as youth group) identity. When teaching phonetics, Tim has often had to ask his non-native MA students to help him with the /ʌ/ phoneme (as in 'cut', 'love') typical of RP and found in many other varieties of English pronunciation. This sound is absent in his own, West Yorkshire vowel repertoire, being replaced by /ʊ/ (as in RP 'put' 'look') and even after decades spent living outside Yorkshire, he still finds it difficult to reproduce the vowel /ʌ/ accurately and consistently (not, of course, that there is much need for him to do so outside a phonetics classroom). The students find this hilarious, naturally, but it perhaps helps to illustrate to them a crucial point – natives do not all speak in the same way, and nor do they know the whole of the language.

When NNESTs come round to focusing their energies and ambitions on being accomplished *language* teachers, rather than worrying incessantly about their lack of native-like pronunciation, range or intuition in English – that is, when they realize there is little point in taking part endlessly in a competition that they can never win – the effect can be dramatic, even transformative. At one university teachers' training course in China in which Tim participated, as the session drew to a close with a strong reminder that the Chinese teachers should feel confident enough to challenge their English-speaking colleagues whenever necessary, one Chinese teacher, who had hitherto been nodding vigorously but silently, simply stood up and began to applaud, alone. This woman, with an MPhil in Applied Linguistics from a prestigious UK university, was actually better qualified than most of her NS counterparts, but had never before had the confidence – and perhaps the explicit institutional support – to own her discipline and assert her identity as a language expert. At a similar point in another training course for NNESTs, this time at a bilingual school in South America, a middle-aged teacher punched the air, and – to the amusement of his colleagues – shouted 'Yes-sss!' In Uzbekistan, meanwhile, one local teacher simply told us, '*I am proud to be a professional.*'

5.4 Being a language teacher

There is so much more to being a professional language teaching expert than, as we saw in Chapter 1, many commentators and institutions would have people believe. So what exactly do we mean when we talk about the knowledge and skills that make for a professional, effective English language teacher, and what do teachers themselves think is important?

5.4.1 Self-perception: What teachers focus on

When we undertook a small survey of ELT teachers we had worked with, both as former students of ours and as colleagues, asking for their thoughts on their careers, we found that aside from their negative comments about class size, the 'anyone can do it' attitude and unrealistic expectations from managers, poor pay and lack of professional recognition, it was what we might call the social and pedagogical aspects of their work that they wanted to highlight. Comments such as *'Teaching allows me to initiate positive change in others'* or *'The opportunity to share my knowledge with others'* or *'Meeting people from different places and who may speak different languages'* were typical of the social, perhaps even vocational aspects they enjoyed. References to pedagogy included *'Being creative with materials design and ways of learning, Creative teaching methodologies, designing my materials'.* Strikingly, the only references to language itself occurred either in the context of student learning (*'Seeing students improve their level of English'*, *'The (rare) occasions that I see grammatical development'*) or in relation to their own proficiency and use (*'I'd like to be super fluent, improve my writing skills'*).

Similar attitudes have been found in other studies. Borg (2006), for example, found that there was a kind of 'blurring of the distinction between teachers and teaching' (2006: 13), by which was meant the interactions between teacher and students, the practice of teaching and learning, methodologies, classroom dynamics and to some extent being a 'life changer' or life guide that is the mark of an English language teacher. English language teachers, it seems, often see themselves as specialists in *teaching* rather than specialists in (English) *language*, and as agents of change with regard to their own students' lives. In other words, they see themselves in the classical role of educator across the board rather than specialist in the field of language and linguistics. Widdowson commented on this more than forty years ago in his ground-breaking book *Teaching Language as Communication*:

> Language teachers are often represented, by themselves and others, as humble practitioners, essentially practical people concerned with basic classroom tactics and impatient of theory. Such a representation is unnecessarily demeaning. Of course the teacher is concerned with practical results, but his [*sic*] practice is based on theoretical notions, no matter how inexplicit they may be. . . . I think it is important to recognise that language teaching is a theoretical as well as a practical occupation. Teaching techniques and materials must ultimately be related to underlying principles. (Widdowson 1978: 163)

We couldn't have put it better ourselves! On very many occasions over years of teaching MA TESOL courses, we have been told by newly arrived students that what they wanted to get from their MA was above all 'something practical', preferably related to methodology. Fairly or unfairly, we tended to gloss this as meaning that what they really wanted, in effect, was a training course, rather than a postgraduate academic qualification. We always set out to persuade them that a large part of the value of an MA lies in the disciplinary knowledge and the relationship between theory and practice: it is an opportunity to evaluate the theory in the light of one's own practice, and to re-evaluate one's practice in the light of theory. But for every student who is eager to embrace that relationship and engage with the ideas, there is another who is, as Widdowson puts it, 'impatient of theory' – even though their day-to-day work is obviously, inescapably, irrevocably rooted in such theory. As we saw in Chapter 1, there are many language teachers who are happy to disown their own disciplinary identity. But what does this disciplinary identity consist of? What is, or should be, the scope of TESOL teachers' professional knowledge?

5.4.2 Teachers' professional knowledge: The essentials

Being a language teacher involves three core areas of expertise: expertise in using the language itself, pedagogical expertise and last but, in our view, far from least, subject expertise – that is, knowledge about language. By expertise in using the language, we mean the necessary proficiency in language production to carry out the teaching required by the context in which it is taking place. By pedagogical expertise we mean an understanding of the interrelationship between learning theory, methodology and classroom practice. By subject expertise, that is, knowledge about language, we do not mean the ability to use a particular language, fluency, proficiency or whatever terms we might choose. We do not mean the implicit knowledge that characterizes native speaker use. We mean the *explicit* knowledge that any subject specialist develops through reading, through study and through research.

Rather than attempt to encompass all the different fields of knowledge relevant to language teachers such as language learning theory, we focus our attention elsewhere. We would direct readers who are interested in theories of learning to others, such as Dornyei's (e.g. 2005 or 2009) work on the psychology of second language acquisition, or edited collections such as Benson and Voller (2013), which focuses on the social-cultural aspects of language learning. Our focus is on what we consider to be the most neglected aspect of the professional identity of a language teacher, the subject matter language itself, using the tools of linguistics and the perspectives of social semiotics (Chapters 6 and 7) to explore it. We hope to show how a grounding in this field can provide teachers with a body of knowledge that will unlock some of the intractable problems that they most fret over, and which characteristically appear as problems of language proficiency and methodology.

5.4.3 Knowledge about teaching

> *I'm the student of Applied Linguistics and ELT is a major subject. In this course, I have studied all methods but still, I become confused while comparing them. So, that's why I want a flow chart to compare them and find the difference between them.*

Fiona received the above request via a website for academic researchers a couple of days before working on this chapter, and we have copied it here because it sums up the way many teachers perceive their professional expertise. For this teacher-student, and indeed, for most of the teachers we have taught over the years, methodology is thought to be the key to the gates of teacher heaven. It is the focus of many teacher training courses and the thing that most students on MA programmes most hope to learn. They are often disappointed, however, as in our view, methodology is not something that can be simply learned, as Fiona's correspondent above has clearly realized but is something to be explored. Fiona's response to the enquiry was as follows:

> *My advice is not to try and learn all methods – but learn more about language itself – the linguistics dimensions about real language in real settings. Methods are useful in offering ways of thinking about teaching, but you also need to take account of who your students are, where they are and what they need the language for. Why are they learning it, for instance? Of course you need to develop classroom strategies – maybe getting students to do things with the language, for instance, as in Task-Based or Goal-Oriented Learning, but learning methodologies in the abstract will probably not help.*

Admittedly, this particular teacher was not asking for Fiona to say what the best methodology was, as many student teachers in our experience start off by doing, but he was trying to learn them as if they were mathematical theorems that can be applied to solve a problem. Of course it is possible to list different methodologies. However, it is not really methodology that will help, but the thinking that lies behind methodology. As Prabhu (1990) argued:

> If we regard our professional effort as a search for the best method which, when found, will replace all other methods, we may not only be working toward an unrealizable goal but, in the process, be misconstruing the nature of teaching as a set of procedures that can by themselves carry a guarantee of learning outcomes. (1990: 161)

> The search for an inherently best method should perhaps give way to a search for ways in which teachers' and specialists' pedagogic perceptions can most widely interact with one another, so that teaching can become most widely and maximally real. (1990: 175)

To Prabhu's 'pedagogic perceptions' we would add the forgotten dimension, linguistics perceptions, because in order to be pedagogically useful you need also to be knowledgeable in terms of discipline. This entails, in the case of language teaching, knowledge of linguistics, and its subcategories, sociolinguistics and social linguistics. In other words, you need to know not just the 'how', but the 'what' and the 'why' – and of course the 'what for' and the 'who with'. You need the revelations from the descriptive tools linguistics provides. You need the insights from sociolinguistics into how people communicate, and you need to understand the interrelationship between the language needed and the context in which it occurs. This knowledge can also help (especially, but not only non-native) teachers overcome anxieties about language proficiency, because it operates at a deeper level than language production alone. You don't need to be fluent in a language to have knowledge about that language or about language per se.

5.4.4 A word about CLT

Before we move on to talk in detail about our consistent, central claim, that knowledge about language is a fundamental part of a language teacher's knowledge base, it is worth saying a bit about Communicative Language Teaching (CLT) because it retains such a powerful position in the world of ELT, yet causes such apprehension among teachers, particularly those working in countries which have long-established pedagogic traditions. CLT developed at a particular time in a particular context when pedagogical and linguistic thinking took what we might call a sociocultural turn. Drawing on social constructivism (e.g. Vygotsky, Bruner) which promoted collaborative and peer learning, pedagogical practice became much more interactive and the student occupied a more central role not just as 'receiver' of education, but as active participant in their learning (see e.g. Barnes 1976). At the same time, the work of sociolinguist Dell Hymes and linguist Michael Halliday, among others, began to have a major impact on our understanding of communicative practice and language learning itself. These theoretical perspectives entered into the world of TESOL in the 1970s, notably via the work of Widdowson with his 1978 book, *Teaching Language as Communication*, which we quoted from above. Widdowson has since said that this title was misleading, and that he wished he had used a different one, more appropriate to his aims, such as 'Teaching language *for* communication' (1983: 30). This is significant, for the book argued that the aim of the language classroom should be to enable students to engage in authentic communicative activity rather than simply uttering instances of language, typified in the audio-lingual, listen-and-repeat methods that had hitherto dominated much of the language teaching going on.

Teaching language for communication, however, is a far more complex and demanding activity than other methods previously used. It requires proactive, and if it is to be effective, language-aware teachers alongside students who are ready to engage in a wide variety of activities. It means working with aspects of other methods such as grammar-translation or audiolingualism, while adopting insights and practices from fields such as pragmatics and even critical analysis in attempting to establish an orientation towards real (or rather, realistic – see Seidlhofer 2003) language work. Unfortunately, though, CLT is usually presented across national-educational cultures in the form of ready-made courses, branded and heavily marketed by global corporate publishers whose interests, though certainly at one level pedagogical, are essentially commercial. And more than that, courses like these can be viewed as promoting a particular, ideological world view, something which has led to serious concern among certain scholars such as Pennycook (1994), Canagarajah (1999) and more recently Gray (2010a), who characterizes the globally promoted 'communicative' ELT course book as:

> a carefully constructed artefact in which discourses of feminism, multiculturalism and globalization are selectively co-opted by ELT publishers as a means of inscribing English with a range of values and associations that include individualism, egalitarianism, cosmopolitanism, mobility and affluence, in which students are increasingly addressed as consumers. (2010: 3)

We are not suggesting that a communicative approach is a bad idea in itself. It is certainly not. What we are saying is that the soil in which it is rooted, its pedagogical inheritance, is different from that of many of the contexts into which it has been introduced. It is, therefore, not surprising that misunderstandings arise about what CLT actually means in those parts of the world where communicative teaching per se does not have a cultural provenance. Nor is it surprising that teachers who are expected to teach it (and it really isn't actually an 'it') find it difficult to make it work in their classrooms. This applies to teachers from the so-called BANA countries (Britain/North America/Australasia) and local teachers alike, though perhaps for different reasons. BANA teachers and local teachers who have studied in BANA countries, try it in classrooms that are filled with students whose educational experience has been very different to the one promoted by CLT courses that have been sold to institutions and governments worldwide. Local teachers find that the 'modern' coursebooks bear little relation to the kind of teaching they have traditionally been doing and so revert to using familiar, but incompatible, methods when using them.

Given these problems it is perhaps inevitable that certain myths have grown up around CLT: (1) that it is all about speaking; (2) that it doesn't involve teaching grammar; and (3) that all classroom teaching must be in the target language. Let's contest each myth in turn.

1 CLT is not all about speaking. Communication or communicative activity, as we all know, takes place in many ways: speech, writing, gesture, diagrams and symbols and so on. It uses different genres according to the circumstances and different materials according to what is most suitable, or indeed, what is available.

2 CLT absolutely involves teaching grammar, systematically but also analytically, so that students not only see and practise the grammatical forms but can also work out what those forms *do*.

3 CLT does not require target language-only classrooms. In fact, in monolingual classrooms, using the mother tongue for analytical activities can result in much richer thinking and deeper understanding than if students (and teachers) are obliged to struggle on in the language being learned (see e.g. Cook 2001).

If these myths are understood as myths (and see Thompson 1996), teachers and students can make far better use of the time spent in the classroom learning not just the language but *about* the language, about how the language is used, and about language in general. These are matters we discuss in more detail in Chapter 9. For now, though, we move on to what we consider to be, if not the solution to all the challenges English language teachers face, then at least the essential knowledge that should inform classroom practice: *linguistics*. In fact, we go further than that. We argue that you cannot have effective methodology without knowledge about language, knowledge about linguistics.

5.5 Why teachers should learn to love linguistics!

In one of the snapshots with which we opened this book, a native English-speaking teacher who was participating in a staff development workshop (and one which made use of the insights of linguistics to aid language teaching) remarked that language was 'not his thing'. His comment might seem rather strange coming from someone who considered himself to be a language professional, teaching English in a university. As we have already had cause to note, though, it is in fact not unusual in the slightest to find TESOL teachers reluctant to engage with linguistics. But why is this? We suspect that it results partly from a very narrow view of the field of linguistics, and one that still prevails in many quarters, in which the subject is understood to be highly abstract, almost mathematical. While that kind of Chomskyan linguistics has been useful in attempting to understand linguistic processing in the brain, and has found a practical place in fields such as artificial intelligence, it has little to do with the pedagogical context in which language teachers operate. Indeed, Chomsky himself famously stated back in 1966 that he was 'frankly, rather skeptical about the significance, for the teaching of languages, of such insights and understanding as have been attained in linguistics and psychology' (cited in Garner 2016: xliii). However, as we pointed out in English and Marr (2015), linguistics is a much broader field than some traditional theoretical linguists might suggest. In that book we argued that like maths, science or, say, literature, linguistics should be part of everyone's general knowledge, particularly since it concerns the most fundamental aspect of human communicative interaction. That being the case, it is no surprise that in this book we are adamant that an understanding of linguistics should be every language teacher's 'thing'.

Linguistics knowledge provides teachers technical resources (such as those offered by phonetics and phonology, with which teachers can explore issues of pronunciation with their students); it also offers the kind of contextual understanding that can enrich the learning experience of their students (e.g. in exploring non-standard usage and comparing it with the standard). It is fundamental to classroom methodology and to effective materials design because it provides both the intellectual and practical resources necessary to understand not just *what* you are teaching but how and why you are teaching it, and, perhaps most importantly, what students can *do* with what you're teaching them. Armed with such resources, a teacher can offer informed perspectives which give students opportunities not only to deal with the workings of the new language, but also to develop their own responses and analytical approaches to the different kinds of language they encounter in their everyday lives.

With linguistics knowledge teachers can develop creative ways for students to think about how they use language, how they think about it and how different choices work in different contexts. They can use their linguistics knowledge to problematize received, but uninformed, understandings about what is 'right' and 'wrong' in terms of language usage. They become less concerned with 'correctness' and more concerned with communicative appropriacy or intelligibility in contexts where lingua franca English is being used. In this way, both teachers and students enhance their social, linguistic and intercultural awareness and skills and instead of teaching 'just' the language, the teacher is also teaching a bit of very basic linguistics. It is in this sense that linguistics comprises the subject matter that language teachers should know and it is in the same sense that it should be part of the subject matter that their students should learn. Otherwise, of course, learning a language remains nothing more than basic functional production, and language teaching, indeed, becomes the kind of 'empty' subject that some people view it as.

We look more closely at different kinds of linguistics knowledge in the next two chapters, together called 'How Does Linguistics Help?'. We want to finish this chapter, though, with a couple of examples which illustrate the kinds of undesirable outcomes that can occur if a teacher lacks even a basic understanding of the subject. This is not to criticize the teachers involved, but to demonstrate how lack of language awareness and linguistics knowledge can undermine not only students' learning but also their respect for their teacher's professional status.

Example one

Some years ago Tim was invited to give a course of lectures in the languages department of a university in Bosnia-Herzegovina, whose head had decided views on how 'correct' English should be pronounced. As part of the assessment for the department's BA in English, students were required to take a pronunciation test. This took the form of a list of recorded words and phrases, all rendered using British Received Pronunciation (RP). Students were required to listen to the list through a set of headphones in the language lab and record themselves repeating the words. In order to pass the test, it was necessary to replicate *exactly* the way the words were pronounced. There was a group of students in the department who, while Bosnian by birth, had been taken to Australia as small children in order to escape the war then raging in their homeland, had grown up in Australia, and were to all intents and purposes native speakers of (Australian) English. The problem was: how was their Australian-accented English to be assessed? When the department head insisted that they attempt to replicate British RP, the students complained that this was not fair: they spoke Australian English with an Australian accent and could see not any reason why they should have to reproduce a foreign pronunciation of their own language. However, from the university's perspective, if the university allowed the Australians to pass the exam using their non-RP pronunciation, all the *other* students would complain of unfairness: why should some students have to reproduce those particular sounds and not others?

A bit of sociolinguistic understanding might have ensured that such a tangled situation would not have arisen in the first place, as the department head would have known something about English variation both nationally and regionally. She would have been able to explain to her non-Australian students that Australian English pronunciation differed from British pronunciation, and what's more, would have acknowledged that English, like all languages, has regional differences even within the same national boundaries. She could even have taken the opportunity of having the Australian English-speaking students in the class to raise awareness about how language varies, and the students could have explored their own language from the same perspective. Above all, what's most likely is that the teacher would never have insisted on such a close adherence to an RP accent in an exam in the first place, and would instead have concentrated on intelligibility (see e.g. Kirkpatrick 2015, Blair 2017). We say more about this in Chapter 8.

Example two

Fiona's niece, who has been brought up in Spain from a young age, had her perfectly legitimate, colloquial use of the present perfect marked wrong in an English lesson at school, because it did not fit the teacher's conception of 'standard' grammar. The girl was quite understandably upset to have her use of

English, one of her mother tongue languages (the other is French) challenged in this way and it led to something of a stand-off between her and her teacher. In the end, Fiona, being the family language professional, was consulted by her sister to provide a 'definitive' answer for her daughter to take back into school while trying to avoid embarrassing the teacher herself. However, Fiona's niece, at the age of twelve, was understandably reluctant to challenge the teacher's authority, so did not take it further. Nevertheless, she herself learned two things from the episode: one, that a teacher is not infallible and two, that a language is not a fixed and immutable entity, but rather a living and dynamic resource which offers flexibility in the process of meaning making.

Heller (2007: 13), after Halliday, refers to 'the messiness of actual usage' – a very apt description of these kinds of real-world English. Indeed, what we see in these examples is what can happen when the 'messiness of actual usage' makes its way unannounced into the classroom – and the teachers are quite unprepared for it, because their teaching is not informed by a wider understanding of how language works. The phenomenon of having native or near-native speakers of a language sitting in a (foreign) language class can be something of a challenge to the professional identity of the non-native speaker teacher. Song (2016) reports on the stress, embarrassment and loss of face felt by a group of Korean teachers when presented with the task of teaching children who had studied in the USA and acquired 'real' American English which did not always correspond to what the teachers were teaching. In Colombia, meanwhile, the Ministry of Education set out to 'strengthen' state school English teaching by bringing in hundreds of native-speaking volunteers between 2015 and 2018 under the 'English Teaching Fellowship Program' of the *Colombia Bilingüe* project. These *formadores* ('trainers'), as they were known, came mostly from the USA, Canada, Jamaica, Australia and New Zealand. The prerequisites for applying for the scheme were to be over twenty-one years of age, to be a native English speaker, to have a degree and to have some experience of English teaching: the applicants were not required to have any teaching qualification (*El Tiempo*, Bogotá, 2 July 2015). They became 'co-teachers' of English alongside several thousand local classroom teachers, among whom, perhaps predictably, it was a fairly common response to feel alarmed, embarrassed and undermined rather than supported.

One local teacher commented to us as follows:

It is undeniable that this program has triggered in students the will to learn English to be able to communicate with people who may not speak their mother tongue. However, teachers' identity has been affected. Local English language instructors are not being considered efficient for this task, and, the most shocking matter of all, they themselves are feeling as not competent for teaching a language without the help of a native speaker. Although the effort made by the Ministry of Education towards the reaching of National Bilingual Program objectives through [this] program is noteworthy, teacher training programs and more resources to public schools could contribute more to the goal of Colombia becoming a country where people can speak English.

This teacher surely has a very reasonable point. However, we would also argue that a language teacher who has had a thorough grounding in linguistics and sociolinguistics, even if their command of English is not native-like, is much less likely to feel confusion, stress or embarrassment when faced with unfamiliar accents, non-standard usages or even a parachuted-in foreigner. They will understand that there is no single, standard form of spoken English (and that therefore the only reasonable criterion for a pronunciation test must be intelligibility). They will understand that language is not merely a system of sounds and structures that can be labelled 'correct' or 'incorrect'. They will understand equally that correctness (well-formedness) is not quite the same thing as standardness (correspondence to a fixed norm), and that in any case, a key aim of English teaching must be to develop students' awareness of some of the extraordinary range and diversity of Englishes. Rather than feel threatened and undermined, therefore, they might make use of the knowledge of the language that bilingual students like Fiona's niece or native speaker co-teachers bring with them by developing activities that encourage reflection on language use itself rather than simply presenting a certain model of native English grammar or pronunciation as fixed, immovable and 'correct'.

In short, linguistically informed teachers would *welcome* non-standard, non-textbook usages and seize the opportunity to let students compare them with the Standard English and idealized pronunciation (Davies 2013) that necessarily forms the bedrock of the curriculum, whether it be American, British, Australian, Irish or perhaps even Nigerian or Indian (see our discussion of the polycentricity of English in Chapter 2). But more than this, teachers would also be able to encourage their students to analyse their own language(s) in relation to English as well as in relation to each other, thereby developing students' own language awareness. In this way, the English classroom becomes a place which embraces and takes delight in the diversity of language, rather than a debate-stifling English-only straitjacket.

5.6 Conclusion

In this chapter we have put teachers in the spotlight and explored some of the issues that their work entails. We have argued that the term 'native speaker' is redundant in the context of the language teacher's professional identity, and in so doing have problematized the term itself and considered an alternative professional criterion, that of *expertise*. This led us to think about what we mean by expertise, and we identified three core areas: *fluency/proficiency* in using the language (the status of 'expert user'); *pedagogical* knowledge relevant to classroom practice; and *subject* knowledge, in other words, *linguistics*. Armed with subject knowledge and supported by the other two core areas, teachers find that their anxieties about their own language proficiency become less acute. It really doesn't matter if a teacher speaks with a non-standard or foreign accent or makes mistakes from time to time, or even doesn't know the answer to a question a student asks. In fact, rather than these being seen as teaching weaknesses, they can be turned into teaching opportunities. Just because someone is good at using the language doesn't mean they can teach it. Being a professional entails far more than that!

In the next two chapters we show how linguistics knowledge can help teachers deal with everyday classroom problems and questions. We overview, with examples, the linguistics tools most relevant to teachers and introduce an analytical framework that helps teachers and students to explore how language works in practice. Chapter 6 discusses the core areas of phonetics and phonology, morphosyntax, semantics and pragmatics in relation to teaching, while Chapter 7 shows how discourse analysis, that is the analysis of communicative phenomena, can reveal taken-for-granted aspects of language that tend to go unnoticed and are therefore often misunderstood. Our aim is to show how such knowledge can greatly enhance how teachers teach, how they can make better use of the materials they are confronted with and how they can reflect on the language needs and language opportunities available to their students and themselves.

Tasks/discussion

For teachers: To what extent do you consider being a native or non-native teacher advantageous or disadvantageous? Why, and on what different contexts and scenarios might your answer depend? Think about this question from alternative perspectives – as both a native speaker and as a non-native speaker of whatever languages you have in your repertoire.

For teachers and students: Think about the different languages (or dialects, or varieties, or registers) that you speak. Who do you use them with? Where, when and why? Do you feel more comfortable or 'at home' speaking one or other of your languages or dialects? Are you more comfortable in different languages in different contexts? If yes, why, and what does it depend on?

Some people report that when they speak different languages they feel and sound different. For instance, they might feel that when speaking English they notice the lack of polite-form pronouns – there is only one 'you' in English, so they feel uncomfortable saying 'you' to people they don't know well or who are senior to them in some way. Think about whether you experience similar phenomena. Do you feel different when speaking different languages, and if so, in what ways?

Suggested readings

Gray, J. and Morton, T. (2018), *Social Interaction and English Language Teacher Identity*. Edinburgh: University of Edinburgh Press.
This book offers a comprehensive discussion about the different ways in which English language teachers are positioned and position themselves institutionally, linguistically, professionally and socially. It reflects some of the issues we have discussed across the chapters in this book, particularly those concerning the particularity of English in the world, its ownership and appropriation and the cultural and social capital it is often thought to bring. The discussion further considers how teachers, both native and non-native speakers negotiate the complexities that the subject itself entails.

Sayer, P. (2012), *Ambiguities and Tensions in English Language Teaching: Portraits of EFL Teachers as Legitimate Speakers*. New York: Routledge.
This is something a little out of the ordinary. It is a substantial case study of a number of local EFL teachers in Oaxaca, Mexico. While it is plain that the teachers see English as being concerned solely with the culture and speech of the USA – the international lingua franca aspect, perhaps understandably, is entirely missing from their perspective – the author manages to establish deep and interesting connections between the teachers' very localized concerns and practices and broader issues in international ELT.

6

How Does Linguistics Help? (1) – Describing Language

6.1 Introduction

As we noted in the previous chapter, many TESOL teachers do not see themselves as language experts, but rather as teaching experts. This implies giving priority to the *how* over the *what*, a view that is encapsulated in a remark from one of our own Master's students during a discussion about teaching who said: *'ELT is a very narrow subject area.'* To be fair to her, though, she was only saying what many people think: that to teach language is to teach an empty subject, one that needs filling with content gleaned from elsewhere to provide the 'substance' of the lesson. It is easy to see how such a view has come about. When we discuss language we need to have examples of it to build our discussions around, because language is always realized as text, as being about something. However, this is no different to, say, the study of history or geography, which nobody would consider to be empty. In those subjects learning about the subject, that is their respective disciplines, arises out of analysis and discussion of 'content' such as maps depicting population hot-spots, or accounts of significant historical events. Surely the same thinking should apply to the language material used in the language classroom. Just as in history and geography, people can enjoy and learn about the *topics* being presented while at the same time learn about the discipline, the study of language (or history or geography) itself. The failure to recognize (or the urge to deny) that the core discipline associated with language teaching is the study of language, has led to the widely held belief among TESOL teachers in particular that knowing how to use the language and knowing how to teach it *is* their subject knowledge. We argue that this is not the case. Language teachers should know about language. We would expect no less from teachers of any other subject, so why should we expect any different from TESOL teachers?

In the previous chapter, we identified three areas of expertise that we consider important to being a professional language teacher: competence in using the language itself, a grounding in pedagogical knowledge, and, in our view most important of all, an involvement and interest in *subject* knowledge, linguistics. This is not to say that we dismiss language competence or pedagogical understanding, but our aim, as we have stated throughout the book, is to redress the balance and argue for teachers to recognize that central to their work is what should be their core discipline, linguistics and the study of language. In fact, we believe that armed with linguistics knowledge, language teachers, and particularly NNESTs, who often feel they have to defer to their native speaker colleagues' supposed greater authority, can empower themselves in the face of the kind of institutional ignorance about language that we saw in Chapter 4 and at the end of the last chapter, and empower their students in helping them to understand why and how they might use the language in their current and future lives. We are not, of course, suggesting that every teacher should be a linguistics academic. What we are suggesting, though, is that even a little knowledge of linguistics can open up new ways of thinking about language, language production and language use. This, we argue, offers teachers, even those who are less proficient in the language, new ways of working with students that can lead to more focused and hence, more effective language learning.

Our discussion about how linguistics helps is carried out over two chapters. In this chapter we introduce the tools that linguistics provides (phonetics and phonology, morphosyntax, semantics and pragmatics), and show, with examples, how these can help teachers deal with practical classroom issues concerning student production and performance. The next chapter, Chapter 7, focuses on an approach linguists use to analyse communicative activity, discourse analysis. Before that, though, in order to provide an overarching frame to these discussions, we want to talk a little about the concept of *noticing*. It is a theme we return to again and again in this and the remaining chapters not just because we believe it to be the first step towards becoming actively language aware, but because we are convinced that it is fundamental to being an effective language teacher too.

6.2 Noticing

Noticing is what language teachers do all the time when they are in the classroom. In fact, it is their *job* to notice. But the problem, as we see it, is that teachers rarely view this particular teacher practice as noticing in the way that we mean it. What teacher noticing tends to entail is noticing when their students get things wrong, and, when they notice something wrong they tend to correct it, sometimes by saying it the right way, sometimes writing it the right way with a laborious red pen. Of course, as all language teachers know, correcting mistakes like this rarely results in students getting it right next time – or even the times after that. Some mistakes just never go away! This is because the kind of noticing that teachers tend to do is constrained by the idea that student errors are problems rather than opportunities and that teaching is about delivery rather than research.

To explain what we mean when we talk about noticing as a starting point, let's take an example. We are walking home from work and look up and notice the sky filled with vibrant colours. We think 'how wonderful!' and take a photo or simply stand there and enjoy it for a moment or two. Then, having had the experience, we continue on our way. In this case it is enough for us just to have noticed. However, if we happened to be meteorologists, we might do more than just reflect on the sunset's beauty. We might also think about the weather conditions that have caused it and what this tells us about weather patterns, environmental effects and so on. To put it another way, if what has been noticed coincides with the specific interests of the noticer, what has been noticed becomes relevant. The meteorologist in our example is not just an observer like you or me, but an *active* observer who simply can't help going beyond simple appreciation.

The same applies to everyone. We all actively notice things when they are relevant to our interests. If you're thinking of getting a new phone or a bag for your laptop, you start noticing the phones and bags other people are carrying. And linguists are no different. For linguists even the most mundane piece of communication can raise questions not only about the given phenomenon itself but about the wider implications that those questions lead to. For example, a linguist might note down a fragment of overheard conversation, or stop and take a picture of some graffiti sprayed on a wall, or hang on to an old newspaper found behind the wallpaper when redecorating a house. The old newspaper might tell us something about how language use changes over time. A small ad might use an unfamiliar script which could tell us something about the readers the advertiser is hoping to attract, and the overheard conversation might provide an example of multilingual speech, or translanguaging (García and Li 2014).

We have foregrounded the concept of noticing and its corollary, research, because we strongly believe that if language teachers develop their own subject knowledge, then they will strengthen their professional and pedagogical expertise as well. A teacher with subject knowledge can use it to go beyond simply noticing and correcting student errors, in the way we have characterized above. She can use it to understand why that error might have arisen and how to turn it into a teaching opportunity that can inform not just the student in hand, but the class as a whole. What's more, noticing is not just an indispensable classroom resource, it is a means with which a questioning and creative teacher can develop her own knowledge about language and that of her students, something we return to in Chapter 9. This is only possible, though, if she has the tools linguistics provides and the understanding that linguistics is not simply a body of knowledge to be had but a body of knowledge to be *used* – every day in the classroom.

6.3 Linguistics tools: A pedagogical resource

In our experience, the word 'linguistics' often causes trainee language teachers and MA students to groan and roll their eyes, presumably because it conjures up images of Saussure's *langue* (but not *parole*), Chomskyan tree diagrams and the complicated-looking apparatus associated with grammatical analysis, all of which offer a somewhat abstract approach to the study of language. By contrast, what we mean by linguistics is the study of actual communicative interaction, and how this takes place.

In order to describe and analyse the 'what' and 'how to' aspects of language, particularly in relation to classroom teaching, we have separated our discussion into the different categories that are typically used in language description: phonetics and phonology (pronunciation), morphosyntax (grammar), semantics (propositional meaning) and pragmatics (social meaning). Dividing them up in this way is useful in that it allows us to consider specific aspects of production, such as pronunciation or grammar, but it is important to point out that the boundaries between them can be quite fuzzy. For example, voice tone is usually considered a part of phonology, to do with the sound system of a language. However, tone can also be part of grammar, for instance, turning a statement into a question, or semantics, in that the meaning of a word or phrase can change according to its tone. In English, 'excuse me' is usually associated with an apology or a polite request. However, the same phrase might mean 'I'm not at all sorry' if said with heavy stress and a high falling tone on the last syllable. (How many other possible meanings of 'excuse me' can you generate just by changing the stress and intonation?) In so-called tonal languages, such as Zulu, Vietnamese or Cantonese, tone has lexical value. This means that a change in tone changes the meaning of the word itself so that, to give perhaps the most celebrated example, in Mandarin the sounded 'word' which we would write alphabetically simply as *ma* can mean totally unrelated things ('mother', 'horse', 'scold' or 'hemp') according to the tone used. In other languages, like Twi and Bini (spoken in West Africa), tone is used to signal grammatical meaning, such as the difference between past and present tense. Nevertheless, despite the fuzziness between the category boundaries, it is useful to separate them out so that we can begin to understand what might be considered the nuts and bolts of language. We start with the most basic aspect of language production, that of sounds.

6.4 Phonetics and phonology

Why can't my students say 'v' properly?

Phonetics is the study of human sound *production*, how humans actually make speech sounds, while phonology is the study of the sound *system* of any given language. Gaining insight into this area of linguistics can be a revelation for teachers and students alike once they get over the idea that it is difficult to learn or make use of in the classroom. Teaching pronunciation can be quite a challenge for teachers, whether they be native speakers of one of the core English varieties or whether they be non-native speakers. As we discussed in Chapter 5 when considering teacher knowledge and identity or Chapter 3 on lingua francas, deciding which model or variety of English to teach is problematic – but perhaps ultimately irrelevant, because although students need models to emulate in terms of pronunciation, it is unlikely that they will achieve what might be considered native-like production. Therefore, in relation to the teaching of pronunciation, the most important thing is to achieve *intelligibility* across as wide a range of different contexts where English is being used as possible. The first step towards achieving intelligibility is to understand how sounds are made (which is the essential subject matter of phonetics) and why students may fail to recognize or reproduce them correctly (which falls also into the ambit of phonology).

6.4.1 Phonology or orthography?

In the next chapter we discuss the many confusions that arise around the ways in which speaking and writing are conceived of. Here, though, we want to pick up on one in particular which is closely related to our present discussion. It arose out of a public lecture on a language-related theme that Tim was giving. He recounts:

> At one point I happened to remark that Hindi and Urdu were in most practical respects the same language. A British-Indian man immediately interrupted me, shaking his head and wagging his finger emphatically. 'No, no', he insisted, 'they're quite different. I'm amazed you don't know that. Don't you realise that they have two completely different alphabets?' I pointed out to him that writing and language were two distinct things.

The thing that was confusing the man in Tim's anecdote was that a script (of which an alphabet is one kind) is only a *visual representation* of a language; it is not the language itself, and as a general rule, it doesn't really matter which script is used. In fact, many languages have gone through changes of script over the centuries, Turkish being a prime example. For almost a thousand years, Turkish writing used a version of the Arabic alphabet but, for political reasons, on 1 January 1929 the use of the Roman alphabet was decreed by law. This does not mean that the language called Turkish disappeared overnight. It means only that the way in which it was written changed. Equally, Croatian, for instance, uses the Roman alphabet, Serbian the Cyrillic, but linguistically they are, to all intents and purposes, varieties of the same language (and were recognized as such when Croatia and Serbia formed part of the same polity of Yugoslavia). Countries may set out to change the way they write their language for reasons that are political or simply practical, but they rarely replace their own language with another one – at least not as a matter of choice. It is worth pointing out here that conceptually at least, speakers of Chinese languages should have little difficulty in understanding that writing is not language, simply because their own writing system (or orthography) is non-alphabetic and is based on the meaning of the various characters, not on sound. Hence, although there are different Chinese languages which are to a greater or lesser degree mutually unintelligible in speaking, they have basically only one written form.

Alphabets of whatever variety (Arabic, Cyrillic, Ethiopic, Hebrew, Devanagari etc.) were designed to reflect the sound system of a language in a visual form. However, as we all know, for historical and other reasons, sometimes alphabets are 'borrowed' into other languages, and sometimes the spelling systems of different languages do not always correspond fully to the alphabetic letters. Some languages have a close relationship with the alphabet they use. Spanish, for example, has a pretty much one-to-one correspondence between the sounds of the language and the letters of the alphabet. But languages such as French or Polish, and of course English, have a less closely associated relationship. It may come as a surprise to some that not all alphabets even within what is essentially the same 'Roman' system, have the same number of letters. The English alphabet has 26 letters, along with French and German, but Spanish has 27, Swedish has 29, Polish has 33, while the Italian alphabet has only 21.

To illustrate the problem, take the English vowel system. In the English alphabet there are only five vowel letters (or *graphemes*), a e i o and u. By contrast, in English phonology (the sound system) there are at least twelve vowel sounds (or *phonemes*) and twenty if we include diphthongs (like the vowel sounds in 'make' or at the end of 'radio'). From this, the English alphabet could be considered inadequate since it doesn't represent every sound in the language, but an alphabet of getting on for fifty letters, taking both vowels and consonants into consideration, would begin to defeat the purpose of having an alphabet in the first place. By contrast, Spanish has five phonological vowels which are matched by its five alphabetic vowels. Spelling in Spanish is, therefore, easier than spelling in English, though that does not mean that *writing* in Spanish is easier or that Spanish as a language is simpler than English. Writing, in the sense of orthography, is not language, as we have already pointed out, although, of course, writing as a *communicative mode* is.

This disconnect between orthography and phonology was famously illustrated by George Bernard Shaw, who considered himself something of a linguist in addition to his literary and political renown. In his call for the simplification of English spelling, Shaw used the example of the word 'fish' to show how illogical, in his view, the system was. He argued that we could, in theory, spell that word as *ghoti* – using the 'gh' as pronounced in the word 'rough', the 'o' as in the word 'women' and the 'ti' as in the word 'nation'. Perhaps fortunately, Shaw's simplification plan failed and we retain the spelling system established more or less during the seventeenth century, reflecting as it does not just the sounds of the language but its etymology too. It is this mix of etymological and phonological elements that gives it its inconsistency, but it is worth pointing out that it also gives it its cultural heritage. There is, though, an obvious truth in Shaw's point about the sound-spelling relationship, which is where phonology comes into play. If we really want to provide a visual representation of the way words sound – and this is of course an extremely useful thing to do when helping students with pronunciation – then we can use a *phonemic* alphabet. These alphabets are derived from the International Phonetic Alphabet (IPA), which provides a symbol for all the linguistic sounds of all known languages, and offer a broad language-specific version showing all the phonemes used in a given language. What's more, drawing on phonetics, a teacher can show how the sounds of a language are produced; the *place* (where they are made in the mouth) and *manner* (how they are made) of articulation. Using the English phonemic alphabet, Shaw's 'fish' would be represented as /fɪʃ/. Note the use of the parallel forward slash lines // to indicate that we are showing phonemes in contrast to quotation marks to indicate orthographic alphabet letters.

6.4.2 Using phonetics and phonology

Sticking with the word 'fish' as an example we can show, using phonetics knowledge, how to produce each of the sounds and the phonemic symbols to visually represent them. We take each in turn.

> The first phoneme /f/ is, in phonetic terms, a *voiceless labiodental fricative.*[1] The *voiced* version is represented phonologically as /v/. Both sounds (/f/ and /v/) are made by passing air through the narrow gap that occurs when you rest your top teeth on your bottom lip. The only difference between them is that you don't use your voice to make /f/ but you do to make /v/; hence voiceless and voiced.
>
> The next phoneme, /ɪ/, is one of two 'i' type vowel sounds in English; in this case it is a short vowel which is made with the lips slightly apart and the mouth stretched a bit into a half smile with the tongue held in a central position in the mouth. It contrasts with the longer /iː/, as in the word 'feet' / fiːt/ made by stretching the lips further apart to either side while keeping the lips in the same slightly apart shape.
>
> The /ʃ/ represents the *voiceless palato-alveolar fricative,* in contrast to /ʒ/ which is the voiced version. If you move your tongue against the roof of your mouth, you will feel a small ridge (the *alveolar* ridge) behind your teeth and

behind that a flat section (the *palate*), you need to place the tip of your tongue between these two spots and then pass air through the space just as you did in producing /f/ as both sounds are fricatives.

While this book does not have the scope to give a full explanation of verbal sound production, Roach (2009), which is designed specifically with TESOL in mind, provides clear descriptions, including practical exercises, as well as other aspects of English pronunciation, and is a book we strongly recommend. What our purpose has been here is to show that a bit of knowledge about place and manner of articulation can go a long way towards helping students. Phonetics and phonology can play a fundamentally useful, even transformative, role in the teacher's resource repertoire and despite oft-heard comments that it would be too difficult for students, in our experience, this is not the case. Students very quickly become familiar with the phonemic symbols if they are used when introducing new vocabulary alongside the spelt representation (e.g. 'summer' /sʌmə/) and they can serve as a quick way of helping students understand which sound they need to focus on, for instance, the difference between a long /iː/ and a short one /ɪ/ to distinguish between /fɪt/ and /fiːt/. This is an example of what we call a *minimal pair* where two words which are different in meaning (semantically different) are separated only by a single phoneme. In the case of 'fit' and 'feet' they are separated only by the two phonemes /ɪ/ and /iː/. This aspect of pronunciation is extremely important in terms of intelligibility and a teacher's familiarity with the basics of sound production, place and manner of articulation, can provide real practical help for students. Equally, where students have difficulty with English consonant clusters such as in the word 'can't', showing that there are two different vowel sounds here, /æ/ for 'can' and /ɑː/ for 'can't', helps eliminate the problem of the consonant cluster. To be able to show students graphically like this that it is actually vowel length that distinguishes these two words (in British English at least), as much as and probably more than the 't' that is so salient in the spelling, is a powerful tool in the teacher's teaching kit.

It is important to stress again here that non-native speakers are unlikely to develop a native-like accent in whatever foreign language they learn, unless they have extended exposure and a very good 'ear'. There are people who achieve this, but for the majority of us, our dominant pronunciation will always be present to some degree. This should not be regarded as a problem. You might argue that it contributes to our linguistic identity, just like a native speaker's regional accent: a skilled teacher, with a solid grasp of the basics of linguistics, will be able to reassure their students of this, and will not worry about their own non-native accent, either. However, when dominant language pronunciation interferes with intelligibility, action must be taken to rectify this.

As we are all humans with the same physiology it is obvious that we share many sounds across different languages. Some sounds are roughly the same while others may be particular to specific languages. A speaker of South Asian languages, when speaking English, will most likely pronounce the English phonemes /t/ and /d/ differently to how a British RP speaker might because in their languages the equivalent sound is produced with the tongue in a slightly different position compared to the English version. To make the English version the tongue rests half behind the teeth and half on alveolar ridge just behind the teeth. Hence the English /t/ and /d/ are *dental alveolar* sounds distinguished from each other by whether we use our vocal cords (voiced) or not (voiceless). For the South Asian version the tip of the tongue rests on the back of the alveolar ridge. Try it out and see how different they sound. With regard to intelligibility, though, it hardly matters if a speaker produces an alveolar instead of a dental-alveolar /t/ or /d/ when speaking English although it may matter if we are trying to speak a South Asian language. However, the Spanish phoneme /x/ (*voiceless velar fricative*), as in the word *jabón* meaning soap, does not occur in most varieties of English (the Scottish *loch* provides a rare exception), just as the English phoneme /θ/, for example, as in 'thank', doesn't occur in French. Not all languages use the same repertoire of sounds and it is this that lies behind the pronunciation question we used at the start of this discussion: Why can't my students ever say 'v' properly?

There are many languages, notably in the Turkic and Persian/Farsi language families, where no clear distinction is made between /v/ and /w/, so that speakers of those languages will tend to approximate the English /v/ by using a Turkish-like /w/. What is more, it is likely that speakers of those languages may not even hear the distinction when listening to English and no amount of teacher repetition will help. If it is important for the student to produce the sound /v/ to avoid confusion in meaning, then showing how the English /v/ is produced in the mouth will be far more successful than the convention of endless repetition. The same applies to the Spanish pair /b/ and /v/ where, although both letters are used in writing for historical reasons, there is a single true sound when the letter is pronounced in most contexts, a bilabial fricative [β],[2] which lies somewhere between the two English sounds.

Raising students' awareness, not to mention teachers' awareness, about such characteristics of language and drawing on the information provided by phonetics and phonology to explain, not only helps in the production of these sounds but also offers the chance to discuss how different languages and dialects draw on different sound repertoires. That is surely an interesting lesson in the making. As we mentioned earlier, many teachers are reluctant to use this approach to pronunciation, arguing that students would never bother to familiarize themselves with it and that it would become just one more burdensome thing to remember. Our impression, though, is that behind this lies another truth, which is that teachers themselves sometimes seem unwilling to try it out. So why does the use of the IPA encounter such resistance? Tim's experience in Spanish-speaking countries suggests that one aspect at least of this resistance might be rooted in the teachers' very lack of linguistic awareness. If you speak a language like Spanish, where, as we noted above, there is a close to one-to-one correspondence between alphabet and pronunciation (a phenomenon sometimes referred to as *shallow orthography*) then you have really very little need for the tools of the IPA. Indeed, you grow up and become literate seeing the alphabet as a transparent, trustworthy and reliable guide to pronunciation: George Bernard Shaw's illustration of how 'fish' could be spelt *ghoti* would be quite impossible to render in Spanish. Hence, perhaps, the mistaken impression that learning to write phonemically is unnecessary and rather pointless.

To learn the basics of phonemic script should not be seen as a chore, but as a sensible investment which will reap large rewards. We are not suggesting that students should learn the entire phonemic inventory of English straight off, nor that they need to know all the technical terms associated with how we produce language sounds. However, we do expect teachers to know about these things, at least in so far as they can be of practical use to them in terms of their disciplinary awareness and classroom effectiveness. Moreover, if you get into the habit of using phonemic representations as a shorthand way of helping or reminding students of what sound they need to be aiming for, a lot of classroom time can be saved in reaching pronunciation goals.

Knowing how we make speech sounds – the position our tongue should be in our mouth, whether air should flow or be stopped, how open or closed our mouth should be, whether we use our vocal cords or not, how the language works rhythmically – and knowing how to represent these sounds accurately and precisely using the phonemic alphabet alongside or instead of the written alphabet, is not just abstract technical knowledge. It can make the difference between intelligibility and unintelligibility: communicative success and failure. And if you understand the reasons *why* your students have such difficulty with certain sounds, based on the differences between the phonology of English and the phonology of their own language, you can go beyond merely saying 'repeat after me'. This is surely where teachers should focus their attention when teaching pronunciation: not on the unattainable and therefore demoralizing goal of acquiring a particular 'native-like' accent.

We have focused our discussion here on the production of language sounds because we are determined to persuade teachers of the value that some knowledge of phonetics and phonology can bring to the classroom. However, of course, sound production is not the only aspect of this area of linguistics that teachers can and must draw on in their teaching. The importance of word stress is often overlooked even though it can make the difference between a word being understood or not, and sentence stress and intonation are also often treated as an incidental rather than the communicative resources they are in meaning making. We discuss these only very briefly because the key thing here is simply to make the point.

Different languages have different rhythmic patterns which characterize how they sound in sequence. Speakers of French and many West African languages, for instance, tend to stress all the syllables of a word more or less equally, (bAnAnA) creating a highly regular rhythm as they speak. English, meanwhile, tends to move between stressed and unstressed syllables (baNAna) which makes the overall sound seem a bit sing-song to some people's ears. The difference between the two systems – the one syllable-timed, the other stress-timed – goes to make up a large part of what is perceived as having a 'French' or 'West African' accent on the one hand, and having an 'English' accent on the other. People's ears are tuned into expecting words to be uttered with the particular stress pattern associated with their language so when someone says a word using a different pattern, it can lead to momentary confusion. For instance, saying the word 'understand' with the stress on the middle syllable 'unDERstand' might cause a native-speaking listener to hesitate because they would be expecting to hear 'underSTAND'. Helping students reproduce the relevant patterns can be highly effective in improving intelligibility, sometimes even helping to overcome difficulties with individual sound production. For example, in the case of 'understand' it can help with the tricky consonant cluster in the middle to realize that in many British accents, including RP, there is no /r/ sound in the word at all. Of course it works the other way round, too – English native speakers speaking a syllable-timed language can sound pretty strange and make their interlocutors stare at them blankly for a moment.

Sentence stress, which can also have an important effect on meaning, is another aspect that teachers should pay attention to. A classic example used to demonstrate this is the following. Take the sentence, 'Newton discovered gravity'. The neutral, or unmarked (Halliday 1985) way of saying it would be with the word 'gravity' (Newton discovered GRAvity) holding the main stress, making this utterance a statement of fact. However, if you shift that stress onto the first word, 'Newton', the meaning changes. The utterance 'NEWton discovered gravity' becomes a kind of contradiction – in other words it was Newton and not somebody else. Placing the stress on the middle word, 'discovered' we get yet another interpretation. 'Newton disCOVered gravity' acts as a kind of correction – he discovered gravity rather than invented it. Sentence stress, then, can also be considered a part of the semantic (meaning making) system.

Finally we mention intonation, which can play both a semantic and a grammatical role. Grammatically speaking, intonation can indicate the difference between a statement and a question, but it is, perhaps, the semantic dimension where most misunderstanding can occur. Take the example of a word like 'please'. We can make it mean different things or rather communicate different meanings according to the intonation we attach to it. It can be neutrally polite with a slight rise at the end or it can be annoyingly whiney if it has fall-rise tone or it can express annoyance and be considered quite rude if said with a flat tone. Consideration of pronunciation and its many different aspects can make for fascinating classroom discussions which encompass not just a focus on how to produce the different sounds, but how those differences contribute to linguistic behaviour in different languages and the cultural meanings that are ascribed to how we say things.

6.5 Morphosyntax

Morphosyntax is the term linguists tend to use when referring to grammar. In other words, it concerns language form or structure. The term is made up of two elements, *morphology*, which refers to word formation or the structure of words, and *syntax*, which refers to the rules of how words are organized into clauses and sentences. This is an area that most TESOL teachers tend to have a good understanding of and are generally more at home with than the area of phonetics and phonology. Nevertheless, for language teachers, an understanding of grammar from a linguistics dimension can be very helpful in getting to grips with not only the English language but also the languages of the students. Just as phonological systems differ from one language to another, so does a language's morphosyntax and the classroom, whether monolingual or multilingual, provides a rich environment in which to 'notice' language use and view it as an analytical opportunity rather than as a problem. We take each aspect of morphosyntax in turn starting naturally enough with morphology.

6.5.1 Morphology

A morpheme is the basic or minimal unit of a language's grammar. It is the core building block, so to speak. For instance, the word 'objectively' is made up of three blocks or rather, morphemes: 'object', which is a free morpheme in that it can stand alone as a word, '-ive' and '-ly', which are known as bound morphemes. We could say that free morphemes have lexical value in that they mean something in their own right, and bound morphemes have grammatical value in that they change the grammatical function (or class) of a word. In this case 'object', a noun, becomes an adjective by adding the morpheme '-ive' and an adverb by adding the further morpheme '-ly'. However, not all bound morphemes are grammatical. Some hold semantic value such as the bound morpheme 'un-'. If we add 'un-' to our original 'objectively', as in 'unobjectively' we are changing lexical meaning as well as grammatical function.

Morphology, then, is one way of describing how we form words and how words can be shaped according to their meaning or their grammatical function. In terms of its morphology, English can be quite flexible as we can easily change the grammatical function of a word by changing its morphological structure. This is not so easily possible in all languages. For instance, in English we can take the noun or verb 'work' and turn it into an adjective by adding the morpheme '-ing' as in 'working practices'. In French this would be impossible and you would have to say something like 'practices of work' (*practices du travail*). Hence for a French speaker learning English, this kind of word transformation might cause some difficulty, just as it does for an English speaker learning French. Some languages have elaborate morphology, like Russian or Polish, with complex verb (conjugation) and noun (case) forms. Languages like Turkish, Japanese and Finnish are known as *agglutinative* languages, meaning that words can be made up of strings of morphemes which can be *prefixes* or *suffixes* with grammatical or lexical meanings based around a *stem*. For instance, if you want to say 'I was at your house' in Turkish you would say '*Evinizdeyim*' which is made up of the morphemes *ev-in-iz-de-yim*, '*ev*' being the stem word 'house'. Other languages, such as most of those spoken in China, have very little morphology, in the sense that they largely lack the property of being able to make semantic change by manipulating the form of a word. Some languages mark tense morphologically (e.g. Italian) and others mark it lexically (e.g. Bahasa Indonesia). Some languages mark whether a noun is subject or object, indirect or direct, while others, such as English, do not.

6.5.2 Syntax

In languages like English, much of what we think of as grammar, such as parts of speech (noun, verb etc.) or tense, is represented morphologically. How we organize these morphological units is the concern of *syntax*, or, in essence, word order. English is considered an SVO language – that is, a language where the subject comes before the verb and the object follows the verb, as in *The farmer* (subject) *bought* (verb) *a horse* (object). If someone says, in English 'Bought the farmer a horse', you know they are unlikely to be a native speaker of English as no such speaker would make a syntactic error of this kind.[3] It is, essentially, a foreign language speaker's error. On the other hand, it is syntactically correct to say 'The horse bought a farmer', but of course it would be semantically unusual, to say the least. The switching of subject changes meaning. In Welsh, by contrast, which is considered a VSO language, the order 'Bought the farmer a horse' would be the normal one for a simple sentence: *Prynodd y ffermwr geffyl*, but you can move the words around if you want to emphasize something in particular. You'd say *Ceffyl a brynnod y ffermwr* if you wanted to stress that it was a horse that the farmer bought, and not a sheep, say, or a new tractor.[4]

English word order is bound by rules like this partly because it does not have an elaborate system of cases like Russian or Polish, as we mentioned above, to tell you which bit of the sentence is which – though Old English did have such a system, and hence a more flexible word order. You can still see traces of this in English syntax, of course: standard written English still distinguishes between subject and object in pairs like 'I/me' and 'she/her'. But it is not at all uncommon to hear 'me' used as a subject in informal spoken interaction ('me and Dave'), for example, and the distinction between 'who' (subject form) and 'whom' (object form), seems to be disappearing rather quickly across almost all genres and registers (e.g. 'Who were you speaking to?'), except perhaps the most formal (e.g. 'To whom were you speaking?').

Where there are well-developed systems of case endings (Ancient Greek, for example, or Russian or Estonian), it is these case endings which indicate subject, object and so on. Where there is no case system, or the system has decayed over time (Swedish, Vietnamese, modern English) we rely primarily on word order, but there are some languages which do not have a particular word order in the sense we have described here. Chinese languages, for example, which lack grammatical morphology of the kind we discussed earlier by which word class or tense are indicated, sequence their words contextually so that it becomes clear, if you are a native speaker at least, who is the subject, when an event took place and so on. Tone, rhythm and metre might also be a consideration for a Chinese speaker in deciding how to order their words – how the words sound when put together, their harmony.

Like morphology, syntax can also have a semantic effect though it tends to be affective rather than propositional (that is, it changes the style or emphasis of a sentence, rather than its lexical meaning). For instance, if we say 'Although he likes Mary, John doesn't like Susan' instead of 'Although John doesn't like Susan, he likes Mary' the change in syntactic arrangement creates a change in the point we are making even though we are using the same words. We discuss this aspect in a bit more detail in the next chapter.

In our discussion of pronunciation we drew attention to the fact that not all languages have the same phonology and some phonemes in one language may not occur in another. Developing the same awareness of how languages differ in their morphosyntax can be equally revelatory for teachers and students alike and can go a long way to explain why different students do or don't get different things right. We have already used examples of some of the ways in which languages differ in their grammar, but here are a few more which can lead to real conceptual difficulties when learning English.

Some languages don't mark verb tenses but instead use adverbs or adverbial phrases to indicate time. A Thai student might say, for instance, 'he come day before today'. If you know this, you will have some idea of why this student has problems with tense, even if you know not a word of Thai. What's more you will realize that no matter how many times you keep saying 'simple past' or 'present perfect' to such a student they will not just suddenly 'get it'. Some languages differentiate in the pronoun system between 'she', 'he' and 'it'; some languages, such as Korean, differentiate even between a senior 'she', an equal 'she' and a junior 'she', while others differentiate between polite or formal address pronouns such as the Spanish 'tú' (informal) and 'usted' (formal). These fall into the area of morphosyntax that merges into *pragmatics* (see below). Some languages, like Chinese or Bengali, don't differentiate linguistically between the sexes at all, so having to use 'she' or 'he' in English when referring to a female or a male may well seem like an unnecessary complication to speakers of those languages. The same, of course, is true for English speakers being expected to mark nouns as either feminine or masculine in French!

In the end, it is this kind of genuine *language* knowledge that enables teachers to respond accurately, helpfully and confidently to classroom questions like 'is it correct to say X?' and treat classroom errors as teaching opportunities rather than problems. A teacher who can show how one language differs from another in its morphology, its syntax and its phonology can not only help particular students with particular questions, but can open up a whole new vista for all the students in helping them realize how varied languages really are.

In the next section we move onto the linguistic category of *semantics* which, as we have seen, is closely associated with the categories we have already discussed. We intend only to focus on those aspects that we feel most useful for teachers to bear in mind rather than the more theoretical issues associated with logic, for instance, which is more relevant in areas of research such as the development of artificial intelligence. In our discussion we link semantics with another linguistic category, *pragmatics* because apart from the classificatory aspect of semantics, they bridge the 'tools' dimension of linguistics (phonetics, phonology and morphosyntax) with the analytical frameworks dimension that we discuss more fully in the next chapter. As we said right at the beginning, the boundaries of these linguistic categories are blurred.

6.6 Semantics and pragmatics

We start with a brief overview of semantics before moving onto a consideration of the semantic dimensions of pragmatics, notably, *implicature*.

6.6.1 Semantics

In its simplest manifestation, semantics concerns the classification of words. At least that's where it all begins. For instance, the word 'tree' can be understood as being a part of the larger group 'plant' and part of the smaller groups 'oak', 'elm', 'ash' and so on. Semantics is also concerned with conceptual meaning, which is where it becomes more complex. For example, do we all perceive things in the same way? If we asked you to draw, say, a tree, would our drawings all look the same? Equally, where words have the same form but completely different meanings, how does it affect our interpretation? An anecdote from one primary school teacher shows how this might be tricky. In that case the teacher had asked the pupils, aged about eight or nine, to draw a picture based on the scene in a story they were reading. The story described a spooky house covered in creepers. One child drew a picture of a house, not covered in the ivy-like plant intended by the story writer but instead with images of burglars climbing (creeping) up the walls of the house!

Meaning, then, depends not just on dictionary definitions of what a word signifies, but also on how we interpret words. What is more, meaning is concerned not solely with lexis (vocabulary), but also with morphosyntax and phonology, as we have already mentioned. Addressing someone in English as 'my friend' or 'pal' can signal friendliness or the very opposite, according to the context and the tone in which it is said. This is the point at which semantics merges into *pragmatics* or the study of meaning in context, which relies on more than purely linguistic factors.

6.6.2 Pragmatics

If words like 'my friend', 'thanks a lot' or 'excuse me' can mean different things depending on the intonation used to utter the words, what does that mean for the language learner? If the phonology of your language has a regular rhythm where each syllable is equally stressed and tends to use a fairly flat intonational pattern, then it is possible that saying the word 'sorry' in that way could come across as rather rude or churlish to a native English speaker. This is because, in most dialects of English, a flat 'sorry' with equal stress on each syllable denotes insincerity. Here we are talking about the social-cultural dimension of language where value is placed not just on what is said but how it is said. This aspect of linguistics is hard to pin down and extremely hard, if not impossible, to teach.

Pragmatic knowledge is quite different to the other categories of linguistic knowledge that we have considered because it is essentially a case of 'it all depends'. In fact, it could be argued that pragmatics fits into the categories of social linguistics and social semiotics which we discuss in Chapter 7. Some aspects of pragmatic knowledge are cultural and become learned over time spent immersed in a culture, and some aspects are contextual. Other aspects have to do with the intention of the speaker and how what she says is understood. Take the following example, Example 6.1, and consider how we get from the question about the keys in line 1 to the offence taken in line 4.

Example 6.1

1 S1: Have you moved my keys?
2 S2: What do you mean?
3 S1: I'm sure I left them there by the phone.
4 S2: Well I haven't touched them!

The next example offers a different kind of meaning association in which the statement in line 1 is taken to be a request in line 2.

Example 6.2

1 S1: It's freezing in here.
2 S2: I'll shut the window, then.
3 S1: Oh great. Thanks

What these examples show is that meaning is not necessarily propositional, as mentioned when we talked about the semantic possibilities of syntactic arrangement above. In both these cases, meaning is based on *implicature*. In other words, it is not what we say but what we are understood to be saying. In Example 6.1 Speaker 2 believes Speaker 1 to be accusing him of moving the keys regardless of whether that is actually what Speaker 1 intends to mean. Such misinterpretation is often the cause of family rows! Example 6.2 shows that intended meaning can be disguised linguistically. Speaker 1 may simply be stating a fact, but her utterance is interpreted as a request and acted upon as such. In neither case can we be sure of the initial speakers' intended meanings since nothing in the words used necessarily leads to the responses from their co-respondents. We cannot know without actually being there and, indeed, actually being the people involved in the exchanges whether the respective interpretations were expected or not. This is the point of implicature. It always relies on context.

The above examples show the contextual importance of meaning, but the following example shows how sociocultural factors are also relevant in making and interpreting meaning. Example 6.3 comes from the research of one of our former MA students (Sarno-Pedreira 2004). In her study, she used the act of offering and refusing among a group of friends, Brazilians and English. From her own experience of living in London year, she had noticed that her English friends responded differently to her Brazilian friends when offered food or drink, and having developed her linguistics lens during her course, she decided to explore this phenomenon by collecting and analysing recordings of different examples of the *genre* of offering (see e.g. Hasan 1989).

Example 6.3

A is Brazilian and B is English

A: Would you like some cake?//
B: I'm OK. Thank you.//
A: Come on . . Just a little bit . . . I'll put . .
B: No, really. I'm all right, thanks.//
A: Are you sure?//
B: Yeah . . Thanks.//

Sarno-Pedreira 2004: 24

Although we cannot quite catch it without seeing or hearing the exchange, Sarno-Pedreira describes how Speaker B becomes increasingly irritated as Speaker A presses him with the offer while Speaker A remains baffled, unable to understand what he's done wrong. She explains that in Brazil it is normal, and indeed polite, to refuse an offer of food or drink on the first and even second asking, even if you really do want to accept. In that culture, everyone knows the routine and plays by those rules. However, Sarno-Pedreira's study also showed the surprise and disappointment felt by one of her Brazilian friends who, having refused an offer of a drink from a British friend, was then not given a second chance.

As a teacher, Sarno-Pedreira wanted to find out whether it was possible to incorporate these different cultural practices in the classroom. Her conclusion was that it was not, partly because it would be impossible to cover everything given the number of contextual and individual factors that might affect them and, equally importantly, because of the risk of stereotyping that ensues as soon as something becomes identified as a 'cultural practice' – not all British people take no for an answer first time and not all Brazilians would continue to insist. What her study did conclude, however, was that having her students explore such examples from the perspective of pragmatics would offer the chance to move away from some of the more mechanical and essentializing exercises which sometimes pass as intercultural awareness raising or 'learning-about-culture'. Gorski (2008), for instance, provides a squirm-inducing account of 'Taco Night' being presented to English-speaking Americans at his elementary school in the USA as an exemplar of Mexican culture, and makes a strong case for moving towards a more meaningful, analytical approach that raises awareness not just of other cultures' practices but of students' own. As Wigglesworth and Yates (2007: 780) point out:

> At the sociopragmatic level, it is important to help learners understand the communicative values underlying interaction, because understanding these values can help them understand why speakers, including them, approach particular speech events in the way that they do.

6.7 Conclusion

In this chapter our aim has been to encourage teachers to develop a linguist's eye and ear, so that they can begin to view the different communicative practices and communicative events that they encounter as data. In the classroom this means that instead of viewing incorrect or inappropriate instances of language primarily as *problems* or as errors to be immediately corrected, they could instead be viewed primarily as *linguistic phenomena* to be explored. By altering their frame of reference in this way teachers can change how they perceive themselves and their work. Instead of being a deliverer of language, as if it were a parcel or a letter, the teacher becomes an observer, and even a researcher of language.

We have shown that even a basic knowledge of linguistics can open up new possibilities in the teaching repertoire in ways that can help address many of the questions raised in earlier chapters.

Our view is that no TESOL teacher can be considered fully professional without this knowledge. However, the tools that we have set out here are just the starting point. We hope that once a teacher starts exploring the actual stuff that they are teaching, language, they will find themselves delving further into other aspects of language and communication. Viewing the world through a linguistics lens, in the classroom and beyond, can change the way teachers think about not only the language they are teaching, but the language that surrounds them and their students in all its diversity and complexity. It reminds us that language teaching is more than the sum of its parts. It offers students the chance to open up their own minds to the many different ways in which language can be realized. We develop this theme in the next chapter.

Tasks/discussion

For teachers: What do you do when you notice student language errors? Think about whether you respond, how and when. For instance, do you intervene at the moment or do you wait? Do you note students' errors or do you correct and move on?

Choose some errors that you have noticed your students making or that you yourself make if you are a non-native speaker. What do you think lies behind these errors? What linguistic tools would be most useful for understanding them yourself, and what tools might you use with your students in helping them get it right?

For teachers and students: Make a note of things about the English language that differ from your own language. By this we don't mean vocabulary – there would be far too much of that – but things like the ways in which sentences are organized and how many tenses there are. What about sounds that you find difficult to produce in English? Why do you think that is the case? And how about some of the social aspects, like greeting people or paying compliments?

When you've chosen a few examples, discuss these with other people in your class. How does thinking about these differences help you with your language learning?

Suggested reading

McGregor, W. (2015), *Linguistics: An Introduction* (2nd edn). London: Bloomsbury.
This book does exactly what it says on the cover. It provides a very useful and clearly explained introduction to the key areas of linguistics including the linguistic tools we have introduced in this chapter as well as other aspects of linguistics, such as neurolinguistics or language acquisition, that we have

chosen not to discuss in our book. It is written in an accessible style and offers a helpful supplement to our own work.

Yule, G. (2016), *The Study of Language* (6th edn). Cambridge: Cambridge University Press.

The fact that this is now the sixth edition of the original publication by George Yule, updated and revised, confirms its popularity and usefulness. From phonetics and phonology through morphology and syntax to sign languages and child language acquisition, it offers a comprehensive and clear descriptive guide to language and linguistics.

7

How Does Linguistics Help? (2) – Analysing Language

7.1 Introduction

In the previous chapter, we discussed the importance of developing a linguistics lens and using it to notice language phenomena, including those associated with student language performance, both in the classroom and beyond. We explained how linguistics can be not only an important resource in the teacher's knowledge arsenal but a practical asset in the classroom itself. Using a linguistics approach to language learning and teaching, we argued, encourages teachers to shift their perceptions about teaching, including their approach to student errors, in as much as they can start viewing these as phenomena to be explored rather than solely as problems to be rectified.

In this chapter we focus on language as communication itself. What does real communicative activity look and sound like? How do people really use language? How do we say what we mean? How do speaking and writing differ, and how does this affect what and how we teach? And how can we talk about real communicative activity in the classroom? In other words, we are talking about the *social* dimension of language, that is, communication.

7.2 What we mean by communication

One of the most important shifts in the history of linguistics and the study of language was, as we mentioned in Chapter 5, what is sometimes called the 'social turn'. Most significantly for the purposes of our discussion, this meant a shift from what had been the dominant focus in linguistics in which language was analysed as an abstract and objective system of structures, as in for example Saussure and then Chomsky's work, to a focus on language as a system of meanings between people in the real world. The work of Halliday on the social interpretation of language and meaning and Hymes on language as social practice, among others, encouraged researchers and educators into exploring not only how language can be described or even what language is used but how, why and in what circumstances. For Dell Hymes, an ethnographer, this developed into linguistic ethnography and for Michael Halliday, a linguist, it developed into social semiotics. The fields are closely interlinked since both are interested in the interaction between the contexts in which communication occurs and the *semiotic*, or meaning-making, resources used in the process.

The first thing to say, as we discussed in Chapter 5, is that communication is not just about speaking. It is not even just about speaking and writing. Verbal communication (literally using spoken or written words), fundamentally important though it is, provides only part of the picture. Often we communicate without words at all – think of embodied communication such as gestures and facial expressions, or visual images such as emoticons or highway code signs, or non-verbal sounds such as 'mmm' or 'shhhhh', and of course intonation and sentence stress as discussed in Chapter 6. Without these dimensions of communicative activity our interactions would be dull indeed, and more than that, they would be severely limited. Try saying everything with words alone! Even when we write, we use non-verbal communicative resources: we use punctuation such as question marks or colons to communicate particular meanings, we might change the font (when and where do people tend to use Comic Sans?) or we might put something in *italics* or **bold** to highlight its importance. We use different cases – capital letters and small letters, and we use font size and sometimes colour too. In fact, all communicative activity is multimodal because it draws on resources beyond the verbal, all communicative activity seeks to be meaningful, and all communicative activity takes place in a context. What is more, the semiotic resources we use in communicative interaction, whether it be speaking, writing or any other mode, are not random but are selected either consciously or subconsciously to shape the meanings we wish to produce and share.

With these criteria in mind, we take a look at some of the widely held myths around communication and consider how those myths are upheld and perpetuated in some approaches to ELT, including certain methodologies and materials. In doing this, we draw on our core methodology, discourse analysis, as a way to encourage teachers to become more language aware and more research oriented than they might otherwise be. As suggested in Chapters 5 and 6, a classroom teacher is, by dint of the work she is engaged in, a natural researcher. It's just that she does not always see herself in that way!

7.3 Analysing communicative activity

In Chapter 6 we looked at some of the tools that linguistics provides to enable us to describe and explain language structures and processes. Now, with our focus on the social, we move onto exploring examples of communicative interaction using the analytical framework (Figure 7.1) we have developed as a guide for analysing communicative interaction and which teachers can use to explore language in the classroom. Our framework is an example of a *discourse analysis* approach which, for us, encompasses *all* communicative modes, not just the verbal ones (speaking and writing). It is a framework that has grown out of a social semiotic view of language (e.g. Halliday 1978, Hodge and Kress 1993), drawing on multimodality (e.g. Kress and van Leeuwen 1996, Kress, 2010, Jewitt et al. 2016), insights from sociolinguistics (e.g. Hymes 1996, Blommaert 2005, Pennycook 2010) and social linguistics and literacies (e.g. Street 1984, Gee 1996, Lillis 2013).

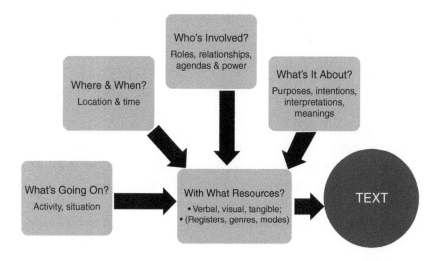

Figure 7.1 A social semiotic framework for analysing communicative activity (adapted from English and Marr, 2015: 121)

What we mean by a discourse analysis approach is, essentially, using a linguistics lens to analyse examples of authentic communication which, for the sake of convenience, we call *texts*. When we use the word 'text' we do not mean what is generally understood by the word, pieces of writing: we mean *any* communicative representation, whether it be spoken, written, drawn or gestured and so on. Kress (2003: 74) describes text as 'the stuff of communication', which we consider to be a useful way of thinking of it. We will use text from now on when we refer to any language phenomenon, whether it be a single spoken word like 'help!', a conversation between two or more people, a WhatsApp exchange, gesture, or whatever else it may be.

In order to analyse a text fully, we need to take account of not just what is said, written or shown (the text itself) but where it is said, what's going on around it, who's involved in it, what it's about and what it's for (the context). We also need to consider how the text is made, what semiotic resources are used, why and what kind of meanings they aim to produce, what Halliday (e.g. 1978) called 'meaning potential'. For instance, choosing to shout at someone can mean different things depending on the context. You could be shouting at someone in anger, you could be shouting at them to warn them of a danger or trying to greet them from across the street, and you would use a different tone of voice for each. It all depends on the context! The framework depicted in Figure 7.1 offers a multilayered approach to analysing communication, which reminds us of the effect of context on textual production and the effect that textual production has on the context. We don't just choose genres or registers, words and structures or gestures randomly, we choose them to promote the particular meanings that a given context gives rise to. Let's now take a closer look at how this might work.

As we have explained, the aim of Figure 7.1 is to show that communication does not occur in a vacuum. It occurs in a context, and that context leads us to make choices about how to 'make' our communications or texts. It makes a difference who we are communicating with and what the communication is about, and it makes a difference where we are and what is going on around us. Let's take the example of being in a college library where there are certain constraints about communicative activity, such as being quiet and not disruptive, which affect your communicative choices. Let's say you spot a classmate working at one of the desks and you notice they've got the only copy of a book that you really want to look at. Given the environmental context, you would not (we hope) shout across the room to that person. Rather, you would abide by the expected norms of behaviour and go up close and whisper your request, or you might instead touch them on the shoulder, point at the book with raised (questioning) eyebrows, point at yourself, wait for a nod from your classmate and then pick up the book and go back to your desk. The 'where' and 'what's going on' have affected the *mode* of communication – whispering instead of speaking out loud, touching and gesturing instead of speaking; the 'who' has affected the *register* chosen, that is how you frame what you say as a result of the social relationship between the participants. And, of course, the 'what it's about' gives us the *genre* that is chosen, the type of communication, in this case, asking a favour. And in turn, these three elements, genre, register and mode, affect what we can call the *textual materials* (English 2012: 76), the words, the grammar, the type of gesture and so on, that are used. So, for example, you probably wouldn't touch and point if you didn't know the other person in the library. You would probably choose a more formal register, saying something like 'Would you mind if I borrowed that book for a moment?', using the mitigating resources of the conditional and past tenses to show that you recognize the potential inconvenience.

Every communication that we engage in involves these kinds of choices. Sometimes, particularly in speaking and other face-to-face interactions, it happens intuitively, but sometimes it happens consciously, particularly in writing where we have the time to reflect on our textual choices. Sometimes we have to adjust the choices we have made when we realize that our co-respondent isn't quite getting what we mean, as we discuss further below. The point is that the relationship between *context* and *text* is fundamental to all communicative interactions and an understanding of this is central to developing language awareness. Language, as Halliday and Hasan pointed out in their seminal book, *Cohesion in English*, 'is made up, not of words and sentences, but of meanings' (Halliday and Hasan, 1989: 10) and we make those meanings by *choosing* the semiotic resources (words, structures, registers, genres, gestures etc.) we find most apt for our purposes and the situation we find ourselves in. It is relevant if we choose the word 'customer' instead of the word 'passenger' when referring to people using public transport. It is relevant whether you say, as I heard on the radio only the other day when referring to the number of people supporting a government policy, 'more than sixty' instead of 'fewer than sixty-five' when the actual number is sixty-three. It is relevant whether you say 'Although I agree that the grass is greener on the other side, I prefer to stay on this side' instead of 'Although I prefer to stay on this side, I agree that the grass is greener on the other side.' And it is relevant if you choose to produce a PhD thesis in the genre of a comic book instead of the genre of a conventional PhD (Sousanis 2015).

The example of 'customer' or 'passenger' is an example of what we call *category change*, whereby the status of a thing is adjusted by using the new term of reference, which in the end becomes normal usage without most people realizing. The term 'customer' implies that we are in a market relationship of buyer and seller – it is a transactional term of reference rather than one of potentially mutual exchange. You can be a passenger in a friend's car, for instance, but you would never use the term 'customer' in that context. Category change, particularly when it involves terms of reference for people, leads to identity change and a shift in the relationship between the participants. This is exactly what we meant when we grumbled about the use of the term 'instructor' instead of 'teacher' in Chapter 1. The example of the use of the different quantifiers (more than, fewer than) demonstrates how we can influence how a piece of information might be understood. If we say 'more than sixty' we are playing up the number whereas if we say 'fewer than sixty' we are playing it down. We call this process *uptoning* and *downtoning* (see e.g. Wigglesworth and Yates 2007). In other words, if you choose either of these two versions instead of simply saying the exact number, you are adding a value judgement of your own – you are showing partiality or bias. The fourth example, with its two versions of the same propositional content, shows that by simply changing *arrangement*, different perspectives are given in each case. The first version (Although the grass is greener on the other side, *I prefer to stay on this side*) emphasizes the speaker's preference whereas in the second version (Although I prefer to stay on this side, *the grass is greener on the other side*), what is being emphasized is the 'truth' of the statement about the grass. This is because of the two clauses in each version, one is *independent* (italicised) and the other, fronted by 'although', is dependent, *subordinate* to the independent clause for its complete meaning. Crucially, what is in the independent clause is the meaning being prioritized. Arrangement is a choice.

The final example, the PhD as a comic book, offers a different way of meaning, not just in terms of using different *verbal* genres (plays, interviews, stories) for writing about academic things as discussed in Fiona's work (e.g. English 2012 and 2015), but using *image* as the primary mode for meaning-making, 'the world shown' instead of the 'world told' (Kress 2003: 1). It matters what genre you choose because different genres afford different textual opportunities for making your meanings.

These four examples demonstrate that choice is always at play when we engage in communicative activity, and it is a key aspect of how linguists view communication. *How* we say or write what we say or write is not only a matter of correctness, or form, but a matter of meaning, of appropriateness and of intent. As Blommaert and Jie (2010: 9) have put it:

> To language, there is always a particular function, a concrete shape, a specific mode of operation, and an identifiable set of relations between singular acts of language and wider patterns of resources and their functions. Language is context, it is the architecture of social behaviour itself, and thus part of social structure and social relations.

An understanding of this is of fundamental importance to genuinely communicative language learning and teaching. Without this understanding, the language classroom remains an entirely self-referencing space in which what is being learned is a series of forms and words which do not act in meaningful ways on the world outside the classroom itself. This in itself is not terrible, but to claim that it is about *communication* is to miss the point. To demonstrate this more clearly, we now examine a language structure that is typically under-analysed and oversimplified in most language teaching settings, and one which every TESOL teacher has to tackle some time or another, the passive voice.

7.3.1 The case of the passive voice

A cursory online search for examples of how to teach and learn the passive voice in English will return a very large number of printable worksheets and other materials, aimed at both teachers and students. The quality is variable, naturally enough, but what is immediately striking is how many of the examples and exercises foreground the form of the passive (i.e. the 'construction' aspect of it) over its meaning in context. In this example we are asked to choose between two possible answers:

Example 7.1

This is the Great Pyramid of Khufu. _____ over 4500 years ago

- It was built by the ancient Egyptians
- The ancient Egyptians built it

Who is to say which of those is the best answer? In terms of structure, both are clearly correct and appropriate. Each is as good as the other. Obviously, then, in order to select the most appropriate for our communicative intent, we must look to the context: but *no context is given*. There is no indication as to why the 'right' answer is right, or why it is better than the 'wrong' answer, except that the exercise requires the student to use the passive form, so the passive form is what the student must use. Nothing is being communicated. There is no recipient of the message and no reason given for sending it. All we have to work with, therefore, is form. At another online teaching site, which appears to specialize in decontextualized structure, the grammatical transformations demanded yield answers which are again structurally 'correct', but often verge on the nonsensical:

Example 7.2

She would reject the offer
   The offer _____ by her

- will have been rejected
- would be rejected
- will be rejected

If we consider our framework in Figure 7.1, who are we supposed to be saying or writing this to? Why, and in what circumstances? At no point are we given any reason why we should want to produce a clunky, context-free, isolated utterance like 'The offer would be rejected by her' – we just have to get on with it, so that the website will reward us with an animated tick or a smiley face. This is the sort of thing that CLT was supposed to have done away with a couple of generations ago, driven by the realization that real language only and always functions in a context of situation (see e.g. Figueiredo 2010), but it lives on, as vigorous as ever, because many material writers and teachers still think of language primarily in terms of correct and incorrect *form*.

Sometimes, to be fair, the writers do give ostensible reasons for the use of the passive. However, often the reasoning must only succeed in confusing the student, as in this example:

> ## Example 7.3
>
> *The painters have painted the room*
>
> In this sentence, we prefer a passive construction:
>
> *The room has been painted*

But why? Who are 'we', and why do 'we' prefer a passive construction? Seeing as there is no context given, how on earth can we judge that the second sentence is preferable to the first? From the same interactive website, if we mark the sentence

> *The dustmen collect the rubbish every day at 7 am*

as correct, as opposed to 'The rubbish is collected by the dustmen every day at 7 am', the answer appears:

> Wrong. We don't need to mention the agent – the dustmen

But perhaps I am right! Perhaps I *do* need to mention the dustmen; perhaps I am telling a story about what happened once when the dustmen came to my house. Where there is no context, how is the student to judge which is the most appropriate linguistic form for the communicative effect that they want to achieve? Ultimately, a fundamental objective of language teaching is to enable students to do this effectively, and to work solely with form is therefore to waste a valuable learning opportunity. Frustratingly enough, some of these online exercises come close to engaging with the embedded social meaning and nuance of real language, only to veer away again. Take this example, where again we have to click on the 'correct' answer:

> ## Example 7.4
>
> *It has been drawn to my attention that some staff are leaving early on Friday. This shall stop.*
>
> - The speaker probably uses the passive as a way of not giving the name of the person who told him.
> - The speaker uses the passive to sound clever and educated.

Now, which is the desired answer? It is of course the first, but given the deliciously self-important and ever-so-slightly-misjudged *This shall stop* (see our discussion of *shall* in public announcements in English and Marr 2015: 11–14) we would suggest that it could just as well be the second. Indeed, this would be a splendid piece of text with which to start a discussion with students about the ways in which English users sometimes employ communicative resources like the passive voice to try to make their pronouncements sound more authoritative, and to compare this with the way it is done in their own language(s). Teachers who are confident with the analysis of language as a social, communicative resource will seize awareness-raising opportunities like this: those who see only grammatical rules will let them slip.

By way of contrast, let us look at what a genuine piece of usage, collected by one of us some years ago, can tell us about the use of the passive and how we might employ it in the classroom in a genuinely language-aware way.

Example 7.5

Members of the Library who are permitted to borrow books should present the books they wish to borrow and their borrower's ticket at the Issue Desk on floor E. Unless a valid reader's ticket is produced, books may not be borrowed. Details of loan periods and the number of books allowed to each category of borrower is given in the Library Rules. Books which are not reserved by another reader may be renewed; this may be effected in person or online, but <u>not</u> by phone.

If you were doing this with a fairly advanced class and wanted to analyse this text in terms of communicative choice, then as a first step – this should almost invariably be the first step – you would ask students to think about the context in which this piece of language was found. The 'where' is a library, of course – but what kind of library? A local, child- and family-friendly kind of library, or perhaps a library of the more staid, traditional sort? How do we know? And who is involved in this textual interaction? Who is addressing who and what sort of relations exist between them? What is the communicative intent of the writer? Perhaps the students will pick up on the use of capital letters (Issue Desk, Library Rules); perhaps they will notice the underlined <u>not</u>; perhaps the presence of behaviour-regulating modals like *should* and *may* as well as verbs like *permitted* and *allowed*. And in what circumstances do sentences usually begin with 'Unless . . .'? At some point, of course, it will be noticed that almost all the verbs are in the passive voice: the deliberately anonymous writer has chosen this grammatical form precisely in order to express detached, unchallengeable authority. Once this has been worked through, a useful task to set the students would be to rewrite the notice using only active forms of the verbs, and then have a discussion about how such a rewriting alters its communicative effect. Depending on the level and engagement of the students, you might end up, after a good deal of discussion and correction, with sentences rather like these:

> You can't borrow books unless you produce a valid reader's ticket
> or
> Sorry, but we can only let you borrow books if you've got a valid reader's ticket

– in which the 'deleted actor' (Hodge and Kress 1993: 21) gradually reappears, and implicit agency becomes explicit (not that one would wish to use those kinds of terms with a class of English learners, of course). The aim, the *point* of such exercises is not to teach technical terms or university-level linguistics or even to practise grammatical form, though that would be an inevitable and welcome result, but to encourage learners to think of language as situated in a social context, within which different choices of words will produce different communicative effects in the way suggested in our analytical framework in Figure 7.1. For learners to engage in exercises like this, which develop their understanding of how and why we use certain structures or words, or indeed any semiotic resource, helps them in a number of different ways. It helps them pay closer attention to the structures of the language because they understand that structural choice is fundamentally relevant. It helps them expand their language repertoire so that they are better able to deal with different communicative contexts. And it helps them develop a deeper understanding not only of the language they are learning but of their own language, and how the choices they make when using it affect how they mean and how they can be understood to mean. This is heady and empowering stuff!

So far we have shown how important it is for language teachers to pay attention to the context in which language occurs and to recognize the close interrelationship between that context and what we say, how we say it. How we communicate, the words, the structures, the tones, the gestures we use shape our meanings in ways that matter. Language learning is not just about whether what we say is correct but about how it means. We now move onto consider the two core communicative modes, speaking and writing, which fall into the traditional TESOL category of the four skills, a concept we return to later in this chapter. Our discussion develops the analytical strand we have set out in this chapter, and in so doing draws on themes from the earlier chapters and tools we introduced in Chapter 6. As is our general aim throughout this book, we seek to encourage readers to go beyond 'common sense' understandings of language, to look below the surface and recognize that many of the assumptions made about language are based on misapprehension and even, sometimes, prejudice. We start off by focussing on common (mis)understandings about correctness.

7.4 Speaking, writing and notions of correctness

Working with our own teacher-students over many years, we have noticed again and again that they begin to shift their thinking substantially about how they teach English when they realize that writing and speaking are quite different communicative phenomena. Of course, that is not to say that our students did not realize before that they are different in their manifestation (oral versus written, listened to versus read), for they obviously did. What we are talking about here is how and where they differ in terms of their production, the resources they make use of and the contexts in which they occur.

The first thing to say is that writing is not speech written down, and speech is not writing said out loud. Now this may seem too obvious to need pointing out, but actually it is at the heart of many of the misconceptions around language, particularly with regard to notions of correctness. Let's take a brief look at this by using the example of one of many blog comments about a particular politician's use of language during a TV interview. The politician involved was the British Shadow Education Secretary, that is to say the spokesperson on education from the main opposition party in parliament.

Blog comment

By improving her English grammar and spoken English, she might have more credibility as Shadow Education Secretary. I cringed a few minutes ago when, on Breakfast Television (BBC) she said, 'There is issues...............' Oops, plural subject and singular verb ......should have been 'There are issues.......' Seconds later she was dropping Hs...

I'm appalled.

Now, this rather condescending self-appointed expert highlights two features which he or she clearly believes to be errors. However, these are not actually so much errors in relation to speaking, particularly conversational speaking, as they are errors more associated with *writing*. Let's take a look at each complaint, starting with issue of the dropped 'Hs' to see how the complainant came to the conclusion she or he did and where they went wrong.

First, we have the common confusion between the two distinct categories of orthography and phonology that we discussed in Chapter 6, where people make assumptions about pronunciation based on the written form. However, in this example, the complaint about the dropping of 'Hs' is not just a comment about the production of a sound, but about social class and education, and therefore reveals rather more about the complainant than it does about the politician. Dropped 'Hs', in British English at least, are considered by some as a marker of low prestige language use. However, a bit of linguistic analysis can show that the complainant rests their case on mistaken assumptions.

In writing, it can never be considered 'correct' to miss out the letter 'h' (we could not write 'the ouse' for 'the house') but in very many regional accents words that are written with an initial 'h' tend to lose it in speaking – or perhaps, rather, gain it in writing for reasons of etymology - (e.g. /æv ju: gɒ̞ mai æt/ for 'have you got my hat?'), especially in informal situations. In the most marked form of Received Pronunciation (RP) some written words that begin with the letter 'h' are sometimes, rather pedantically, pronounced without a corresponding /h/ and preceded by 'an' instead of 'a'. 'A hotel' becomes 'an hotel' /æn əʊtel/, for instance. In fact, the sound /h/ in English, particularly in rapid, connected speech, is often dropped simply because, as an aspirate, it requires some effort to produce in its fully aspirated form. Most of us drop our 'Hs' from time to time. Perhaps if the politician had been a speaker of a language which does not use the sound /h/, like French or Italian, the blogger might have thought she sounded quite charming, speaking English with her 'dropped Hs'!

The blogger's second misconception is to assume that the politician's use of 'There is issues . . . ' is an error of grammar. Without the actual recording it is difficult to say, but it is more than likely that what the politician actually said was 'There's issues . . . .' rather than the fully expressed 'There is issues . . . ' simply because in rapid speech /ðəz iʃu:z/ (there's issues) slips off the tongue more easily than /ðɛr ɑːr iʃu:z/ (there are issues) and is an extremely common usage for British English speakers (e.g. 'there's lots of people here', 'there's times when . . . '). Indeed, the construction [*there's* + plural noun] is so common that many corpus linguists consider it to be actually *standard* for spoken – not written – English: 'The form *there's* is used standardly in spoken English irrespective of whether the following subject is singular or plural' (Carter 1999: 157). Tellingly, it even appears in writing where the context of the writing means that people express themselves as if they were talking (as in 'as long as there's enough seats for paying customers', from the online discussion site Mumsnet – and see our discussion of spokenness vs writtenness below). Neither the 'dropped H' nor the supposed grammatical error are signs of ignorance or lack of education on the part of the politician; rather, they are evidence only that she is a native speaker, with a regional accent, whose spoken language reflects the normal characteristics of spokenness. Example 7.6 is a nice illustration of how even 'prestige' speech is still speech-like. It is a transcription, that is, a word-for-word written record, of the opening section of a lecture given by a popular university professor who makes frequent appearances on radio programmes as an expert on environmental issues, and whose written publication record is distinguished and extensive.

Example 7.6

Now what I've what I want you to imagine at the start is a core community what I want us to imagine is a core community eventually and I'm going to talk about everything in relation to this core community that will be in a moment the key divisions er the the of this formation um of this classification begins as follows.

What, we wonder, would our fault-finding blogger make of that?

The problem is, as we have already hinted, that most people's notions of correctness are based almost entirely on *written* language despite the fact that speaking predates writing by several millennia and is, along with other embodied modes of communication such as gesture, our primary communicative resource. As Carter (2003: 6) notes,

> For many centuries, dictionaries and grammars of the English language have taken the written language as a benchmark for what is proper and standard in the language, incorporating written and often literary examples to illustrate the best usage. Accordingly, the spoken language has been downgraded and has come to be regarded as relatively inferior to written manifestations. Both in the teaching and learning of English and modern foreign languages and in educational institutions and in society in general, oral skills are normally

valued less, with literacy being equated almost exclusively with a capacity to read and write. In this respect, the similarity of the words 'literature' and 'literacy' is revealing. What is written and what is literate is accorded high cultural status.

The prestige attached to writing has been so great, historically speaking, that writing systems come almost to represent language itself – the language in its most correct form, its most prestigious form and its most fixed and authoritative form. It is its visual manifestation that makes this possible (writing is a visual mode) and, as Halliday points out, 'it is only after language is written down that it becomes an object accessible to conscious attention and systematic study' (1989: 96). This does not fully explain the process of standardization, however, which develops through a combination of chance, some academic or literary interest and, very often, a large dose of ideology and political involvement. For instance, in English, before spelling became more or less fixed, it did not really matter whether the word 'take' was spelt 'teik', 'teyk' or even 'tek' as it would be said in some dialects. How it ended up, in English, as 'take' is largely the result of certain publishers gaining market dominance and the development of dictionaries such as that of Dr Johnson in 1755. Standardization of English grammar developed equally organically, largely through biblical translation and literary composition rather than (as we noted in Chapter 2) through the establishment of a language academy to codify the language and lay down norms. This can come as a surprise to people from parts of the world where official bodies monitor the language to decide what is acceptable or not, often quite regardless of people's actual usage. Nevertheless, as we have seen, English has its fair share of language police!

But while in the public mind correctness is felt to reside in books, for linguists (and linguistically-aware language teachers) this is far from being the case. With the advent of audio and video recording, followed by the construction of computerized corpora (that is, collections of speech samples), spoken language can now be extensively analysed in the way that written language has always been, and the different affordances of each mode can be identified and explained. Basing opinions of what is 'right' and 'wrong' on just one of these communicative modes while ignoring the reality of the other is a mistake. This is particularly so when opinions and attitudes about 'speaking properly' are used unreflectively to damage other people's credibility and confidence. If only our language police would record and transcribe examples of their own naturally-occurring speech! We suspect they would be as appalled by some of their own grammar and pronunciation features as they are by those of others.

So are speech and writing always quite different from each other? Before moving onto the next part of the discussion, we would like to throw a small task your way in preparation. We call it the Spokenness-Writtenness continuum task. Everything written goes on the right-hand side of the continuum and everything spoken goes on the left. But *where* on the continuum? If a piece of writing seems to you to be very characteristic of the idea of 'writing', or a spoken text to be highly representative of spoken communication, then you would put it right at one of the ends. If, though, a written text has some of the characteristics of speech, or a spoken text has some of the characteristics of writing, then you would put it closer to the middle. So we're going to give you four different kinds of text, and ask you to place them on the continuum. Are they more towards the spokenness side, or more towards the writtenness side? We'll return to this later in this chapter but we want you to start thinking about it now before reading any further. See how you get on.

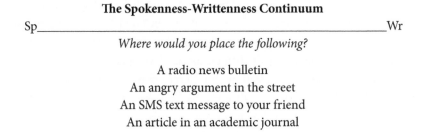

The Spokenness-Writtenness Continuum

Sp_____Wr

Where would you place the following?

A radio news bulletin
An angry argument in the street
An SMS text message to your friend
An article in an academic journal

7.4.1 Speaking and writing have different characteristics

Now that we have established that most people's notions of correctness tend to be derived from how we write rather than how we speak, let's now take a look at some of the characteristics of each of these two communicative modes. A good place to start is by thinking about how we experience doing writing and doing speaking.

7.4.2 Writing and speaking let us do different things

Writing and speaking are not only different modes of communication done in different ways, they are also used for different purposes and in different contexts. There are things that we do with writing and there are things that we do with speaking, and this is because writing is very good for some things but not for others, and the same goes for speaking. They each let us do different things.

Writing allows us to keep a record of things, which is, of course, why it developed in the first place. Record keeping plays a crucial role in the development of civilizations and the maintenance of cultures, whether it be recording the moon's cycles, cataloguing herbs used in healing, reporting the events surrounding a famine, sharing stories and myths and so on. We use writing to pass on information to other people who may not even yet be born and of course we can read for ourselves what was written before we ourselves were born. Writing helps us to not forget. But more than that, writing is a resource for thinking and creating with because it involves slow thinking and reflection as we shape and reshape our thoughts, and sometimes the process takes us along paths that we hadn't previously intended to go down. This is something novelists often report on but which academics find themselves doing too. Finally, writing allows us to shape our thoughts through the process of editing. We have the time to seek the most apt items of vocabulary or play with the order of things, to go back over what we have written and reframe things that don't quite say what we want them to say. And it is this process of editing which ensures (we hope) that the end product appears whole and complete, in other words, *composed*. Hence, written language is seen to be or expected to be more 'correct', more 'polished' than its verbal counterpart, spoken language and this, perhaps, explains some of the outrage expressed over alleged falling standards in relation to social media interactions such as Instagram, which, as we discussed in our last book, can be seen as having some of the characteristics of spokenness which we discuss below.

Unlike solitary writing, speaking almost always involves other people being present (unless of course you are speaking to yourself!). It is a collaborative mode, a co-production between people who are always present in one way or another (in person, on the phone, Skype) and because of this it has a quality of spontaneity as participants respond and react to each other in real time. Even formal speaking such as a lecture has a collaborative dimension with regard to audience reception and intervention, unless, of course the speaker reads out loud a written piece, in which case it cannot really be described as 'speaking' in the way we mean it here. Some might argue that writing has lost its record-keeping status because we can audio or video record people speaking. This is, of course, true, but it does not change the point that speaking and writing let us do different things. Think of watching a YouTube video of, say, David Crystal giving a talk on one of his many linguistic topics and then think about reading one of his books on the same topic. They achieve different aims. The lecture does not replace the book. It cannot contain everything that is in the book and it cannot discuss what is in the book in the same way as the book does. What the lecture does is draw out certain aspects of the book. It offers more examples, perhaps. It adds in some anecdotes or new examples that the speaker has come across since writing the book. It might unpack some aspects of the book but leave out many others. Have a think yourselves about the different experience of writing a lesson plan and teaching the actual lesson. They are not one and the same thing.

So far we have only been able to scrape the surface of ways in which writing and speaking are used to do things and we would recommend that readers refer to other books on the subject, such as the collection edited by Barton and Papen (2010), which focuses on some of the various things people do with writing. A small task that you might undertake yourselves, as readers of this book, could be to spend a bit of time noting down the sorts of things you do with writing and the sorts of things you do with speaking. That way, you will get a better sense of how we use the two modes. In the meantime, we move on to look at specific aspects associated with writing and speaking in order to get a little closer to understanding their different configurations and uses.

7.4.3 Writtenness and spokenness

As we have just pointed out, doing writing and doing speaking let us do different things. But, of course, it is more than that. They let us do different things because of the contexts in which we do them and the semiotic resources available to us when engaged in each (see Figure 7.1). For example, in the spoken utterance "Look at that!" we cannot know what 'that' is unless we are actually physically there with the person who spoke. If we were writing this we would have to describe in words what 'that' was (a strange-looking vehicle, a beautiful sunset) but the fact is, this is something that would occur only in speech and not writing unless it was part of a written dialogue in a story or a play. Speaking lets us do this while writing does not. This is one of the characteristics of spokenness that differs from writtenness.

In the following, in order to investigate how writing and speaking differ, we have organized our discussion under four parallel descriptors which help us to see the differences and then understand why it is relevant to pay attention to them. However, we want to stress that these descriptive categories are not to be taken as firm differences. For instance, with our first category, speaking as collaborative versus writing as self-contained, sometimes writing is a collaborative co-production between two or more people working on the same document and sometimes speaking is self-contained as in individually preparing a speech to give to an audience. Our aim here is to encourage readers to think about how speaking and writing are different and the different communicative strategies we use when we write as opposed to when we speak and, as a result, avoid making errors of judgement about correctness. We take each in turn.

Speaking is collaborative/writing is self-contained

One characteristic of spokenness is the way speakers share the meaning-making process. Sometimes, particularly between people who know each other well, one person finishes the point that the other is making as shown in Example 7.7, taken from a radio programme in which two young men (S1 and S2) are talking about how they first became friends at school.

Example 7.7

S1: You were in one class and I was in the other, so just by our class we were in . . .

S2: . . . we were sworn enemies

S1: Yeah and it was when you gave me

S2: . . . that black eye, yeah

S1: . . . . we became friends

This particular characteristic of spoken interaction is, essentially, what makes a conversation flow and is arguably one of the most important advantages of having a conversation in the first place. It is often in the to-ing and fro-ing between participants that ideas are formed or, as in the case above, memories evoked. It also plays a role in promoting social cohesion. This kind of collaboration is not available in writing which, because it is a more or less solitary activity and lacks the shared immediacy of conversational speech, needs to be a self-contained, stand-alone text. This does not mean that writing is not social or that it does not enable ideas to be formed. On the contrary, by its very nature, it requires thoughtfulness, as we have already pointed out, and its very existence implies social interaction because writing always involves readers.

Speaking responds/Writing anticipates

The second distinguishing category can be understood by looking at Example 7.8, which illustrates the responsiveness of speaking. It is a transcribed extract from a conversation between two people discussing an artwork representing a scientific process and which is made out of a combination of materials, primarily glass. Both speakers are standing together besides the artwork which is hanging on a wall.

Example 7.8

S1: And why did you use those particular materials?
S2: Oh I used to work with neutrons all the time.
S1: No but I mean the actual materials for the painting for the picture.
S2: Oh because glass has the quality of translucence.
S1: Ah I see.

In this example, there is a momentary breakdown in the flow of the conversation which stems from a misunderstanding about what is being referred to by 'those materials'. From the artist's perspective 'those materials' refers to the materials he is *representing* in his work, in this case 'neutrons' but from Speaker 1's perspective, as the clarification in line three confirms, 'those materials' refer to the materials he used in making the artwork. But no matter. Because of the possibility of instant feedback in spoken interaction, either verbally as in the example above or non-verbally, such as a facial expression, the misunderstanding can be quickly repaired and the conversation can proceed. In writing, which does not allow for such instant response, this would not be possible as there is almost always a physical and temporal gap between the writer writing and the reader reading, even in instant messaging interactions such as WhatsApp. We cannot repair readers' misunderstandings as they occur, so we try to anticipate what those might be in advance and cater for any potential confusion, even if we are not always successful. When we write, we have to pay more attention to the communicative choices we make, the words and grammatical structures we use, how we arrange our ideas and even the non-verbal resources we include such as italics or bold for emphasis or emoticons to communicate feelings. As we have remarked, writing is a slow mode of communication which gives us time to think about how best to write what we want our readers to understand.

Speaking can be verbally vague/writing needs to be verbally explicit

We have already alluded to the significance of the type of participation involved in any communicative event. In the case of speaking, the co-presence of the interlocutors is fundamental to the range of resources speakers can draw on. In writing, the separation between the co-respondents, the solitary writer and the absent reader, similarly influences the semiotic choices available. Both speaking and writing draw on context, and both are socially situated in that we have to take account of audience or readership when engaged in either communicative mode, but only speaking can enlist the physical world in its meaning-making. We can use vague verbal references to things, as we have already mentioned, saying 'Look at that' or simply 'Look', but accompanied by clarifying non-verbal references such as pointing or indicating with a movement of your head. In writing we need to name or describe what we are referring to though, as we pointed out earlier, we wouldn't use writing for this kind of communicative activity. It's not one of the things we do with writing. In fact, if we were to reproduce it as dialogue in a story, say, we would need to provide an explanatory context for it: ' "Look at that!" she cried, pointing to a strange-shaped cloud in the sky.' To reiterate the important, but not always recognized point, we use writing and speaking for different things.

Speaking is loose and open-ended/writing is compact and complete

It is undoubtedly these characteristics of speech and writing that have led to some of the misconceptions that we referred to above about what is correct and what is not. Indeed, this aspect is the effect of the other aspects that we have just outlined. Writing, by its very nature has to stand in its own right, it has to be a complete entity so to speak, no loose ends. A piece of writing is essentially a 'finished' item, at least once it has been put out into the world. Of course, there are written genres that are not intended to be read by anyone other than the writer herself, private diaries and journals, notes taken at a meeting, for instance. But in general, the concept of standard language is based on written language rather than spoken for reasons we mention later on in this chapter. Speaking, as is clear by now, is quite different. Because of its of-the-moment, interactive nature, it allows us to leave things open, to throw out ideas without having to square them off. If you were to do this in writing, the reader would get pretty fed up with you because they want to know what you think and you would not be there to clarify. However, what is perhaps more important in relation to the structure and organization of these two modes is the looseness of speaking, essential for listener accessibility and information processing and the compactness of writing, essential for readers to follow narrative threads. Let's take another look at Example 7.6, the extract from a professor's lecture, repositioned here for convenience.

> Now what I've what I want you to imagine at the start is a core community what I want us to imagine is a core community eventually and I'm going to talk about everything in relation to this core community that will be in a moment the key divisions er the the of this formation um of this classification begins as follows.

If we put this into writing it might look something like this:

Example 7.9

In a moment I want you to imagine a core community, which is central to everything I am going to discuss, starting with the key divisions of this classification.

All that has happened between the two versions is that the written version has, essentially, been cleaned up. All the hesitations and repetitions have been removed and the core information has been differently packaged into a single sentence which uses a clause subordination (which is central) and participial phrasing (starting with) as a means of organizing the points in a kind of hierarchy of relevance. In the spoken version (Example 7.6) we can identify *eight* clauses and their respective verbs and it is precisely this open, loose shape of speech that renders it suitable for being listened to compared to writing. Hierarchy or salience of information is achieved more by intonation and voice pitch, pauses and hesitations than by structures such as subordination and nominalization which are more typical of writing, particularly formal writing. For a final comparison, take a look, now, at

Example 7.10, which is an extract from a published article by the same geography professor on the same topic.

Example 7.10

These distinctive formations, the canopies of which are dominated by six leaf-shedding members of the Dipterocarpaceae, have been much neglected by ecologists, although they often comprise the most important single formation over much of the region, and play a significant role both in the ecology of the area's distinctive forest wildlife and in the economy of many local peoples.

If the professor had read, out loud, the whole article as it is written here, it is likely that the students in his lecture would have quickly fallen asleep or logged onto their Facebook page. You have all probably been in that very position yourselves, and we certainly have! This kind of communication is designed to be read, not read out loud.

These examples show some of the ways in which we can think about what characterizes spokenness and what characterizes writtenness and give some insight into how misconceptions arise about what constitutes correct language. Using writing as the basis of standardness is one thing, but using it as the basis of *correctness* is quite another. So when self-appointed experts such as our fault-finding blogger above complain that people do not speak properly or proclaim, as one academy school in the UK did in their behaviour manifesto, that 'Students must always speak in complete sentences!' they are making the category error of thinking that writing is the model for all language. Halliday firmly insists that the term 'sentence' is only relevant with reference to *writing*. A sentence is 'that which extends from a capital letter following a full stop up to the next full stop' (1989: 66). Speaking, as we all know, does not have capital letters and full stops. More recently, using the evidence provided by spoken corpora, Carter and McCarthy demonstrate that ellipsis as in *Sounds good* or *Hope so* is entirely normal – it is, in fact, standard – in spoken English (McCarthy and Carter 2012: 337). To start from the base of the sentence as the key unit is to get the wrong end of the stick. Normal speech is not really made up of sentences at all! Those who insist on 'complete sentences' would perhaps benefit from some self-reflection, not to mention linguistics knowledge, before they start policing the speech of others.

We now want to return briefly to the small task we asked you to do earlier on in this chapter to see whether your opinion has shifted in the course of reading so far. Let's take each piece of communication in turn.

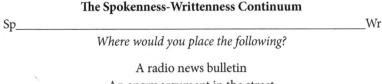

The Spokenness-Writtenness Continuum

Sp_____Wr

Where would you place the following?

A radio news bulletin
An angry argument in the street
An SMS text message to your friend
An article in an academic journal

The argument and the academic article are pretty straightforward, are they not? The argument (spontaneous, open-ended, with lots of overlapping, interrupting and repetition) goes well over to the left, and the article (planned, highly structured, lexically dense) well over to the right. What about the other two? At first sight, a radio news bulletin goes immediately well into the spokenness side of the continuum – it is presented in spoken mode, and we listen to it. But is it speech? Is it spoken communication? A bit of a clue lies in the name we give to the person giving out the news. They are called a 'newsreader' and are often introduced by the phrase 'the news is read today by . . .'. This may be oral communication, but it is not actually speaking as such. Of course, to render it accessible to listeners, what has been written to be read out loud will have adopted some of the qualities of spokenness, so the question remains: is it more towards the spokenness side or the writtenness side? It is up to you to decide.

Moving onto the next item, an SMS to your friend, this is clearly a written text made with letters rather than sounds, so it goes on the writtenness side. But where on that side? Does it have the major characteristics of writtenness? An immediate response might be that it is more like speaking, despite being in written form. But consider, do you write in sentences with capital letters and full stops? Do you include hesitancy (ers and ums) or repetitions? Be careful here, because we are not necessarily talking about formality and informality, though that might affect the productive aspects of an SMS. Your answer may be that it all depends on who is writing the SMS, and that some people follow the conventions of writing in SMS, or some of them, whereas others do not.

Looking at speaking and writing from a linguistics perspective enables the teacher to get to grips with the fact that they really are *different*. This fundamental insight should inform every decision the teacher makes with regard to what is correct, what is authentic, how speaking competence is assessed, and whether a supposed error of speaking is actually more an error of writing.

7.5 TESOL and representations of communication

Since the introduction of CLT there has been, as already mentioned in earlier chapters, a proliferation of coursebooks available for use all over the world. Each new publication or series claims to be 'groundbreaking', with an ever expanding array of digital materials to accompany them (see Gray 2010a). However, what we tend to find is that although the materials offer increasingly up-to-date content in terms of the topics included and the range of text types, there is a remarkable similarity between them. This is not surprising, as human communicative interactions do not vary that much over time. People still buy things in shops, they still take trains and buses, they still give and accept invitations and so on. We want to draw attention to how communicative activity is represented in these coursebooks and how the concept of the 'four skills', so beloved of so many initial teacher training courses, can actually militate *against* effective language work. We go into more detail in Chapter 9 about how we can work with both 'found' and coursebook materials; but here we focus on some taken-for-granted concepts and assumptions. The first relates to representation of communicative interaction, the second to the teaching of the so-called four skills.

7.5.1 Representations of communicative interaction

Let's take a look at how speaking is typically represented in ELT coursebooks and compare it with natural speech. Using the act of 'asking for directions' we compare two examples: one taken from *New Headway Elementary* (2006), one of a highly successful series of books which has been updated regularly since the 1980s and the other collected live out on the street.

The coursebook example is part of a listening exercise in which students are provided with a 3D sketch of a town map with buildings labelled with their names (bank, post office etc.). The students are given a gap-fill script of several conversations all concerned with asking for and giving directions and their task is to fill in gaps as they listen to the people having the conversation. We are not particularly interested here in the actual exercise in hand but rather in the representation of the conversation itself. Here it is.

Example 7.11

A: Excuse me! Is there a newsagent's near here?
B: Yes. It's in Church Street. Take the first street on the right. It's next to the music shop.
A: OK. Thanks.

On the face of it, this seems a perfectly acceptable and unproblematic dialogue, typical of ELT coursebooks from almost any period and almost anywhere in the world. It is pitched at a level of complexity that elementary level students could handle, and uses classic expressions of direction (the first street on the right) prefaced by the imperative form 'take'. Giving directions or instructions is typically encountered in coursebooks in relation to teaching the use of the imperative, a structure that is, incidentally, rather rare in spoken English as corpus research confirms (see O'Keefe et al. 2007). People actually tend to prefer to use alternative, less direct, ways of telling people what to do such as 'if' clauses (*If you turn right at the traffic lights* versus *Turn right at the traffic lights*), an issue of pragmatics rather than of grammatical form, as a linguistically aware teacher would immediately recognize. However, despite this example being apparently uncontroversial, there are some anomalies that stand out for the linguistically thoughtful teacher and student, particularly if they take account of our next example (Example 7.12) which is transcribed from a recording borrowed from Howard (2008: 15).

Example 7.12

A: Excuse me, do you know how to get to Victoria Park from here?
B: Sorry?
A: Victoria Park.
B: Um, yeah it's but whereabouts in Victoria Park do you want to go do you know?
A: Just generally where it is.

B: Just the park.

A: Yeah.

B: Um . . . if you go . . . actually because you're here it probably just go down there just walk along the road.

A: Yeah.

B: On the right you'll see a pub called the Victoria Park.

A: OK.

B: Park's behind it you're right on top of it the park park's basically behind all these buildings.

A: Ah OK.

B: You'll probably get to quick quicker by walking through the estate I don't know but definitely you have to go down turn to your left when you see the pub on your right there's actually big gates that's the entrance.

A: OK, alright thank you.

We do not have to go into any detail when comparing these two examples, as the differences between them are patently obvious. There are, though, one or two features that we feel are worth drawing attention to. At the level of interaction, we can see that Example 7.11 displays none of the thinking-while-speaking behaviour of Howard's Example 7.12 in which the speaker takes a few seconds to orientate herself both metaphorically and geographically before starting out with her instructions. There are obviously many other features present in the authentic conversation, the reiterations, the reference to visible and invisible landmarks and the uncertainty or rather lack of the seamless certainty that is shown in Example 7.11 in which speaker B unhesitatingly proceeds. We leave you to make the comparisons, but for now imagine your student, having learned how to ask and follow directions from the coursebook, finding himself confronted with speaker B's explanation in Example 7.12. You may even have been in just such a situation yourself!

Such comparisons are somewhat unfair because in the case of the coursebook, the aim is simply to introduce learners to *ways of saying* rather than to engage in authentic communicative activity. This is something Howard himself explored when he discussed with a group of ELT teachers the use of authentic recordings such as Example 7.12 in the classroom versus using cleaned-up coursebook examples. He found that on the whole, teachers preferred using coursebook examples for a number of reasons, most of which concerned the issues of standard 'correct' language and clarity with regard to pronunciation which, he suggests, are 'expectations of spoken dialogues that have been conditioned by using language textbooks' (Howard, 2008: 49). Or we could put it another way and say that very often, coursebook examples of *speaking* actually carry many of the characteristics of *writtenness*. If you were to put them on the Spokenness-Writtenness continuum which we introduced above they might sit somewhere in the middle, just slightly on the side of Spokenness.

Our final example (Example 7.13) comes from a more recent coursebook, *Empower* Starter level, published by Cambridge University Press in 2016.

Example 7.13

A: Excuse me, where are the shops? Are they near here?

B: Yes, there are a few shops in New Street. That's just near here. There's a small food shop and there's also a good bookshop. It's really big and the people there are very nice. Oh, and there's a nice Italian café in New Street near the station. They have very good cakes and great coffee.

A: What about a bank?

B: Bank? Yes there's a bank in Old Street. It's near the school.

A: And restaurants?

B: Well there's a new Chinese restaurant, that's in Old Street, but it's expensive.

When we consider the relationship between speaker A and speaker B, who are apparently strangers on a street as indicated by speaker A's use of the typical attracting-the-attention-of-a-stranger phrase, 'Excuse me', we might wonder why B launches into such detail ('It's really big and the people there are very nice'; 'there's a new Chinese restaurant . . . but it's expensive'). Some people are more naturally effusive than others, but it is extremely unlikely that anyone would list and even evaluate such an array of shops in this way. And just as in Example 7.11, speaker B uses specific names of landmarks (in New Street, in Old Street, near the station, near the school) that A could not possibly be expected to know. There is no suggestion of any of the non-verbal communication that typifies Example 7.12, not even an 'over there' or a 'that way'. What's more, poor speaker A never really gets a proper answer to his question, 'where are the shops?'!

Are we saying that coursebooks are wrong to present fragments of pretend-authentic dialogue such as these? No, of course we're not. Part of the work of a coursebook is to provide examples of language which can be used for the purposes of demonstration and analysis of language learning aims such as particular grammar points, vocabulary items, as in Example 7.13, or aspects of pronunciation. Relying entirely on authentic language samples would not provide the clean focus that 'manufactured' coursebook samples offer. In fact, invented dialogues, simplified reading passages and suchlike aids to learning have been successfully used in language teaching materials for millennia: Dickey (2016) reproduces some of the texts used in the ancient world by Greek-speaking lawyers, soldiers and merchants who needed to learn Latin. Simplification happens for a good reason. Normal spoken interaction is often just too context-dependent and its structure too deeply buried for it to be used as a model for learners, especially less advanced ones. Even people who have made an academic specialization out of pointing out the inauthenticity of much coursebook speech, and its quantifiable distance from real speech, have accepted that some measure of artifice is inevitable (see e.g. Gilmore 2004). What we are saying, though, is that teachers need to be clear about what these 'dialogues' are and what they are not. In fact most students will realize, particularly if a teacher raises the issue as a classroom activity, that most people use language differently to coursebook representations. As we have already pointed out, being a beginner in English does not mean you are a beginner in language!

7.5.2 Rethinking 'the four skills': Three contentions and considerations

The final issue that we want to raise is that of 'the four skills', a concept so well used that every language teacher who has ever been on a TESOL course has it fixed firmly in their mind. We believe that this concept is problematic because it focuses more on communicative activity as something that we *get* than on communicative activity as something that we *do*.

Our first contention is that the term 'the four skills' implies separateness, self-containment, such that they can be taught or learned in isolation. Coursebooks are often divided into sections each dealing with one of these four skills (speaking, writing, reading and listening) and some courses are even organized institutionally into separate classes dealing with each. However, you cannot separate out communication into such neat packages as the four skills concept might imply, and some coursebooks are beginning to acknowledge this. For a start, speaking always entails listening, even if it is listening to your own voice, and writing always entails reading. Although we can 'do' listening and reading in isolation (listening to a podcast, reading a novel), these would not normally be the sort of thing we would do in a classroom situation without having some kind of associated 'language learning' activity to do. Reading can involve writing, note-taking for example, and it can also involve speaking – like when you summarize snippets from an article or a blog you might be reading while in the company of a friend. Writing may well involve speaking – think of planning a celebration meal with a friend. You might discuss the things you need to buy and write them down as a list. In TESOL, these kinds of activities are typically known as 'integrated skills': we would simply call them communication!

The second thing that we take issue with is the widely held notion that there are active or productive skills (speaking and writing) and there are passive or receptive skills (listening and reading). This is a misleading and ultimately false dichotomy. *All communication is active and all communicative activity is productive.* As readers and listeners, even if we are alone or do not interact directly with those we are listening to or whose work we are reading, we do not passively receive information, we *engage* with it on many different levels – emotional, intellectual, imaginative, analytical and so on. In fact all language work is active, all language activity is social, all language activity is purposeful and all language activity is situated (that is, it does not exist independent of a context, as we showed in Figure 7.1).

Our final point is related to how 'skills' activities are conceived by coursebook designers and made use of by teachers. This very much depends on how learning itself is understood both socially and culturally. Sometimes, as we have already suggested in our discussion of Spokenness and Writtenness, what is labelled 'speaking' is not speaking at all but more like reading out loud. What is labelled 'writing' is often more to do with practising a grammar point than developing actual writing. Listening is often presented as a task in which you eavesdrop on someone else's conversation to hear how things are pronounced, and reading is sometimes no more than a basic vocabulary checking exercise. There is nothing wrong with these learning activities. They can be useful and students enjoy them because they can see their learning advance. However, they are more about performance and display than about the thing they purport to be. Real speaking, listening, reading and writing are dynamic and highly contextualized activities and unless this is taken into account in the classroom, they will tend to remain largely mechanical and abstract exercises.

The question that needs really to be asked is what can be taught and what cannot. Can we really teach speaking and listening? Can we teach students reading and writing? Or is it that we can only teach students to recognize and produce specific spoken genres (ordering in the café, introducing yourself, asking for directions), grammatical structures, vocabulary and pronunciation with some pragmatics along the way? Is this what we are really doing when teaching the four skills? Our suggestion is that it is and we should be aware that this is what we are doing. Essentially, what the 'skills' provide is the *content* for all those other learning activities, the texts and the topics with which to explore, learn and develop the linguistic aspects of the new language. Our students do not need to learn how to speak, listen, read or write as such: they need to learn how to do these things in English.

7.6 Conclusion

In this chapter, we have shown the value to teachers of engaging in detailed analysis of different language phenomena using a framework that views communication as multimodal and context oriented. We have invited teachers to appreciate that language use is not random, but a matter of choice and encouraged them to share this with their students so that they, in turn, can better see the relevance of learning different linguistic forms and actually getting them right. As the pioneers of CLT realized, the mastery of form without an equivalent understanding of function is close to useless. This is why teachers need *linguistics* knowledge, not just grammatical knowledge, or knowledge of English, as we argued in Chapters 5 and 6. The approach we have used here allows us to challenge taken-for-granted beliefs about language and communication and move towards the kind of teaching that encourages analysis and reflection in which students learn what is useful, what is effective, what is appropriate and why, instead of focussing only on what is correct. Importantly, and as we will see in the next chapter, it also helps displace and diffuse the focus on NS norms that still characterizes so much – though not quite all – TESOL practice, and encourages the teacher to think about the already-existing language knowledge that the learner brings to the classroom.

Tasks/discussion

For teachers: Try doing the experiment devised by Ivanic et al. (2009) in which they asked their research participants to track their own 'literacy practices' for a single day by noting every single instance of writing, hour by hour. Then consider what type of writing it is, what language you are using, what register, who you're writing to, what about and why.

For teachers and students: Analyse a course book dialogue structured around a social interaction such as ordering a meal in a fast-food restaurant or introducing a new person to a group of friends. Then start paying attention to such conversations in real life (you might need to do some YouTube research). Make a list of the differences you notice. What kind of differences are they?

Suggested readings

English, F. and Marr, T. (2015), *Why Do Linguistics? Reflective Linguistics and the Study of Language*. London: Bloomsbury.
Our first book set out to show how viewing the world through a linguistic lens can help us to understand how we communicate and what resources we need to do it successfully. In it, we argued that the study of language, or linguistics, really should be a fundamental element of everyone's education, and that the first step in understanding how language works is to become a 'noticer' of language – of the communicative activity that surrounds us all, every day, wherever we are.

O'Keeffe, A., McCarthy, M. and Carter, R. (2007), *From Corpus to Classroom: Language Use and Language Teaching*. Cambridge: Cambridge University Press.
A book which builds on the huge advances of recent decades in corpus linguistics to show how the study of real, unmediated language can be brought into the classroom. It moves from demonstrating how to develop and use a corpus of (mainly spoken) language to analysing communication and designing effective, authentic language teaching materials.

8

What Does the Learner Bring to the Classroom? Students' Linguistic and Cultural Capital

8.1 Introduction

In the preceding three chapters we have argued that 'language expert' or 'language professional' should be a fundamental aspect of a language teacher's professional identity, and set out some of the areas in which linguistics can help inform classroom practice. Our contention is that a wide, rounded conception of the notion of language and a solid grounding in language study should be regarded as indispensable in TESOL teacher training and professional development. We have suggested, in line with our broadly social semiotic view of language, that language learners learn most effectively when the *context* of a communicative event (who? why? in what circumstances? with what intent? using what communicative resources?) is accorded much the same importance as its *form* (see Figure 7.1). Our belief is that an approach to TESOL which is rooted in this kind of language awareness, informed by the practice of linguistic ethnography, can radically transform teachers' and students' idea of what can or should happen in an English language classroom – and that this kind of approach goes some way towards answering the challenges posed by the unique role of English in the twenty-first century.

In this chapter, we take the process of linguistic and cultural awareness development a step further. We argue that, if we are to embrace the notion of the English language classroom as a site for the informed study of language, and if we are to acknowledge the variety of ways in which English is learned and used, to say nothing of the multilingual contexts worldwide in which English is situated, then we should welcome the linguistic capital that learners bring in the shape of the language(s) that they already speak. The L1, in other words, should be regarded as a teaching and learning resource. And not only the L1. If we once make up our minds to start from where the learners are, building on what they already know, then we are led inescapably into a process of engaging seriously, respectfully (though always critically) with globally diverse cultures of learning and teaching. Let's begin there.

8.2 'Vocabulary Camp': Educational culture and linguistics knowledge

Consider these two scenarios, presented here in the form of research notes taken during a visit Tim recently undertook to a university in China.

Daytime

On a university campus on the outskirts of Beijing, the summer's Vocabulary Camp is in full swing. In each of twenty or so classrooms all the way down either side of a long corridor, the scene is identical. The class is full of eager, attentive pre-teens and young teens, their desks arranged in a horseshoe pattern. At the front stands a notably attractive, stylishly dressed young Chinese woman – probably an undergraduate or recent graduate in English. With lots of laughter, smiles and encouragement (in Chinese), she is pointing out words on the PowerPoint display on the screen, and having the children repeat them as they appear. Sometimes the words are grouped along with other words with a similar syllable structure or stress pattern – though they are never grouped into sense or context units. '*Image . . . imagination . . . invention . . . repetition . . . politician . . . specified . . . unspecified . . . specialised . . .* ' Sometimes the words give the appearance of being simply random, as if picked by an electronic vocabulary generator. At the back of each class sits a monitor – also, it would seem, a student or recent graduate, wearing a Vocabulary Camp ID badge and looking at the stopwatch function on their phone. The job of the monitor is not only to keep order in the room – it's hardly a problem, to be honest – but to make sure that the PowerPoint display ticks along at the required rate. Every hour, a certain number of words must be shown and repeated in chorus.

Evening

In the evening, after dinner (which Chinese people tend to eat early), the outside balconies of the accommodation block of the university present a curious sight. At any given moment, two or three of the balconies will be occupied by a lone girl of perhaps twelve or thirteen (it's always a girl, not a boy – do the girls tend to be more studious?), pacing up and down as she attempts to memorise the next day's words for Vocabulary Camp. The light of her smartphone illuminates her face – an ancient Chinese tradition of memorisation mediated through the most up-to-date technology – and random, decontextualized words float across the evening air in a meaning-free stream as each of the girls chants rhythmically to herself: '*Variable . . . pressurized . . . architect . . . Christmas . . . candlelight . . . orange juice . . . interesting . . .*' Each girl spends a good hour out on her balcony, presumably to avoid annoying the other students staying in the apartment. They must be memorising hundreds of items. It doesn't stop till midnight.

Now, few western-trained teachers would consider Vocabulary Camp to be a model of good practice. It is axiomatic in modern TESOL theory that language items should be presented within a meaningful context, and that learners should assimilate them through communicative activity – the very opposite of what is happening here. And yet, as we will see in a little more detail in Chapter 9, memorization is a key element of Chinese learning culture, and Chinese learners tend to feel comfortable with it. It has been pointed out repeatedly by Chinese academics and practitioners alike that simply imposing a western-derived 'communicative' model of teaching in local classrooms is likely to meet with discomfort, incomprehension or outright resistance (Hu 2002, 2005; Rao 2002, Zhang et al. 2013). To be able to engage with these students, one must first understand them – and the understanding begins with language knowledge of the kind that we argued for in Chapters 6 and 7.

Let's take some of the basics. The Chinese writing system, of course, is not an alphabet. It is an ideographic system which consists of more than fifty thousand characters, of which about twenty thousand are usually to be found in dictionaries. To be considered functionally literate, you need to learn between two and three thousand of the most common ones (Ding 2007, Dong 2014). You can't tell exactly how a character is pronounced just by looking it, and while there are recurring root patterns or 'radicals', often you can't even guess, either. So the process of becoming literate in Chinese essentially consists of long hours of repetitive rote learning, repeating and copying, hour after hour, day after day, year after year, until a specified number of characters have been thoroughly memorized. As an aid to memorization, even the direction of each stroke of the pen is taught, as is the order of the strokes that make up each particular character (Knell and West 2015, Everson et al. 2016). At the same time, classic texts such as the three hundred Tang Dynasty poems are read, recited and memorized, an exercise in literacy development so familiar to so many generations of Chinese speakers that it has given rise to a popular saying reproduced in Zhang et al. (2013): 熟读唐诗三 百首, 不会写诗也会吟 ('If you have been reading and are familiar with three hundred Tang Dynasty poems, you will be able to recite a poem even though you cannot compose one').

In short, and even given modern digital tools and devices, the *only* way to learn to read and write in Chinese is by memorization, and *all* Chinese-speaking children are therefore taught to respect and try to develop this fundamental intellectual capacity. Along with recitation and obedience to the teacher, it forms the bedrock of the so-called Confucian educational culture. Official discourse, at least, regards memorization and recitation of the classics not as dull and repetitive but as a key learning tool and source of inspiration, as is suggested in the following extract from an article entitled 'Ancient texts not a burden on students', which appeared in China's leading English language newspaper:

> The newly revised senior high school curriculum includes more ancient Chinese poems and prose for recitation, sparking a public discussion on whether it will increase the burden on students. A Ministry of Education official has said recitation should not be regarded as a burden, as it will make students more familiar with traditional culture.
>
> Some people consider an increase in the number of subjects, texts or homework raises the students' burden, while reducing them eases their burden. But they fail to identify the real source of students' burden. By learning something they are interested in or something that is inspiring, the students will actually gain in knowledge and resolve, so such content cannot be an additional burden on them. (*China Daily*, 1 February 2018)

Chinese students, then, do not rely on rote learning and memorization because they are passive, or because they lack creativity or individuality, or whatever cultural stereotype might sometimes be invoked by frustrated western teachers – it is because this style of learning is held up to them as the ideal. Above all, it is because it has been their experience of their own successful attainment of literacy in Chinese (Starr 2012, Ding 2007). That is, they 'believe that repeated reading, imitating the teacher, and reciting can be helpful to English learning since it has long been proved by their L1 learning' (Zhang et al. 2013: 2).

A teacher who wishes to engage with Chinese students needs to acknowledge, respect and work with this cultural background. But to understand the cultural background, it is fundamentally necessary to understand the linguistic context within which it is rooted – that of a non-alphabetical writing system. We argued in Chapter 5 that the professional language teacher should combine pedagogical expertise with linguistics knowledge; and it is in areas such as this that it becomes clear how closely and vitally the two are related. There is an obvious need here for expert pedagogy: having ideas about how to make a class accessible to 'Confucian-heritage' learners; adapting methodological approaches in order to play to strengths such as memorization; being able to explain persuasively to these learners how and why communicative techniques might help them as much as traditional ones; and so on (we look at some of this in Chapter 9). But what underlies the pedagogical expertise – in fact, what makes it possible at all – is knowledge about the students' language. *One is of little use without the other.* And while the case of Chinese script and the Chinese tradition of memorization is perhaps an extreme one, the principle holds good for all linguistic-educational contexts: effective language teachers do not necessarily need to speak the language of their students, but they do need to have an informed interest in their students' linguistic and educational-cultural backgrounds. They can then begin to work with what the learners bring to the classroom – not just in terms of their prior learning experiences, but their linguistic knowledge and language practices too.

8.3 Working with local norms

It is inevitable (and quite rightly so) that a large element of what is taught in classrooms will be recognizably 'Standard English', broadly defined. However, as some of the proponents of ELF have argued, and as we noted in Chapter 4 during our discussion of learners' expectations, it is legitimate for learners, who as a general rule are investing substantial time and effort in their language learning, to demand that what they learn should equip them with the ability to communicate effectively (see Lock 1996, Figueiredo 2010). In the case of English particularly, with its role as the world lingua franca, this means that the teacher needs to go beyond the mere teaching of standard grammatical structure and lexis, and engage with wider questions of intercultural interaction and the deployment of a range of communicative resources. To put it another way, we think it indispensable that some of the reality of contemporary English use and usage be reflected in what teachers teach.

Now, this first means not only acknowledging, but actively valuing, and bringing into the classroom whenever appropriate, some of the immense variety of NS English, including regional varieties and what has been called World Englishes (see e.g. Galloway and Rose 2017). However, it also means incorporating into day-to-day teaching some of the characteristic features of NNS English use, along with some of the insights into intercultural communication which have arisen from research into ELF (see e.g. Kirkpatrick 2006, Alsagoff et al. 2012). It means valuing what the learners already know, starting from where they are, and resisting the temptation to test them always against a native-speaking ideal. Let us acknowledge immediately that this is a highly contentious area for many teachers, as Blair (2017) or Swan (2017) note, and may well meet with resistance, too, from educational managers, schoolchildren's parents and so on (the 'stakeholders' in TESOL that we identified in Chapter 4), to say nothing of students themselves. Certainly, the exposure of students to this kind of language must be carefully and persuasively explained to all involved, and it demands technical expertise and considerable professional and pedagogic confidence on the part of the teacher. It has, though, begun to happen in a systematic way in a few areas, and in a more informal way in others.

There is one English-using context in particular where the notion of working with and through local (in this case, NNS) Englishes in the classroom is quite well advanced, and this is the project currently under way in the Association of Southeast Asian Nations (ASEAN) countries. Kirkpatrick (2010, 2011, 2012) has described in some detail how, as part of the process of 'localizing' southeast Asian ELT, coursebooks, curriculum design, assessment, pedagogy and topics of classroom discussion are all designed to revolve around the communicative needs of southeast Asian learners, with no reference to NS norms and goals other than the requirement that 'standard' English be used for formal writing (e.g. in exams). Code-mixing, translanguaging behaviour (see Section 8.4) and use of L1 are regarded as unremarkable; students are encouraged to express their national identities (Burmese, Laotian, Filipino and so on, as well as numerous local cultures and identities) through English, and southeast Asian cultural norms are expected in conversation and classroom discussion rather than the ones associated with, say, British, Australian or North American native speakers.

It is the overwhelming primacy of *communication* as opposed to the attainment of NS-like fluency or 'standardness' that comes up again and again in discussions of lingua franca contexts such as the ASEAN one. Clayton (2006: 233) quotes a Cambodian government minister as saying, quite explicitly: 'You know, when we use English, we don't think about the United States or England. We only think about the need to communicate.' The point is not lost on people from other parts of Asia studying English in ASEAN countries. Kirkpatrick (2015) found, for example, that Chinese engineering and civil engineering students typically have little interest in acquiring prestige NS norms, cultural models or standardness, other than in order to pass written exams (which, granted, are of course no small thing). Beyond the necessary exams, as we can confirm from personal experience, as a general rule they simply want to learn to communicate effectively in English in work-related contexts, which, given their area of professional specialization, often involves ESL- or EFL-using Africans, either in Africa or in China. It was even noted that groups of Chinese students who went to study in the Philippines made better, faster progress than their counterparts who had gone to a UK university. Perhaps, surmises Kirkpatrick, they felt more comfortable surrounded by other Asian lingua franca users and learners of English, who were less likely to appear judgmental about their competence in the language, and more likely to have well-developed intercultural communicative skills, than British native speakers. This model of ELT, where Standard English is demanded in formal written contexts and students are introduced to specific written genres, but no particular reference is made or privilege accorded to the speech, cultural norms or discourse conventions of the traditionally English-speaking countries, has been referred to as 'post-Anglophone' English teaching (Clayton 2006, Kirkpatrick 2012). Galloway and Rose (2017) doubtless mean something very similar by their suggested term 'Global Englishes Language Teaching', or GELT.

Interestingly, it appears that there has been some resistance to the ASEAN project from teachers themselves, some of whom argue that only 'Standard English' (i.e. NS-derived norms) should be used in the classroom: in Thailand, to pick on just one of the countries involved, it has been noted that there has been rather slow progress in moving away from traditional NS norms (Kirkpatrick 2015). In considering why this should be, we should perhaps note first of all that in most parts of the world it takes a good deal of personal, emotional and financial investment to become a qualified, professional teacher of English in the state educational system. Teachers might then have a vested interest in maintaining standards, in every sense, and may feel that their position is compromised if what is seen as a less prestigious or less demanding model of language is allowed into the classroom. In this, of course, they may actually be being more conservative than their students (see Galloway and Rose 2013 for Japan). However, we would argue that it is also (in general, rather than in the particular context of ASEAN) because too many teachers have little or no sociolinguistic awareness of the kind we have highlighted throughout this book. Indeed, even the most basic grounding in sociolinguistic issues is routinely absent from teacher training in great swathes of the world, even though its relevance to what is taught in English language classrooms, and how, is *direct and inescapable*.

8.3.1 Why sociolinguistics?

What we mean by sociolinguistics in this context is principally knowledge about how English is distributed and used in the world – how it functions not only as a native language in the 'core' Anglophone countries, but as the world's lingua franca in the way we saw in Chapters 2 and 3. We mean who speaks English, who they speak it to, how many of them there are, what are the characteristic domains and functions often associated with global English use, and so on. Now, this kind of information about the use of a language might be interesting if you were learning Italian, or Afrikaans, or Greek: but as we pointed out in Chapter 2, for the learner and teacher of English it is of crucial import. Once you grasp that most English spoken in the world is used between non-native speakers, and that the *primary* role of English is that of the world's lingua franca, then everything suddenly looks very different. It has implications for *what*, exactly, you teach (British English, American English, Indian English, ELF, something else?), and for *how* you teach it. You might want to think about intelligibility and comprehensibility rather a lot, for example, and consider replacing traditional 'knowledge-of-other-cultures' coursebook content with reflective, pragmatics-oriented intercultural awareness exercises of the kind we suggested in Chapter 6. It is the knowledge of the wider context that drives change, innovation and renewed focus in the classroom. Some sociolinguistic awareness is therefore not an optional extra: it is a basic necessity for the English teacher in the twenty-first century.

We make no apology for coming back to this point repeatedly during the course of this book, for the lack of awareness has deleterious effects at every level. Are most English teachers really aware that most interaction in English takes place between non-native speakers (Seidlhofer 2005)? We are now years on from when Jenkins (2006a) first noted that the objective sociolinguistic reality was barely beginning to creep into the world's English language classrooms. And still, most learners and teachers remain trapped in a world of syllabuses, exam systems and coursebooks where English is either 'British' or 'American' (but anyway always NS-centred), and students are assessed on how well they can emulate supposed NS-like structures and norms, rather than by a 'performance model' which privileges international intelligibility and successful intercultural communication (Blair 2017; and see among others McNamara 2012, Gray 2010a, Kirkpatrick 2015, McKay 2012).

In our experience of global TESOL teacher education, in very large parts of the world, teachers who have imbibed a traditional view of language and languages (starting with their own), and who have not had the good fortune to have travelled widely overseas, are potentially working with two levels of misconception about the way English operates today. First, the default conception is that those their students will be using English with will be native speakers, which is presumably one of the reasons why so few teachers feel it necessary or useful to expose their student to NNS varieties of English. Second, it is sometimes thought, or imagined or just hazily assumed, that 'English-speaking countries' are places where everyone speaks English and that, in the capital city at least, lots of people speak standard English (see Marr 2005 for Chinese teacher-students). Again, this might help explain why so few teachers feel the need to expose their students to native but non-standard language. In both cases, though, the teachers' reluctance also clearly owes a great deal to assumptions and prejudices about what is 'correct' or 'good' usage, which have never been challenged in a linguistics class (Blair 2017, Sewell 2013).

Global TESOL at the classroom practice level is, then, shifting at an agonizingly slow pace – that is if it is shifting at all – partly because many teachers feel an ideological attachment to the idea of the standard language. But many also feel that teaching anything other than a traditional, codified, NS model of English is too difficult, confusing or unstable, especially when it comes to the matter of assessment (Newbold 2017). And of course, they have a point. There is little in most teachers' training or experience that would enable them to handle with confidence non-standard and non-native Englishes in the classroom, and lack of understanding about language can create distress and anxiety, especially among NNS teachers already faced with a daunting, idealized NS standard.

The proponents of ELF as an alternative model are, it seems to us, heading in the right direction with their emphasis on educating teachers about variation in English, but the larger target is perhaps coming only gradually into focus. What must drive the change is not just training in variation in English, and the role of English globally but 'the nature of language itself' (Dewey 2015: 191). In other words, teachers need core linguistics knowledge, with the crucial element of sociolinguistic awareness, indispensable for the lingua franca context in which global English is today positioned, as an integral part of it. One of the wholly positive effects of the (albeit very slow) diffusion of ELF-derived ideas into the ELT mainstream has been a new and welcome emphasis on language in language teaching (Jenkins et al. 2011, Sifakis 2014). But unless this new emphasis is accompanied by an understanding of such fundamentals as the distinction between correctness and standardness, for instance, then it rests on very shaky ground indeed. Increased linguistics and sociolinguistics awareness provides the key to opening up the classroom to a rethought, remodelled kind of ELT, in which NS standards and cultural norms lose their primacy and the educational backgrounds and linguistic and cultural inheritances of the students come to the fore.

8.4 Focus on the learner's language and culture

Once we approach working with Englishes with this kind of sensibility, three (at least) related issues of classroom practice very quickly come into focus. They are, first, the place of the learner's first language in the classroom; second, the use of locally appropriate goals and models of language; and third, the acknowledgement of local cultural practice and the pragmatics of transcultural communication as legitimate subjects for classroom discussion. We'll look at them briefly in turn.

8.4.1 The place of the learner's L1

We say a little about translanguaging in section 8.5. But well before translanguaging theory became widespread it had already been pointed out by Vivian Cook, with the use of an engagingly apt metaphor, that languages cannot exist in isolation from each other in the learner's mind: 'Learning an

L2 is not just the adding of rooms to your house by building an extension at the back: it is the rebuilding of all internal walls. Trying to put languages in separate compartments in the mind is doomed to failure since the compartments are connected in many ways' (Cook 2001: 407). And it is not only useless to try to keep the other language at bay: it is actively counterproductive. Comparing communicative strategies in English and in your own language, for example, is a hugely illuminating and revealing learning device, as we suggested in Chapter 6. How do you apologize? How do you compliment? How do you agree politely, disagree strongly, make jokes, swear, hesitate, back-channel, repair? The L1 is also naturally associated with the learner's regional, ethnic or national culture. Linguistically confident and culturally sensitive teachers will engage with the culture and welcome it into the classroom, validating the learners' own experiences and resources and turning them over time into sophisticated builders and organizers of their own communicative repertoires. This kind of language education can be genuinely *transformative*, in the sense of encouraging the emergence of new perspectives and ways of thinking that are both inclusive and discriminating, reflective and emotionally open to change (Mezirow 2000: 7). In short, we must be both realistic and constructive with regard to the role of the L1, encouraging a view of the students' own language(s) as a resource to be drawn upon, rather than as a barrier to learning which should be shut out of the English language classroom (see e.g. Machaal 2012 on the use of Arabic in a Saudi Arabian university). In Chapter 9 we show in some detail how this can work in practice.

Unfortunately, however, despite the best efforts of many academics over a number of years (see especially Cook, e.g. 1999, 2001), many ELT classrooms worldwide remain no-go areas for the student's L1. Indeed, use of the L1 in the classroom is regarded by many teachers and managers as simply unacceptable in *any* circumstances. One teacher from a Spanish-speaking country told us in some detail about how this orthodoxy was enforced in her bilingual secondary school.

> *[There were] instructions given about the use of Spanish. I didn't have the opportunity to use Spanish at all, not inside of the classroom or even outside of it [. . .] It was impossible to use Spanish or make use of the code-switching. Actually, the worst thing, I didn't have the opportunity to listen my students when they were crying and they wanted to share with me what happened. I had to ask them in English and they just looked at me like if I were crazy and finally gave up trying to explain. My bilingual coordinator always said that students were more than able to express their feelings in English even if that was not*

their L1, and that speaking in English all the time, teachers could guarantee that English learning would be meaningful and successful. We have to push students to use more English and less Spanish but never through the use of code-switching.

Very reasonably, you might think, this teacher did not feel that a total ban on the students' L1 was a constructive way to approach L2 learning. Having finished an MA in TESOL, she was confident in her knowledge and grasp of the issues and was keen to explore the dynamics of bilingualism in a creative way. She therefore began allowing a certain amount of Spanish by her students, in appropriate contexts and domains. However, this led only to a series of increasingly acrimonious meetings with the school's 'bilingual coordinator'. Shockingly but not entirely surprisingly, she was eventually fired from her job. There is much that is noteworthy in this distressing story, but perhaps the most striking element of it, for our purposes, is the background of the bilingual coordinator:

The most frustrating thing was that my bilingual coordinator has an amazing intercultural competence because she has travelled around the world, but she didn't study any degree that has to do with education or teaching, she has never taught in a classroom and her background is directly related with business, not teaching English. What she transmits is her level of English, not her experience being a teacher, and the most disappointing fact is that she doesn't want to be part of the educational field in terms of be inside the classroom or learn more about education.

This links directly back to our discussions in Chapters 1 and 5 of what particular field or fields of expertise tend to be associated with the discipline of language teaching. Once again here we see that the *only* qualification regarded as essential for taking on a professional pedagogic role as crucial as the coordination of bilingual policy in a bilingual school, is high competence in English. This particular individual had no qualifications or experience related to teaching or to language, and no interest in acquiring any. What is worse, she was not only uninformed of or indifferent to the disciplinary core underlying language education: she was *actively hostile to it*, whatever she thought it was, and terminated the employment of someone who was well versed in it and took it seriously. '*At the end of the day,*' the teacher told us, '*I lost my job because I was trying to transmit ideas about how capable and good are the non-native models to teach English.*'

As we saw in Chapter 4, all too often, it is the retrograde and ill-informed opinions of other stakeholders that carry most weight in language teaching contexts, over and above the opinions of teachers. This is likely to continue for as long as language teachers as a whole fail to own their own disciplinary identity and establish their expertise and right to be heard on matters pertaining to language. Until then, capable and progressive teachers like this one will remain isolated and vulnerable, and 'bilingual coordinators' like this one will continue to prove the truth of Goethe's dictum that 'everyone thinks that because they can speak, they can speak about language'.

8.4.2 Attainable goals and relevant models

While the bulk of commercial ELT coursebooks still tend to privilege UK and US voices (Lopriore and Vettorel 2015), some 'new generation' coursebooks, such as Cambridge University Press's *Empower* (2016), do feature some more NNS voices (and see Harmer 2015). However, even in quite recently published books, NNSs, when they appear, still often appear only as early-stage *learners*, rather than competent English users, and then often in a wearily hackneyed way (the heart always sinks at another 'My name's Michiko. I'm a student. What's your name?' opening chapter conversation). And of course, most coursebooks in use around the world, and especially in state schools and in poorer countries, are not in any sense 'new generation'. It was noted decades ago that there are psychology textbooks which feature lists of celebrated bilinguals such as Gandhi, Picasso, Marie Curie and Samuel Beckett (Grosjean 1982: 285). Given the potentially powerful motivational effect of such models of bilingual success, why, then, do so many ELT coursebooks still predominantly feature NS models from the UK and United States? It certainly does not have to be that way. Murphy (2014), for instance, lists a variety of 'intelligible and comprehensible' NNS models of English use, ranging from novelist Isabel Allende to footballer Thierry Henry and World Bank director Sri Mulyani Indrawata, and suggests a series of noticing and imitating tasks to help students make constructive use of them. And of course, for every country on earth there will be people from that country who can speak English and who are recognizable and popular or well respected. Bangladeshi university students might find it motivating to hear Nobel Prize-winning economist Muhammad Yunus speaking English, for example. Korean teenagers would surely enjoy hearing K-Pop band members like SF9's Inseong, or Monsta X's rapper I. M. (or whoever the star of the moment might be – it is *very* important to be up to date), communicating successfully in English-speaking environments.

Increasingly easy access to the internet, and the existence of YouTube in particular, opens up vast, indeed inexhaustible possibilities in this area: as Murphy remarks (2014: 267), this was 'unimaginable a mere decade ago'. Why would teachers *not* avail themselves of this resource?

We would in fact suggest that even speakers with quite limited competence can serve a positive and constructive purpose in the classroom. Here is the Colombian footballer Falcao, on joining Manchester United in 2014, in a dressing room interview with the club's TV station:[1]

> **Interviewer:** *What is your name? What should I call you? What do you like to be called?*
>
> **Falcao:** *I, I like, er . . . call me Falcao, because Radamel was my father, you know, my father's name. Is not my name. Some – somebody, some peoples told, or think, is my surname, but no. Is my second name [. . .] I . . . always . . . I always worked to er, to arrive a club like this. This club, this club, fight for the Premier League – eh . . . umm . . . every . . . bueno, this year don't play the Champions League but er, every year fight for to win the Champions League also . . .*

And so it goes on. Written down, it is pretty excruciating. Speech usually is – and that includes native speech, as we showed in Chapter 7. But watch it on YouTube and you are struck not by the poor English, but by the skilled use Falcao makes of the limited amount of English he has at his disposal. He is calm and collected, he takes his time to think and prepare what to say, he uses paraphrase and repair strategies, he gestures, he concentrates on the interviewer's questions. He is, in short, a natural communicator, and is highly motivated to achieve his communicative goal. As we have tried to show throughout this book, once we start to think of language as essentially a (quite possibly limited) set of communicative *resources*, rather than as essentially a matter of correct or incorrect linguistic *form*, this kind of text becomes available as valuable language learning material. Learners might well be motivated by seeing a model they can relate to, whether in terms of culture or of level of proficiency. And most importantly, in our view, the classroom becomes a place where communicative activity is thought about, analysed and discussed.

There is another aspect, too, to the over-representation of NS models and under-representation of NNS models in the classroom. As Cook (1999) pointed out twenty-odd years ago, and as has been confirmed since by much empirical research (see e.g. Derwing 2010, Munro and Derwing 2011), classroom learners are highly unlikely ever to attain the goal of native-like pronunciation – and to insist on this goal is therefore to condemn them to inevitable failure (see Chapter 6). Even to lead learners to believe that they might one day reach that standard is, claims Murphy (2014: 259), 'unfair' and 'perhaps even unethical'. So what goal should in fact be set? Davies (2017: 186) insists that there must be a 'described and assessable model' if learners' pronunciation is to be assessed effectively. His strong implication is that this can only realistically be a native model. However, as we showed in our little anecdote about the Bosnian-Australian students in Chapter 5, this apparently straightforward approach has its own problems. There are very many NS varieties of English, and 'Standard English', insofar as it exists at all, exists only as a *written* standard (Hickey 2012).

This circle can only be squared if it is clearly understood by all involved that, given that English is being taught primarily because of its role as the international lingua franca, it should be *intelligibility* and *comprehensibility* that are foregrounded in assessment rubrics rather than adherence to native norms (see McNamara 2012). At the end of the day, the goal (and therefore the assessment benchmark) of language teaching and learning cannot really be anything other than successful language use. Meanwhile, and naturally enough, a speaker who uses two or three languages will sound like a successful multilingual: there is little point in evaluating them as if they were two or three native-speaking monolinguals (Kirkpatrick 2009, García 2009, Li 2017). In François Grosjean's famous phrase, 'the bilingual is not two monolinguals in one person', and to judge their competence as if they were is to perpetuate a fundamentally mistaken 'monolingual view of bilingualism' (Grosjean 1989: 4).

Nevertheless, it is undeniably the case that teachers themselves can be resistant to this kind of approach, in which language teaching and learning are contextualized within a multilingual social environment, especially if they have been trained in educational cultures which place great emphasis on grammatical correctness and standardness in language. One Chinese teacher told Tim that her head of department, whom we shall call Mrs Wang, would never allow the use of English-using Chinese models like the businessman Jack Ma or the basketball player Yao Ming in the classroom, as he had (perhaps naively) suggested in a teacher-training workshop. The grounds for this were that they not only did not represent 'good' usage, but did not give students a challenging enough target to aim for. In Mrs Wang's mind, these models offered a substandard (for which, read non-native) model of speech which would encourage the students to be content with communicating in 'Chinglish'; and this she perceived not as creative translanguaging behaviour (as argued by Li 2016), but as lazy and sloppy. On the occasions that she (reluctantly) allowed supposedly relevant and familiar models to be used in the classroom, these were restricted to American-Chinese or British-Chinese bilinguals. That this entirely missed the point of offering attainable models of second language learning, such people having by definition been *born into* English-speaking societies, appears not to have occurred to her. It is in large part the dominance of these kinds of entrenched, ultimately ideological attitudes to language that is preventing the routine use worldwide of this most liberating and motivating of tools. Such attitudes can only be shifted, as we have argued throughout this book, by teaching teachers the fundamental tenets of linguistics, and especially sociolinguistics.

8.4.3 Studying culture/studying communication

Once the link is broken between the idea of correctness and adherence to (standard) NS norms, the astonishing diversity and fluidity of global English becomes available, for a suitably skilled teacher, as a classroom resource. The interrelatedness of language and culture has been a given in much TESOL discourse for a very long time, and has been a focus for serious academic attention in language teaching at least since the mid-1980s (see Byram and Feng's 2005 review of scholarship and research in the field). However, notions of 'culture' often still tend to get stuck at the national/ethnic level, causing needless anxiety among those many teachers who, for the very best of reasons, have had limited exposure to other cultures. 'How can I be expected to teach my students about the culture of English-speaking countries?' one teacher asked Fiona on a visit to Lahore: 'I have never been out of Pakistan.' But as Halliday (2007) reminds us, we 'have to go beyond the popular notion of culture as something defined solely by one's ethnic origins. All of us participate in many simultaneous cultures; and language education is the principal means by which we learn to do so' (2007: 284). Culturally and linguistically aware language teaching does not demand that global teachers know when Americans celebrate Thanksgiving, or why. It certainly does not require the rehashing of tired tropes about British people supposedly taking tea at four o'clock. Rather, it asks teachers to pay careful attention to how people interact, to consider how things like community, identity and power are played out in language, to look at why, for example, people might choose to speak standardly in one context and non-standardly in another, or why some speakers feel they have a greater right to interrupt than others.

A broader conception of culture(s) and communication goes some way towards repositioning the language classroom as a place where language behaviour is *noticed* and *discussed*, not just a place where structures are taught and norms imparted (though this is certainly also important). How do international users of English, NSs and NNSs alike, set about the task of understanding each other? Why don't conversations always go right? What can we learn from them when they go wrong? Look, for instance, at another slice of real-life conversation, recorded in London by our postgraduate student Sarno-Pedreira (2004) whose study we referred to in Chapter 6. Speaker A and speaker B are a gay couple who have been living together for four years. For context, A is a British flight attendant aged twenty-eight, and B is a Brazilian doctor aged thirty-three.

> **A:** Would you like some coffee, Paulo?
> **B:** Are you making for you?
> **A:** Say yes or no. Would you like some coffee?
> **B:** If you're making for you . . .
> **A:** Why don't you give a straight answer? [*irritated*]
> **B:** I just . . . OK . . . I'll have some.
> **A:** Thanks, darling . . . [*ironically*]. Sugar?
> **B:** A little [*hurt*].

This is very far removed from the scripted, perfectly sequenced interaction to be found in most coursebooks as we discussed in the previous chapter. Indeed, the language is in places not even formally 'correct' ('Are you making for you?'), and in terms of grammatical form the links between the utterances can be rather obscure. But a language teacher who had some knowledge of pragmatics, one of the key areas of linguistics that we outlined in Chapter 6, could surely make confident and productive use of this little exchange. And why should a text like this not have its place in the classroom? Why should we not consider and discuss real intercultural communication – the kind of interaction the learners are very likely going to be engaged in, one day – alongside scripted interactions? Why not compare the two? In considering how and why British and Brazilian norms of offering food and drink differ, and therefore why speaker A was irritated and speaker B hurt, the point is not really to compare British and Brazilian behavioural norms, fun though that may be. The point is, first, to encourage students to *notice* communicative behaviours, and second, to encourage them to reflect upon their *own* communicative needs and behaviours, and how language facilitates these behaviours.

This approach leads to the very heart of what it means to use, teach and learn 'the world's lingua franca'. It leads us inescapably to the consideration of questions which until very recently have been invisible in most English classrooms, and which in the vast majority remain invisible still. To what extent does an ESL-speaker who is Malaysian, say, or Ghanaian, need to adjust their use of English when in the UK or Australia rather than at home? Does it depend, apart from anything else, on who they are talking to – and should they automatically assume that a fellow NNS (perhaps even a compatriot) will accommodate to them? Why is it that NSs are often less intelligible to NNSs than their fellow NNSs are (Jenkins 2017), and how should NS–NNS encounters therefore best be approached? When NSs do accommodate to NNSs by attempting to make themselves more intelligible, is this always welcomed or does it risk coming across as condescending (Margić 2016)? How do we set about negotiating meaning and preventing misunderstanding in NNS–NNS encounters, where there might be few mutually understood cultural and conversational norms? When is prescriptive correctness considered important and desirable, and when do speakers tend to overlook anomalous usage or 'let it pass' in a spirit of communicative cooperation (Firth 1996, Kimura 2017)?

To make the larger question: why is all this ignored in most ELT classrooms? By being introduced to language variation and questions about language variation (core issues in sociolinguistics!) at an appropriate level, which effectively means 'as soon as they are ready' (Sewell 2013: 7), learners go beyond simply 'learning English' to become reflective learners and users of language, noticing the language and culture around them and monitoring their own and others' communicative strategies. Some years ago, during one of the periodic pushes (the second? the third?) for the foregrounding of language in language teaching, Wright (2002) identified two crucial aspects of teachers' language awareness: first, that teachers should develop their own sensitivity to language, their 'language radar' (a nice phrase), and second, that they should routinely oblige students to work with authentic language. In our view, the dual advance of digital technology and of English as the global lingua franca in the years since has only served to reinforce, in spades, the fundamental soundness of this approach. Indeed, the approach is indispensable, and the need for it urgent. As we shall see in the next chapter, 'What makes a classroom authentic?', the available resources for teachers to begin to do the kind of work that we have suggested are virtually limitless.

The key which will unlock them all is the teacher's own language awareness and linguistics knowledge.

8.5 Is translanguaging the future?

One area where a teacher's language awareness, and their knowledge of how language is used as a resource for meaning-making, might impact on classroom practice is that of translanguaging. While there has been work towards developing a practical theory of translanguaging (see e.g. Li 2018), it is perhaps more easily understood, at least for now, as an *approach* – a way of thinking about bilingual language use. Seen through a translanguaging lens, bilingual or multilingual speakers tend to use the language systems or parts of language systems that they have in their repertoire as a single, integrated system. So rather than focusing on how bilinguals move from one language to another (as, arguably, terms like 'code-switching' encourage us to do) a translanguaging approach focuses on the dynamic, fluid combining of linguistic resources in order to achieve a particular communicative goal. As we noted when we cited Grosjean (1989) in section 8.3.2, it is perhaps not terribly helpful to think of a bilingual person as a dual monolingual.

There is currently much interest among applied linguists in the implications of translanguaging theory for classroom practice. It is undeniable, though, that more attention has been and is being paid to the question of translanguaging in the context of bilinguals in mainstream education (see e.g. García and Li 2014, Creese and Blackledge 2010) than in ELT. The term, in fact, originated in the context of bilingual (Welsh/English) schools in north Wales in the 1980s (Lewis et al. 2012), and it is principally those who work and research in EAL and related areas who have been quickest to see its immediate relevance to their work. This does not mean that nothing is being done in the area of TESOL: Moore (2017), for example, makes an attempt to demonstrate to practitioners that the approach has applications, and can bear fruit, in TESOL environments, too.

Our emphasis throughout this book on issues such as the 'situatedness' of language in a cultural context, the value of the learner's own linguistic repertoire and the primacy of meaning over form will obviously, and rightly, suggest that we lean towards finding translanguaging a persuasive and productive way of thinking about language use. Sadly, we do not have the space to present here a comprehensive guide to what can be done with it in the ELT classroom. However, in Chapter 9, and especially in Section 9.2.3

'From out on the street to inside the classroom', you will find some examples of translingual practice and suggestions of how to use them. The logic, after all, is inescapable. If we agree that it is important to engage with, value and build upon learners' linguistic capital, and if the learners have access (even in a small or limited way) to multiple linguistic resources, then why would we shut these other languages out of the classroom? If we accept the L1, why would we not accept whatever other languages are used in the society that surrounds us?

8.6 Conclusion

As will be clear by now, when we talk about the English classroom as a site for learning about language, we mean pretty much all types of language, including non-native English and non-standard English, and including consideration of the learners' *own* language(s), properly contextualized, as a tool to aid understanding. To this end, we think the inclusion of non-native models of English, especially culturally appropriate and relevant ones, and explicit reference to the learners' own language and culture increase learner engagement and enhance motivation and aspiration.

The implications of this are large, and will worry some. However, stepping away from a NS-dependent, standard-only, English-only model does not mean chaos. It means the opposite: an observant, focused, rigorous and analytical approach to language, which considers how communicative behaviour and form interact, and uses key analytical concepts such as those of register and genre to help teachers 'to identify and focus on whatever aspect of language in use the learner needs most help with' (Painter 2001: 178). To see language as a set of communicative resources is to encourage learners to think about how language is suited to situation (Figueiredo 2010), rather than reaching for an 'off-the-peg', standardized (in every sense) set of words or structures. And we think that learners of English who also learn something about how language and communication actually work in the real world (for this is really what we mean by authenticity, as we show in the next chapter) will become better users of English, and better users of their own language.

Teachers should push themselves to go beyond the assumptions about nativeness, standardness and correctness which underlie most coursebook design and 'English-only' classrooms. They should, in short, embrace linguistic difference and diversity in all its shades, and value (and be seen to value!) the students' own linguistic and cultural capital. As we argued in Chapter 5, this takes self-confidence, which can only come from professional disciplinary knowledge and awareness. It needs a language specialist, or someone who is willing to work towards becoming one. In the next chapter, we show how teachers can engage with the language phenomena that they encounter, from signs in the street through to coursebook English and non-standard and non-native Englishes, and make use of these in their day-to-day work using some of the techniques of linguistic ethnography. For now, though, we finish this chapter with an anecdote from a teacher which sums up the failure of so many institutions to understand the educational value of developing language awareness and making use of the language that students bring.

8.6.1 The 'banned words'

In our previous book, *Why Do Linguistics?*, we wrote about the depressing fashion in the UK for banning certain colloquialisms, regionalisms and other non-standard words and pronunciations from schools, on the entirely spurious grounds that 'slang' usages harmed children's acquisition of Standard English. In criticizing this linguistically ignorant, intellectually incurious and counterproductive practice, we cited the example of a south London 'academy' school[2] with a large African-Caribbean student population, which saw fit to erect notices on its premises announcing 'Banned Words: *COZ, AINT, LIKE, BARE, EXTRA, INNIT, YOU WOZ and WE WOZ . . .*' (English and Marr 2015: 215). A year after the book came out, we met a former teacher at the school in one of our workshops. He had, he said, been so depressed by the 'Banned Words' policy and what it suggested about the mindset of the school's management, that he had finally resigned and taken a job elsewhere. But he still dreamed of subverting the policy. He wrote to us later:

> It would have been funny to create a subversive prohibitive sign with terms the teachers might not understand: Positively no **chirpsing** or **jamming** on the stairwells, do not wear the **creps** from your **drum** in these **ends**; **extra** behaviour in the corridor will not be allowed.

These, of course, are words associated primarily with young, black Londoners. Indeed it would have been funny! It would also have been original, thought-provoking, constructive, and a splendid way to get these pupils (and their teachers) thinking about standard and non-standard forms, language and identity, ethnic/regional variation, register, context, appropriacy and many other features of language. But another school employs that teacher now, and its gain is the academy school's loss. At the end of the day, it doesn't really matter whether the language we are talking about is standard or non-standard, native or non-native, formal or colloquial, or whether it is derived from an EFL context or a mainstream one like this. Teachers who have an interest in language tend to be interested in *all* kinds of language, including the language – and the culture – that the learners bring to the classroom, as we will see in the next chapter.

Tasks/discussion

For teachers: Think about the institution in which you work, or other language teaching contexts that you have experienced. Do they have a policy or attitude (stated or unstated, explicit or implicit) with regard to the use of the students' L1 in the classroom? What does it consist of? Most importantly, on what basis do you think it was developed, by whom, and with what assumptions or beliefs in mind?

For teachers and students: In small groups, decide on a specific cultural practice in your country (not a traditional or 'folk' practice – it could be something as simple as getting into a taxi, greeting your workmates in the mornings, or ordering a drink) which requires at least some use of language. Describe it in detail for the benefit of a visitor from another country who has never been to your country before and knows nothing about it, so that armed with your instructions, the visitor would be able to negotiate the encounter successfully.

How does this kind of sustained thinking about communication help your language learning?

Suggested readings

Pennycook, A. (2010), *Language as a Local Practice*. London: Routledge.
In this thoughtful and challenging (though accessible) book, the author uses the notion of 'language ecology' to highlight how language, far from being a

matter of decontextualized form, replicable anywhere at any time, is actually always a matter of repeated social practice. The book offers case studies from various countries, and takes an approach which is highly sensitive to multilingualism and influenced by the developing theoretical concept of translanguaging.

Hua, Z. (2018), *Exploring Intercultural Education: Language in Action* (2nd edn). London: Routledge.

A revised and expanded new edition of a popular book, which offers a series of varied, useful discussions and activities based around the idea of cultural diversity and language practice. Hua considers not only the classroom, but contexts such as the workplace, study abroad and even tourism, raising awareness of intercultural practices and challenging stereotypical and essentialist views of cultures.

9

What Makes a Classroom Authentic? English Inside and Outside the Classroom

9.1 Introduction

In the previous chapter we made the case for not only valuing students' linguistic and cultural background for its own sake, but actually drawing on it as a resource to be used in the classroom. As we have argued throughout this book, a sole focus on standard forms is not a sufficient response to the communicative demands that are likely to be faced by international learners and users of English in the twenty-first century. We have suggested that awareness of native and standard forms, while necessary and desirable – we should be careful not to throw the baby out with the bathwater – needs to be balanced with an equal awareness of how language works in different contexts, including non-standard and non-NS contexts, and how different communicative effects are achieved with a range of communicative resources.

As we have consistently argued (and we are far from alone – see e.g. Byram et al. 2002, Byram and Feng 2005), learning a language requires more than acquiring mastery of language forms. Long gone are the days when the listen-and-repeat of the 'audio-lingual' approach dominated language teaching, encouraged, no doubt, by behaviourist theories of learning and the technological developments that facilitated the method. This is not to say that repetition is an entirely useless way of learning or that memorizing prefabricated chunks of language is wholly without merit. But, as we pointed out in Chapters 6 and 7, learning language without reference to context (and that includes the contexts that the learners bring with them as discussed in Chapter 8) is unlikely to translate into communicative success. Researchers such as Kramsch (2009), Canagarajah (2013) and Jenkins (2015) have argued that being able to function effectively in what is an increasingly interconnected world, at least in terms of communicative activity and particularly via social and digital media, requires an understanding not only that people speak different languages, but that, even when a lingua franca such as English is used, different rules of engagement will be in play. In a lingua franca context things like accommodation to other speakers' variety of the language or level of fluency, negotiation of meaning and tolerance of difference become not desirable add-ons but fundamental, primary aspects of language learning. But how are they best developed?

We suggest that the process of developing this sort of competence (or rather, this bundle of linguistic and communicative competences) gains traction when learners themselves are invited to explore communicative activity themselves, to think and talk about the language examples they are provided with, supported by a series of questions and prompts supplied by a language aware, linguistically knowledgeable teacher. In this way we approach a situation where what happens in classrooms is not just a reductive 'teaching English', but a process of encouraging learners to becoming active and thoughtful observers of language, and just as importantly, skilled global communicators.

The aim of the present chapter, then, is to examine ways in which teachers might work with English language phenomena that they or their students encounter and interact with in their everyday lives – social media, YouTube channels, online gaming, advertising notices, care labels in clothes, newspapers, even coursebooks – the list is almost endless. Using examples that have caught our attention, we show that even quite mundane texts can be used to generate classroom activities that enhance students' English language learning along with their knowledge of language and communication more generally. However, before moving on to that discussion, we need to establish two ground rules of our own, which may not sit entirely comfortably with some teachers and some institutions.

9.1.1 Ground rule number one – use the language you come across in daily life

As will become clear in this chapter, like Sayer (2010) or Scollon and Scollon (2003), for instance, we are strong advocates of using found texts in the classroom. Some teachers might be worried about using texts that have not been authorized within the frameworks of their teaching context. In order to establish the legitimacy of using found texts, they may have to argue their case with managers and other stakeholders (see Chapter 4), which is why they need to have the confidence that comes from the kind of professional disciplinary identity that we discussed in Chapter 5. Some teachers may shy away from using found texts because they consider them to be too difficult for their students' level of English, particularly beginners and elementary levels. However, it is important to remember that beginners in English are not beginners in *language*. It is not precisely the difficulty of a text that should be a deciding factor in whether to use it, but what you can get your students do with it. If your activities are pitched carefully, you could even use the same text from beginner to advanced level students. It all depends on what you want your students to do with it. There is no such thing as a too-difficult text – only a too-difficult task!

9.1.2 Ground rule number two – it needn't always be English

Even more controversially than our first ground rule, if you want to get the most out of certain activities (and we show some below), if you want your students to really get their teeth into a discussion, it may be more productive to have them do it in the language they feel most comfortable with rather than always insisting on them using English. Think of all the times you have watched your students struggling to 'discuss' when being restricted to using only English. Unless they are pretty advanced in the language, one of two things is likely to happen: virtual silence or muttering sub voce in whatever home language the students share, looking up from time to time to make sure that the teacher doesn't notice. What a waste of an opportunity for students to fully engage with the language and develop their own language awareness!

9.2 Outside the classroom: Doing linguistic ethnography, or, 'noticing'

To start our main discussion, we revisit the practice of noticing that we introduced in Chapter 6. We offer two examples: the first is presented as a case study and the second as a classroom activity. Both examples show how even the most ordinary incidences of language can stimulate the linguistic imagination and even lead to the kinds of theoretical discussions that are to be found in, for instance, Scollon and Scollon (2003) or Jaworski and Thurlow (2010), who explore communicative phenomena in the 'linguistic landscapes' in which we live.

9.2.1 Example one: The case of the polite notice

It all began when Fiona was standing in the queue at her local post office and noticed the sign shown in Figure 9.1 placed to one side of the queue near the counter. Having to hand her smartphone, an essential tool for a linguistic ethnographer, she took a couple of photos, an act which aroused curious looks from other customers in the queue. What was it about this innocuous sign that made it worthy of notice?

Figure 9.1 In the post office

The answer is, that by labelling it 'Polite Notice', the post office staff were positioning it as a very particular kind of sign belonging to what we might call the 'polite notice' *genre*, which, like all genres, fosters expectations of what it should look like, what and who it is for and how it is supposed to be understood. What made Fiona notice this particular 'polite notice' was that it did not fit with the familiar image of the genre like the one shown in Figure 9.2, attached to some railings outside a large building on a London street (Try Googling 'polite notice' to see other similar examples). In fact, she noticed and photographed the one shown in Figure 9.2 precisely because she had previously noticed the post office version and wanted to add it to her collection of language phenomena. One of the unforeseen consequences of noticing is that once you start you can't stop! But of course this is not simply a case of collecting, but of collecting in order to move onto the next stage, that is, analysing.

Figure 9.2 On the street

By juxtaposing the two versions it becomes clear that although they share the core purpose of the genre, which is the regulation of other people's behaviour, they differ in the way they seek to achieve this. Let's take a closer look at them using the analytical framework we introduced in Chapter 7, reproduced here as Figure 9.3, to unpack the different elements that combine to make up each of the two notices.

We start off by considering the context questions set out in the framework to establish the circumstances in which each of these notices occurs, taking each question in turn.

What's going on? In Figure 9.1, the post office sign, people are queuing up for a specific purpose. They are fixed in place so to speak, waiting their turn to reach the post office counter where they will be served. With regard to Figure 9.2, what's going on is fluid and random. Cars and buses are moving along the road and people are passing by on the pavement, most unaware of the sign since it is unlikely to be significant for them unless, of course, they are on a bicycle and are looking to leave it somewhere.

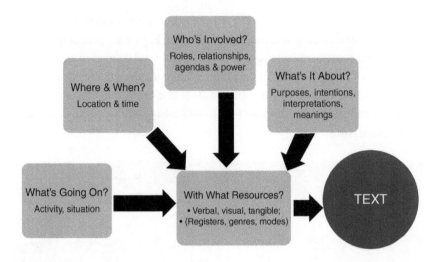

Figure 9.3 A framework for analysis

Where and when? Both signs are in publicly accessible locations, one an interior location and the other exterior. However, both these locations are actually privately owned – the post office is a small franchised branch and the railings, though not the pavement, belong to the property that they surround.

Who's involved? In the case of the post office, the participants are the people who work there who also happen to be the holders of the franchise lease. They are present and therefore known, unlike the 'owners' of the railings example who are anonymous. The other participants involved are, in the first example, the post office customers who have gone there to make use of the service offered. In the second example, they are whoever happens to pass by and read the sign. The relationship between the participants in the post office, the customers and the staff/owners, is a largely transactional one, with neither party having the upper hand, so to speak, although the staff have authority over the premises and manage the service they are providing. This is what gives them the right to have a 'polite notice' in the first place. In the second example, there is no relationship at all between the passers-by and those with their assumed rights of ownership of the railings until a cyclist comes along planning to attach their bike there. In that case, a relationship is established, one in which power and authority play a key role. Does the cyclist ignore the sign and risk chaining up her bike or does she accept the authority of the sign poster?

What's it about? In each of these two cases, what it's about is regulation of behaviour and particularly undesirable behaviour, at least from the perspective of whoever put up the polite notices in the first place.

The question that remains is why it is, given that the signs are similar in their aim, that of regulation of others' behaviour, that they come across so differently. The answer is, of course, because of the differences in their contexts that we have just noted. This particular post office is run as a family business in which the counter staff are family members. Most of the customers are local to the area coming and going as they carry out their different, often regular, transactions: paying bills, withdrawing cash, posting letters and parcels. It is a social space where the participants communicate in face-to-face interaction and as such there is, perhaps, a reason to maintain social harmony. By contrast, there is no direct interaction between the participants in our second example. The people (or institution) who are responsible for the sign are not present, you can't see them or talk to them: they might be out of the country, they might even be dead! Social harmony is not on their radar. These differences are reflected in and promoted by their respective design. Let's see how.

The conventional sign on the railings promotes and reflects the highly *anonymized* relationship between the addressor (the person who put the sign there) and addressees (cyclists seeking to leave their bikes). It does this through the use of the passive voice, with its agentless verb forms, but also with its bland, off-the-peg design. This, taken together with the uncompromising 'without further notice', which seems to have been borrowed wholesale from legally binding, regulatory documents such as final demands for unpaid bills, adds a tone of legitimacy even though the legal authority of such notices is ambiguous. This contrasts strongly with the approach adopted in the post office, which draws on a very different range of linguistic and design elements. It has a deliberate, unabashed, home-made quality, enhanced by the quirky decorative elements of a colourful border. Unlike the railings notice, which seeks to *intensify* the message with its legalese threat, the post office one seeks to *mitigate* it. The filled-in letters of the polite notice heading could be seen as a visual 'downtoner', similar to the verbal ones we discussed in Chapter 7. The use of 'please' makes the message seem more like a request even though it is actually a demand. (They're not really asking you to pay for things before you use them, they're telling you). There is no explicitly stated punitive element, unlike in the railings sign, and there is no obvious attempt to sound official. Legitimacy, in the case of the post office sign, is taken for granted. It is socially understood that people should pay for things before using them. Out on the street, though, where railings are often thought fair game for cyclists to attach their bikes to, a more authoritative tone might be thought to be more effective.

Of course, there is also the question about what is actually polite about a 'polite notice', a question that may never satisfactorily be answered. For British people at least, the very term 'polite notice' has a passive-aggressive tone to it, verging on the threatening. It tends to be used to reflect a sense of annoyance, of being fed up with certain, usually recurring, behaviours by other people that have a negative impact on you. Perhaps, the post office franchise holders borrowed the concept but felt reluctant to go the whole way. By using the name, they claim the authority of the genre, but by providing the downtoning, decorative elements and the mitigating 'please', they feel they have rendered it more palatable to their customers.

9.2.2 Example two: The mystery of the unknown maker

Now let's take a look at another example of found text (Figure 9.4, overleaf), which is a sign in a shop window in a busy street in a highly multicultural part of north London. We don't know who designed it. This kind of communication rarely finds its way into traditional English language classrooms – and it's easy to see why. If the primary goal of language teaching is to instil a mastery of correct form and standardness, then this notice fails at pretty much every level. It is awash with grammar and spelling errors; the punctuation is idiosyncratic; one error has been crudely 'corrected', but wrongly. It is, in short, far from being a model of good English, and we would hardly want our students to reproduce it.

But if we look at this text through a 'linguistics lens', using the frameworks that we discussed in Chapters 6 and 7 – that is, if we consider it first and foremost as a communicative phenomenon, put together with the resources that the person or people who produced it had to hand, then it has much to teach us about how English is used as a lingua franca in multilingual environments. Now, we haven't got space here to do an analysis of this sign, so we'll leave you to think about it yourself. Instead we will move on and look at it, along with the Polite Notices, from the perspective of how it might be used as a classroom resource.

Figure 9.4 Shop window poster

9.2.3 From out on the street to inside the classroom

There are several ways in which teachers could make classroom use of these examples. Doing discourse analysis with students is an effective way of raising their language awareness – not only in relation to English but also their own language(s). An exploration such as with our first example, shows how grammatical choice can promote feelings of inclusion or exclusion, of intimacy or distance. In this way, students can more easily understand why we might choose one structure over another in composing our meanings. Discussion could also be had around *register*, that is the way we adjust our language choices to suit a given situation, the use of formal and informal language for instance. The norms of interaction in connection with the making of requests or demands could make for a fascinating class discussion, particularly in considering whether these travel effectively across cultures or even generations. Is 'politeness' universal and if so is it represented in the same ways in different languages and cultures? (See e.g. House 2007 in relation to German and English speakers, Cheng and Warren 2006 on the failure of an imported British TV quiz programme which clashed with Chinese politeness practices).

Alternatively, the Phone Unlocking sign gives the opportunity to discuss lingua franca English and some of the sociolinguistic issues that it involves. The teacher could provide questions to stimulate classroom or small group discussion in order to engage students in some deep-level thinking about language use. She could even get the students to produce their own questions. In this way, students would develop the kind of language awareness that incorporates thinking about language from the perspectives of both form ('How would this be written in Standard English?') and context. The questions might be along the following lines:

- Where do you think this photograph was taken? Who do you think wrote this? With what aim? Can you guess anything about the writer? Are they native speakers of English? What language(s) might they speak?
- Who do you think is the intended audience? Can you guess anything about them?
- Who do you think made the 'correction' and why did they do it? What can you say about them?
- How does the language used resemble or differ from Standard English? If this were rewritten using Standard English grammar, punctuation and spelling, what would it say?
- Do you think the text is successful as a piece of communication? How do you think it might be improved?
- Have you ever seen notices like this in your country, or in your language?
- Where do you see notices in English in your town or city? What do they say? Who writes them? What kind of English do they use? Who is the intended audience?

Discussions like these can be carried out with students of any level, even with quite low-level students, provided there is no insistence on them taking place in English. The point in this case is to have the discussion rather than to practise the language!

As a follow-up, students could be invited to do a bit of linguistic ethnography themselves by bringing in examples of public signs, notices and social media that they find in their own environments, whether in English or other languages. For example, they might bring in something like the screen shot (Figure 9.5) from a Facebook posting by one of our

Figure 9.5 Facebook comments

(anonymized) postgraduate students, which could open up a discussion about translanguaging. (A rough translation is: Got your thick coat for outside? Sweater? Scarf? Ha! I'm changing shoes. Summer shoes will be boxed, winter boots coming out.)

You might get students to think about why two friends who share a mother tongue, in this case, Bengali, would choose to use English for parts of their interaction. Is there a difference between the kind of words written in Bengali and those written in English? Bengali uses a non-Roman script (বাঙালি 'Bengali') so why are they using Roman letters here?

Or look at Figure 9.6, also from Facebook, where one of a group of Serbian football fans has posted a jokey comment in Roman script even though Serbian uses the Cyrillic script (Српски 'Serbian'). Why?

Figure 9.6 Facebook post

These kinds of texts could also open discussions about the way English is used in the world, its social as well as linguistic function. Sayer's (2010) discussion of using the linguistic landscape as a pedagogical resource makes precisely this point using examples found in Mexico, where he lives and works. He was interested to understand why Mexican advertisements for products and services incorporated elements of English language and how this approach was received by Mexicans themselves. He identified different social and cultural meanings that the language seemed to promote, the kind of things that we discussed in Chapter 2, but he also discovered that the use of English was not simply a case of showing provenance or prestige, but rather that these elements were viewed as just another communicative resource that could be drawn in to enhance existing repertoires (see Blommaert 2010). Sayer concludes:

> We can see that as English becomes increasingly globalized, it also acquires new, local meanings as people in those contexts take it up, learn it, and begin to use it for their own (whether global or local) purposes. (2010: 151)

This is just the kind of research and practice that we, along with Sayer, feel should be incorporated into the ELT portfolio. And if students are encouraged to bring in examples that they themselves have found interesting, inspired by those provided by the teacher, it changes the classroom dynamics. Direct action like this, where students do linguistics work for themselves, puts them in the driving seat for a change and, rather than simply responding to what the teacher presents, gives them ownership of their learning. After all, as we pointed out in Chapter 4, language learning is about so much more than just language production and display.

9.3 Inside the classroom: Why we do what we do

In the previous section, our examples demonstrated how a linguistic ethnography approach can offer teachers and students the chance to explore and analyse communicative interaction in a spirit of curiosity and speculative enquiry. We now turn our attention to the question of why we do what we do in the classroom. Our focus is on teaching materials and their design and what use teachers can make of them. Rather than talk about teaching methodologies, something that we find problematic for reasons that we have already touched on in earlier chapters, we prefer to talk about *guiding principles* that emerge out of the kinds of professional and disciplinary knowledge that we have argued for throughout this book. Basing what we do on a set of principles offers flexibility in how we do our teaching because it moves the focus away from teachers seeking *how to* methodologies towards developing *why to* approaches.

Whether you are using a published coursebook, materials prepared for your particular institution or materials that you yourself have designed, you need to be completely on top of whatever it is that you are teaching. You need to know what you are doing and why, and your students need to know this too. We suggest three core principles – authenticity, validity and relevance, which we discuss in turn below. We have separated and itemized these principles for the sake of clarity but it is important to stress that they are really overlapping and inseparable in practice. They should, we argue, become a way of thinking, an epistemology, that can inform everything you do as a teacher, whether you are inside or outside the classroom yourself.

9.3.1 Principle 1: Authenticity

The issue of authenticity has been long discussed in TESOL fields (see e.g. Widdowson 1979, Breen 1985, Lee 1995, Guariento and Morley 2001, McDonald et al. 2006). For some, authenticity refers to the texts that are used in the classroom. Are the texts used naturally occurring ones or have they been adapted or produced for the teaching context? For others it refers to provenance, which usually means a native standard variety of the language. Is this the 'authentic' English or some other kind of English? And for others, the focus is on whether authentic interaction is taking place; for instance, are the students engaging in 'real' communication? Such considerations are, of course, fundamental to choice of materials and classroom activity, but how we respond to them depends very much on context itself. For us the issue of authenticity is first, whether what we are asking our students to do can be justified in terms of whether it is something that we actually do; second, its validity both inside and outside the classroom and, last but not least, its relevance to students' own interests, values and concerns.

Take a look at the set of questions below and spend a few minutes thinking about each of them. We do not imagine it will take you long to appreciate what they are about, but we encourage you to consider each one carefully to think of possible reasons for doing each activity.

In 'real' life do we ever:

- Read something and then answer a set of questions about it?
- Translate a list of words into a different language?
- Describe what we or others are doing at a particular moment?
- Listen to somebody speaking and fill in gaps in a written text?
- Read something out loud?
- Ask people we know questions about things we already know the answers to?
- Memorize and then repeat something that has been written?
- Change sentences from one grammatical form to another?
- Write down word for word what someone else is saying?
- Eavesdrop on conversations between strangers and note down what they are saying?

As you have undoubtedly realized, these questions describe the sort of activities that are commonly used in language classrooms all over the world. You could probably even label some of them under some kind of 'language teaching' heading: reading or listening comprehension, grammar practice, speaking and so on. The point of thinking about this list is not particularly to say that you must never do anything in class that would not be done outside. The point is to use it as a tool to think through your own classroom practice and the ways in which you work with the materials you use. The framework in Figure 9.3 is helpful in this.

If we take the last item on the list, eavesdropping and noting down, for instance, this is something a linguistic ethnographer might do if they overhear a linguistically interesting use of language. This might be an example of 'youth speak' such as 'bro' or 'fam', or it might be a use of a local dialect term such as 'snicket' in Yorkshire or 'dricht' in Scotland (we leave these unexplained here for you to find out the meanings if you don't know them!). However, we would be most unlikely to listen in on a conversation between a couple, sitting together at home, talking about what to have for dinner or a customer buying flowers in a florist's. Yet fragments of such conversations pepper our coursebooks. Of course, we are not saying that you should never use conversational fragments or longer pieces as listening texts. They can be useful ways of presenting and even practising conversational language. What we are saying is that teachers need to be critically aware of the nature of the 'conversation' (Is it realistic? What is it supposed to be doing? Could it offer more learning opportunities than its stated description?) and need to be explicit with their students in relation to these questions. In this way students can know the reasons why you want them to listen to a particular conversation, not fictional reasons (you're a spy, you're an undercover police officer) but language learning reasons (a grammar point, politeness intonation). This leads us on to our next principle, *validity*.

9.3.2 Principle 2: Validity

Do I know what I'm learning and why? Do I know what I've learned and how? It is a well-documented fact that students rarely spontaneously use the structures and vocabulary that the teacher has just been teaching (e.g. Ellis 2003, Kumaravadivelu 2003). There are many reasons for this, including how we process information in the brain (e.g. Dekeyser 2009) but one of them is that students, all of whom are different from one another, do not necessarily interpret things in the same way or in the way the teacher assumes that they do (Dornyei 2005). Often little attention is paid to ensuring that students really know what they are learning (and why, and how) since they are rarely asked to reflect on classroom activity. To ignore this aspect of the teaching and learning relationship is to miss an important opportunity for both students and teachers, as a small anecdote will illustrate. In this case, when students were asked to give feedback on a short EAP course they had undertaken, several reported that they had done no grammar work. This surprised the teachers concerned as, from their perspective, grammar had featured in almost every session. The mismatch arose because the students' view of grammar work (e.g. exercises in putting verbs into the 'right' form) differed greatly from the teachers' view, which involved analytical work exploring grammar in context. To respond to the misunderstanding, the teachers were encouraged to incorporate reflective activities into the course so that there could be a space for open discussion about what students had been learning and how. This helped both parties. It helped the teachers understand that not everything they do in class is self-evident and it helped the students to recognize the validity of each of the different classroom activities.

9.3.3 Principle 3: Relevance

By relevance we are not only talking about usefulness in terms of the world beyond the classroom, though of course that is an important dimension of this principle. We are talking also about relevance within the context of classroom learning itself. For students to be persuaded to want to learn a particular thing, they need to be invested in it. They need to know how it will help them in relation to other things they are learning and other things they are doing or will be doing. It's no use drilling the stress patterns of English if you don't also point out the relevance of this in terms of intelligibility or of social aspects such as politeness. It is no use changing active sentences into passives, as we discussed in Chapter 7, unless you understand how such a transformation would change the meaning of what is said and the intentions behind it. It is no use having students read aloud without thinking about occasions when they might actually do this in 'real life', occasions which require specific *ways* of reading out loud, such as bedtime stories for children or snippets from a newspaper over breakfast. Mechanical learning only goes so far. We all need to know how something fits into our social and intellectual worlds, whether it be in the classroom or beyond.

Taking these three principles together, it is easy to see how closely they interact. Relevance is an integral part of validity since something can only be valid if it is seen to have relevance. Likewise, to be relevant, something needs to be authentic which, in turn, gives it its classroom validity. Teachers therefore need to view their teaching, not just with a linguistics eye, but with a critical eye. In other words, they need to properly analyse what they use in the classroom (Is that activity labelled 'speaking' really about speaking or is it about something else?), whether it be coursebook materials or things they have created themselves, to make sure they are themselves aware of what they are asking their students to do and why. If they do not do this, then how can they expect their students to appreciate what they are doing and engage in their learning?

To demonstrate what we mean by adopting a critical eye, we consider two examples of classroom activities taken from published coursebooks. The first is from a widely used Chinese coursebook and the second from a well-known British one. Our aim here is to explore them using the principles outlined above as our overarching philosophy, combined with the language awareness that comes from the different branches of linguistics we have been discussing throughout the book.

9.3.4 Reading aloud

We start with Example 9.1, which is from the 2007 edition of *New Horizon College English*, produced for Chinese university students. This particular activity is the first in a series of what are labelled 'exercises' and it follows a longer listening-while-reading activity based on a written text from which Example 9.1 is the introductory paragraph. We want you to focus specifically on the exercise shown in Example 9.1. Drawing on our 'do we ever' questionnaire above, can you think of any circumstances in which you would naturally do what is being asked here? (This is the whole of the exercise, by the way – not an extract).

Example 9.1

Reading Aloud

1 Read the following paragraph aloud until you can say it from memory.

In most parts of the world, environmental awareness does not exist. The great majority of nations concern themselves with economic development, regardless of its effect on the global ecology. But in recent years, as environmental damage has increased, signs of change have sprung up in various pockets around the world. The following are a few examples of countries undertaking new environmental initiatives.

Before looking more closely at the activity itself, we need first to consider the context in which it has been produced. For some readers, the idea of using this in their classrooms with their students might seem appalling, while for other readers, it might seem perfectly normal and valid. Remember, this is a coursebook produced for use with Chinese students in China where, as we saw in Chapter 8, reading aloud and memorization is a highly valued teaching and learning strategy, so that literally millions of students undertake exercises like this every day. Certainly, to be able to memorize and recite a chunk of text is a skill, but is it really a *language* skill? Some Chinese learners report that text memorization helps develop their 'language sense' or *yugan* (Yu 2013) and given the nature of Chinese languages, it may well be the case that memorization is a valuable resource for language learning, particularly if language is viewed as a series of fixed forms. We would argue, though, that while custom and tradition may be enough in itself, in order to make a classroom activity valid, relevant and authentic there needs to be mutual understanding on the part of teachers and students about what constitutes these criteria. Using this exercise in the Chinese context might work because it fits expectations, but insisting on it in a different cultural setting would undoubtedly cause consternation among teachers and students alike! However, just because a classroom activity is familiar, it does not necessarily mean it is good. Let's now take a look at Example 9.1 as a teaching resource.

In terms of authenticity, Example 9.1 is an exercise which corresponds exactly to what it says – *Reading Aloud* – it is not masquerading as something other than what it is and reading aloud is not necessarily a useless exercise. Given the right circumstances and the relevant, explicit teacher input, it might help with developing word and sentence stress, which are of course key factors in English intelligibility. There could be a focus on, say, consonant clusters which can be hard to get right in connected speech, and this extract provides several examples of where students might have difficulty. For instance, the opening phrase, 'in most parts' could be tricky as students might try to pronounce all the sounds represented by the letters rather than use the mix of assimilation and elision that occurs in natural speech. In English it would be more usual to say something like /ɪm məʊs pɑːts/ where the 'n' in 'in' assimilates to the 'm' in 'most' and where the 't' in 'most' is elided to make the transition between the two words (most parts) flow more easily; and in most British English varieties at least, there is no /r/ sound in the word 'parts'. Using a reading aloud exercise in this way provides the validity and relevance for students – but only if they fully understand *why* they are doing what they are being asked to do and, of course, only if the teacher knows something about phonology.

We have already mentioned the relevance of memorization in Chinese learning; it is, after all, how Chinese people learn to read, as we pointed out in Chapter 8, so applying the same thinking to language learning makes some sense. One of our own MA students, a highly proficient user of English who came from a remote rural area in China, told us that he had learned his English by systematically memorizing the contents of a dictionary that his teacher had given him. In Example 9.1, we can certainly identify examples of fixed-form *nominalization* chunks based around the word 'environmental' (environmental awareness, environmental development, environmental initiatives) which would be prime candidates for this approach. In fact, research into recurring language chunks has a long pedigree in the context of linguistics and language learning (e.g. Hoey 1991, Francis and Hunston 2000). However, if the teacher does not make the learning point explicit, the exercise remains empty of linguistic relevance and derives what validity it has from nothing more than custom and practice.

Another way in which a teacher could use this example, given that it is part of an EAP course, is to use the text as a catalyst for discussion about oral presentation, which is an integral part of much university study. What is the difference between reading a paper out loud and speaking from a series of prompts on a PowerPoint slide? How can you render a written paper accessible to a listening audience? A creative teacher, that is a teacher who has the confidence that stems from disciplinary knowledge, analytical reflection and an understanding of pedagogical principles, can go beyond even the most mechanical materials and turn them into something that offers meaningful and engaging learning.

9.3.5 Manipulating grammar

Our second example (Example 9.2) comes from the pre-intermediate level general English coursebook *Global*, which was first published in 2010. It involves manipulating a grammatical structure and will look familiar to most language teachers as such things are standard fare, part and parcel of the language teaching repertoire. In this instance the activity is located early on in a unit which is based around the topic of 'Health & Fitness'. The activity is preceded by an exposition box showing what reported speech looks like and its mechanics, and it is followed by an activity which entails turning direct speech into reported speech.

Example 9.2

Change the sentences to direct speech. Then check your answers in the conversation on p. 108.

For example, The doctor told me she had the test results.
'I have the test results.'

1. I said I was fine.
2. She said that I wasn't very fit.
3. She told me that I couldn't eat any more red meat.
4. She told me that I also needed to do some exercise.

The purpose of these kinds of exercise, as we all know, is to practise the mechanics of structure, the form rather than the meaning, and there is nothing wrong in that. However, what is often ignored, and reported speech is a good example, is that the mechanics and forms tend to be foregrounded and overstated while the semantic aspect, the *meaning*, is usually ignored (see our discussion of the passive voice in Chapter 7). In this coursebook, we are told that we use reported speech 'to say what another person has said' and that 'the verb <u>often</u> goes one tense back.' But nothing is said about why that happens; and if it does not happen all the time, what happens in the times when it doesn't go one tense back? In fact, according to corpus-based research into spoken communication (Kettemann 1995), reported speech that follows this format is really rather rare. In most interactions we would tend to choose the tense that is relevant to the situation in hand. For instance, it would be more usual to say 'She said *I'm* not very fit' rather than 'She said I *wasn't* very fit' because the condition of 'fitness' is current.

Questions we might ask of this exercise include: do the students know why they are doing this (validity)? How does it fit in relation to everything else (relevance)? Would we normally do this, and if so, when and why (authenticity)? Who is talking to whom here and how does that affect what we say (context)? These questions then lead to consideration of language choice and the effect of using one form or another. Choosing direct speech instead of reported speech is not just a mechanical shift: it is a semantic one, too. Correspondence between the meanings produced by each of these two structures is by no means exact. Saying 'I'm not very fit' is not the same as saying 'She told me I wasn't very fit.' The fact that someone else says something about you does not mean that you believe it or accept it, or even that it is true, so the likelihood of anyone making this kind of syntactic conversion is fairly remote. If direct speech were to be used it might go something like this: 'I'm not very fit, apparently/according to the doctor/so she said.' Reporting someone else's words is quite different to reiterating them as if they were our own.

As with the previous example of reading aloud, we are not saying that mechanical exercises are useless or a waste of time. In fact we think they are actually very helpful for students as they can be quite satisfying in their own right, giving students the chance to get to grips with the forms and sounds of the language (so long as they realize that this is all it is). However, using these kinds of exercise *only* for the purpose of form is a missed opportunity. What is the purpose of reported speech? Why might we change the tense or not? What other ways can we do it? How is it done in students' own languages? These are just some of the questions that could be asked to generate classroom discussion about language and language use so that the exercise, mechanical though it is, becomes an integral part of learning *about* language and not just an add-on to practise form. In other words, it becomes a valid, authentic and relevant part of the whole.

9.3.6 Principles or methodology?

In concluding this section on using principles rather than methodology to drive your teaching, it is important to clarify our position. We are not saying that methodology is not useful, but that the emphasis that teachers and many training courses place on methodology ignores an important point. Methodology without principles is just an empty frame, a set of procedures to be followed with the hope of replicating in some way the aspirations of the methodology being used. In fact, the reason why so many teachers understandably complain that CLT does not work in their classrooms (e.g. Tsui 2007) is precisely because they are trying to apply a methodology without context. As long ago as 2003, Stephen Bax argued in his discussion on CLT:

> This implicit focus on methodology leads us to ignore one key aspect of language teaching – namely the particular context in which it takes place. When we emphasise what the teacher must do, and start our list of solutions with methodological issues, we thereby give off the message that the solution to the problem of teaching is a methodological one – and therefore, by extension, the solution is not to do with the context in which we happen to be working. (2003: 280)

Bax's argument for context to take priority over methodology is certainly one that we endorse. However, using context alone as a guiding principle is not enough. Without subject knowledge, by which we mean, of course, linguistics, teachers will find themselves stuck in a methodological rut. Our solution is to start from a position of principles, informed by subject knowledge and accompanied by the kind of curiosity that challenges taken-for-granted thinking. If a teacher starts from there, everything else falls into place and the need for a discrete, identifiable methodology is replaced by second-nature practices which continue to shift and develop over time, space and experience.

In the next part of this chapter, we bring together some of the points and suggestions we have already made concerning the use of texts found both inside and outside the classroom. Our aim is to demonstrate how some of the basic principles behind materials design connect with our invitation to teachers to make use of the environments in which they are working. We follow our motto 'one text, many tasks' to show how a single text can be used for a variety of pedagogical purposes and even have great longevity. This develops our 'principles' approach into concrete classroom activity, as we consider how these principles can be used to inform approaches to working with texts.

9.4 Working with texts

The starting point for all materials design is a combination between what you are intending to teach in terms of specific language and communicative practices and behaviours, the particular students you are teaching and the text you choose to build your teaching around. It does not necessarily happen in that order, but these three elements are always present in the process. You might start with the text itself – a public notice of the type we discussed above, an article from a newspaper, a part of a radio phone-in programme or a podcast – and analyse it in terms of the different learning opportunities it affords. On the other hand, you might need to be teaching students about something as specific as giving opinions or evaluating something, in which case you might look for a text that does that kind of communicative work. Teachers need not only to be active noticers of language, as we have pointed out, but active noticers of language that could be useful in the classroom. In fact, once you develop this skill, you will find yourself unable to view almost anything without thinking of its pedagogical potential. And even if you do not have the opportunity to develop materials of your own, it is nevertheless possible to develop ways of filtering, explaining and expanding the materials you are expected to work with, in ways such as those we discussed with our two coursebook examples above.

9.4.1 Everything must be useable, everything must flow

Assuming the pedagogical principles we outlined above, look at the following design checklist which we have used on our programmes with teachers who have gone on to produce either their own creative and pedagogically effective classroom materials or adaptations of existing coursebook materials that they have found unsatisfactory or ill-suited to their context.

1 **Think beyond the single focus.** If you have collected a text that you think would be good to use in your teaching – an article from a magazine, a YouTube video, a notice in a shop window – exploit it for all it is worth. Why did you collect it in the first place? Does it offer any particular language use opportunities (grammar, vocabulary, pronunciation)? How about language awareness discussions? What is interesting or relevant about it in its own right (topic, content)? What kind of analytical or research opportunities does it offer students?

2 **Think about authenticity.** For instance, you might think a YouTube video would make a good listening/viewing comprehension so maybe you think you must devise a series of comprehension questions. But stop there. Would you ever answer a set of comprehension questions while watching a YouTube video? Of course not. But you might watch a YouTube video to learn how to do something (change a plug, do a hairstyle, make a kite) or decide whether you like something (a music track, a film trailer). In that case, those reasons provide guidance as to the kinds of activities and tasks you could develop for your students.

3 **Analyse your text.** What else can it offer? Are there any specific language points that it could be used to demonstrate? How about a grammar point? Maybe you decide to use a YouTube of someone showing how to do something, as above. Perhaps this could be used for showing ways in which instructions can be given. Are imperative forms used, as often indicated in coursebooks, or are there different instructional forms – and why is that? What else does it offer? Pronunciation points perhaps. Is the accent easy or difficult? Is the YouTuber a native or non-native speaker? How can you tell? Could this lead to discussion about dialect, variation, lingua franca English?

4 **Make sure everything flows.** When putting the materials together each phase must be stitched together so that there is a meaningful thread from one thing to the next. This way the materials will have an inbuilt sense of purpose, validity and relevance. Even if the students will never actually use this language in their everyday lives it must be seen to be useful and relevant within the context of their classroom learning. Think also about how one set of materials can springboard into another set.

5 **Build in cycles of learning**. This encourages reflection as students revisit points they have previously encountered, but in a different context or for a different purpose. This further enhances the sense of purpose, validity and relevance within the classroom.

6 **Make use of everything**. Avoid any redundancy in your materials. Everything must be useable and purposeful and not just there for effect or decoration. If there are images, make them work for you. And remember, the same text can be used multiple times for multiple purposes and at different levels. As we said right at the beginning of the chapter, there's no such thing as a too-difficult text – only a too-difficult task!

7 **Pay attention to visual design**. Good product design combines appearance and function. The same applies to teaching materials! If they look scrappy, they lose validity even if they are pedagogically sound.

8 **Be aware** of what you are asking students to do with every activity, sub-activity, exercise and task. Students can be kept in the dark for some of the time (though not ultimately) if you want there to be an element of discovery, but the teacher must always know what's happening and why!

Now let's take a look at a complete sample set of teaching materials and consider how they fulfil the criteria set out in the checklist.

9.4.2 One text, many tasks

The example we use to illustrate the way in which one text can be used for many different activities is built around what could be considered almost a TESOL cliché, the newspaper article. Often teachers find an extract from the news media, whether print or online, solely because of its topical relevance and they use it, as a written text, for reading comprehension and perhaps to provoke discussion of the topic of the article itself. The obvious benefit of using such a source is that it can be current, and although, in reality, the topic doesn't really matter in terms of language focus, it makes sense to choose things which resonate with students' own interests and which offer the opportunity to develop into further classroom activity.

The subject matter of the cuttings used in our example are, to all intents and purposes, fairly mundane. They do not concern the grand themes such as 'saving the environment' or 'how the pyramids were built' typical of coursebook readings, but instead offer a glimpse into everyday local life, the kinds of things people might read about wherever they are in the world.

In this sense there is topical potential, though, as you will see, this is not the focus of the activities that we have developed around these news items. Our purpose is to show how much can be done with very little and how each activity flows naturally into the next in a way that ensures inbuilt validity and hence relevance. The materials are presented as a set, complete with instructions, activities and explanations. This means that the students have everything they need in order to work through the different activities so that, when they leave the class, rather than having separate sheets of different handouts, they have everything there in one place. This is an important aspect of all teacher-designed materials: they must look good in terms of visual design to avoid undermining their validity, as we noted in our materials design checklist. As you look through these materials, consider the level of students these materials might be used with and think about how you could replace the texts with others more relevant to your own students, yet keeping the same set of activities. We suggest that it is not just a case of 'one text, many tasks', it is also the idea of devising tasks that can be used with or adapted for different texts. In this way, teachers can build up a portfolio of flexible, interchangeable materials. Let's go through them activity by activity, noting that each one has its own label explaining what it is about. This is part of helping students see the relevance in what they are doing.

Activity 1 is a lead-in activity with a twist. The invitation to use whatever language students prefer means that we are expecting a real discussion about reading habits rather than simply warming the students up or preparing them for what might be considered the 'core' work of the session. In these materials, everything is core.

Activity 1 – Talking about reading habits

In a moment you're going to read a set of short newspaper articles, but before you do that, spend a few minutes talking in your group or to a partner about your own newspaper reading habits in any language. (Use whatever language you prefer for this discussion).

- Do you ever read newspapers? Why? Why not?
- What kind do you read? How? Where? When?
- Do you read everything or do you choose particular articles?
- Do you ever respond to what you read? How? To whom?

Talking about reading habits may be something students have never really done before, so an activity like this serves to raise students' awareness of their own interactions with written texts. For instance, they may not recognize online news such as Buzzfeed as being, essentially, a newspaper. They may not even think of online reading as actual reading, in much the same way that Lenhart et al. (2008) found that teenagers did not think of social media interactions as writing.

Activity 2 (no dictionaries) – Reasons for reading

Now look at these headlines from a newspaper and choose the one that interests you most.

- **Kids Saved From Fire**
- **Pirate Radio Operator Fined**
- **Thieves Asked to Return Jewellery**
- **Vandals Caught Red-handed**

Tell your partner which one you chose and why.

This is another discussion activity based around the authentic practice of skimming through newspaper headlines to select what attracts your interest most. Giving reasons for choosing one rather than another is in itself a comprehension activity, as students need to identify what they think the article might be about based on the headline. They may not know all the vocabulary in the headline, but they may be intrigued by them nevertheless. It leads into the next activity (Activity 3), which is to find and match the article that goes with their chosen headline and read it to see whether it matches up to their expectations. The choice factor, despite the limitations resulting from what is on offer, gives students some autonomy which is further emphasized by Activity 3, a self-directed comprehension activity in which the 'questions' are the students' own rather than the teacher's.

Activity 3 (no dictionaries) – Comprehension check

Find the article that matches your headline and read it.

Is it about what you thought it would be?

John Davies of Candler Street, South Tottenham has been convicted of aiding the operation of the unauthorised radio station "Ruud Awakening 104.3" which broadcasts in East London.

Mr Davies admitted supplying apparatus and allowing his premises to be used by the pirate radio station when he appeared at Haringey Magistrates Court on June 29th.

He was given a one year conditional discharge with £250 costs.

Mindless thieves have stolen jewellery from an exhibition being held at Crouch End Arts Centre.

Organisers of the exhibition say the jewellery, which was designed and made by local art students, was going to be sold to raise money for the Red Cross. They are begging the thieves to return the jewellery so that the charity does not lose out.

Police say the thieves must have entered the building through a window in the roof which had only recently been repaired.

Two women were arrested after emptying a can of red paint over a neighbour's car. Amazingly, they were caught on camera by a local photographer who was taking pictures of a house for an estate agent.

A bystander said, "They just opened the can and poured the paint all over the front of the car. I couldn't believe my eyes!"

The women were questioned at Hornsey Police Station, but refused to give any explanation about the incident.

Courageous fire-fighters rescued two infants from a blazing house in Tottenham. Both firemen and the children, aged 18 months and three years, suffered burns in the fire in Courtman Road on Saturday morning. One of the youngsters remains in hospital after suffering 20 per cent burns.

Firefighters were called to the blaze at 10am and arrived to find the first floor in flames and the children's' parents outside. When they were told children were still inside a back bedroom on the first floor, two firemen entered the house using breathing apparatus.

While their colleagues fought to quell the flames, the brave pair located the bedroom and carried the youngsters to safety.

The cause of the fire is still being investigated.

You might have noticed that thus far there has been no point at which the teacher has tested students' comprehension of any of the reading, nor any explicit feedback to the teacher. What is more, there has been no demand that students speak in English. However, the materials are in English and they have therefore been doing English language work. The next activity, though, moves onto more conventional territory as students are asked to find someone who chose a different article so that they can tell each other about what they have read. Retelling, with regard to newspaper reading, is a natural thing to do and may even involve reading bits out loud. At this point in the lesson, students are expected to use English in their retelling. In this way, the comprehension check is undertaken by peers rather than by the teacher, although, of course, the teacher is there to intervene if necessary.

Activity 4 (no dictionaries) – Comprehension and summarizing

Find someone who read a different article. They can tell you about theirs, in English, and you can tell them about yours. Ask your partner questions if you don't understand.

Now read your partner's article and see if you agree with how they told it to you.

Finally, read the other two articles and then decide which of the four is the most interesting to you.

Throughout these four activities dictionaries, including those on students' phones, have been forbidden. This is to encourage students to work with the English that they already have and to try to guess meanings from the context. Reliance on dictionaries is a difficult thing for language learners to overcome, and of course, the usefulness of phone dictionaries cannot be disregarded. However, overreliance militates against fluency, and students need to develop a sense of self-reliance when it comes to reading. There will always be a point at which it becomes necessary to check the meaning of a word, but that point does not have to be at the time of encountering it – and certainly not at the first encounter point. With respect to the articles that we have been discussing, there will undoubtedly be words and phrases that the students are unfamiliar with, but despite this, the associated activities do not require understanding of every word. Students have not been tested on their detailed understanding. In fact, all they have been asked to do so far is show what they do understand, not what they do not. This is an important distinction. What's more, following the 'two heads are better than one' adage, working with another student improves the chances of figuring vocabulary out.

This brings us neatly on to Activity 5 which concerns this very issue, vocabulary. It is designed to make vocabulary work in the context of reading, an explicit part of the learning process, and as before, it is a self-directed approach. Students choose the vocabulary that they feel they need not only for understanding the text more fully but also for use beyond the text. They also get to use their dictionaries in class time, something that is often discouraged, particularly in 'English only' classrooms.

Activity 5 – Vocabulary work

As you read through the articles, you will have seen several words and phrases that were new to you. By yourself select five words or phrases that are new to you.(Choose ones that you really want to know). Compare your list with your partner's.

- Are they the same or different?
- Discuss what you did when you came to the new words.
- Can you help each other with understanding them?

Read through the articles again.

- Do you understand the meanings better after talking about them?
- Would you feel confident to use the words yourself?

Together choose just five words or phrases that you would like to learn properly.

- Check their meaning and use in a dictionary.
- Teach your words to the whole group using a method that you have found helpful.

Finally, having reached a point where the students are familiar and comfortable with the content of the articles, there is a move towards a focus on grammar. What that issue is depends on whatever the teacher thinks the text naturally gives rise to. In the case of newspaper articles, which report on things that have happened, this might include use of past tenses when narrating a story, reported speech when referring to what witnesses might have said when interviewed by journalists or, as here, the use of passive forms. Take a look through Activity 6 to see how this structure has been treated and compare it to some of the examples given in Chapter 7 or, indeed, to the exercise with reported speech that we discussed above.

Activity 6 – Language awareness and language choice

'the passive' – review (be) + past participle
In each of these articles there are several uses of the 'passive'.

- With your partner, see how many passive constructions you can find.

Be careful, sometimes we don't use the auxiliary verb – 'be' – even though the construction is a passive. We call this type an 'elided' form.

- Which are full passive structures and which are elided?
- Compare the examples of the passive with those of the active verb forms?
- Why do you think the writers chose these two different forms?

Try rewriting one of the articles but this time exchanging the passive forms for active and the active forms for passive.

- What differences does that make to the flow of the article?
- What effect does it have on meaning?
- What about the impact of the article?

In each phase of this activity, students are once again being encouraged to work things out for themselves. It is analytical work involving grammatical analysis for the sake of form but also discourse analysis for the sake of meaning. The rewriting exercise gives students the chance to see how grammatical choice changes the way something can mean as well as allowing for more precision in writing. By working with another student, they are encouraged to discuss these issues while they work. And because this is a language awareness-raising activity, it does not matter which language they use for their discussion.

The final activity (Activity 7) in this set of materials returns to social matters, and is focused on encouraging students to consider transcultural factors as well as issues of discourse and register in talking about the newspaper genre. It is a return to broader issues about how information is produced within specific contexts and for specific purposes. Depending on the students, it could develop into a wider discussion of bias and perspective and the role of news media in shaping our understanding, or a further discussion about genre, register, discourse and textual choice.

Activity 7 – Open discussion

Discuss the following:
- What kind of newspaper do you think these articles came from? How do you know?
- Do you think newspapers in your country are different from other countries? In what ways?

Because this is a final phase in relation to the original text, the set of newspaper articles, it might work well as an open discussion in class. Context would need to be taken into account here when considering language choice. In a multilingual class, English would necessarily be used and would probably affect the quality of the discussion, but in monolingual contexts it would be quite possible to use the local language. If the teacher does not speak the local language well, an additional task could be added whereby two or three students are allocated the role of rapporteur with the job of reporting back to the teacher, in English, key elements of the discussion. Whatever the case, it is up to the teacher to decide what matches the interests of the students, what fits with the classroom culture and how best to ensure that students (and potentially other stakeholders) understand the choices that the teacher has made.

We recognize the difficulties that teachers may encounter, particularly in terms of resistance to using other languages in the class or for there to be activities in which the teacher seems to take a back seat. Teachers themselves sometimes feel that they should be doing things all the time, inputting, checking and testing that input. The materials we have shown here seem to encourage the opposite. Our view is, though, that much of the work of the teacher is in the design (or, in the case of coursebooks, redesign) of the materials themselves: the finding of the text, the thinking through each phase, the decisions about where to focus and how, not to mention the importance of ensuring students themselves understand what it is they are doing when they are working through them. It is not as if the teacher is absent in any way, but rather that she has the ability to bring her students with her even when she appears to be taking a back seat. This is something that all teachers must learn how to do if they are to succeed: teaching the students how to be *your* students. This requires being open with them, being explicit in your purposes so that they understand what it is they are learning. As we mentioned earlier, one way to achieve this is to introduce reflective tasks at the end of every session or once a week. For instance, with the materials discussed here, a small reflection task (Activity 8) could be added which not only reminds them of what they have just done inside the classroom but which also takes their learning outside.

Activity 8 – Research and reflection

We focused on the use of the passive in these newspaper articles as a commonly used structure. Your task is to have a look at newspapers in your own language to see if there are similar structural choices.

The point of presenting an entire set of teaching materials as we have done, is to show the sorts of things that can be achieved using a single textual artefact. We chose a very conventional text, a newspaper, as our core, but you could choose almost anything, including the examples from our discussion about 'noticing' at the beginning of this chapter. Think about the texts that your students interact with on a daily basis, on Instagram, YouTube, WeChat, WhatsApp, Facebook or whatever they use in the social media world. Think about commercial sites such as Amazon with its easy access to English language via the 'purchaser comments' sections. What we want to stress here, and you have doubtless already noticed it, is that the approach we advocate is concerned primarily with matters of *language* rather than with the subject matter of the texts themselves. Our activities are designed to raise and develop language awareness, that is, linguistic, sociolinguistic, intercultural knowledge and, of course, knowledge of English language itself. Nevertheless, choosing texts that are relevant and interesting to your students is always going to be a strong added plus, and letting them bring in their own texts offers a further motivational dimension.

9.5 Conclusion

This chapter has been about encouraging teachers to open their teaching up to the world around them by thinking not just about what people say but who they say it with, where, for what reasons and to what effect. We have made the case for moving away from a methodology-driven approach to teaching, drawing instead on fundamental pedagogical principles which are informed by the kind of linguistics and sociolinguistics that we have discussed throughout the book. We know that what we are suggesting is difficult to incorporate into an already busy teaching load, in which teachers are obliged to cover certain materials and certain language points (and we know it might be challenging to get it past the beady eyes of institutional overseers). Obviously you have to teach the course you have been given to teach, and students may have to pass exams at the end of it. Our contention, though, is that even small adaptations to the materials you use can make a big difference in the kind of learning that students experience. It may seem risky, perhaps, but letting the outside into the classroom and giving students more autonomy over their learning makes for happier, more motivated learners – who, we suggest, are more likely to become effective users of the language and, perhaps, better at passing their exams.

Tasks/Discussion

For teachers: Take a course book that you are familiar with. Analyse all the activities in a single chapter or unit from the perspective of the list of 'authenticity questions' we laid out in this chapter. To what extent do the activities demanded by the course book reflect authentic communicative activity? If you were to adjust them in order to better reflect 'real' communication, how might you do this? What might be gained and what lost in doing so?

For teachers and students: Bring in some examples of English that you have come across (they might be e.g. photos of billboard advertising, screenshots of social media posts, song lyrics, snatches of speech from film or video blog). In small groups, analyse these examples and then develop tasks or questions for the rest of the class to work on as a language learning activity.

Suggested readings

Pinner, R. (2016), *Reconceptualising Authenticity for English as a Global Language*. Bristol: Multilingual Matters.
A theorized book, though one which developed out of the author's thinking about his own classroom practice, this is an attempt to reconsider what 'authentic' might mean in the context of globalized, often lingua franca English.

Jaworski, A. and Thurlow, C. (2011), *Semiotic Landscapes: Language, Image, Space*. London: Continuum.
This edited collection explores ways in which people make their mark on the global landscape through texts as varied as graffiti, billboard signs, monuments, shop fronts and home-made vernacular signs of the kind you see stuck in windows or pinned on trees. With a focus on the interaction between the texts observed, the physical locations in which they occur and the sociocultural context that gives rise to them, the different contributors analyse the ways in which these combine to produce meanings that can tell us a lot about language, language use and sociocultural practices as well as provide insights into contemporary issues such as the movements of peoples. It's a book that can be dipped into for inspiration into the many different ways that texts from the outside can be enlisted to generate discussions ranging from multilingualism to lingua franca English.

10

Conclusion: What Do I Teach When I Teach English?

I feel all the time more like a language teacher (Non-native English speaker MA student on studying linguistics as part of her course).

10.1 Introduction

This will be a short chapter. If you've kept with us this far, it's probably because you agree with us that the study of language should underpin language teaching. If you disagree, then we're unlikely to persuade you at this late stage (though we'd still like to try!) So we won't restate our case for the umpteenth time, but we will try to draw together some of the different strands of the argument that we have developed thus far.

10.2 Why English teaching is different

We started this book by arguing that English, by dint of its exceptional (and in some ways rather strange) role in the world, is a little different to other languages – even other big and widespread languages like Spanish, Hindi-Urdu, Chinese and French – in the way it is perceived and valued. We are quite aware that not everyone agrees with this, and some will resist the idea passionately, but in the end we are convinced that, as Ostler (2010: 8) flatly states, there 'is little point in trying to treat English as "just another language" '. We want to finish the book by discussing the corollary of this proposition: that teaching English, the '*de facto* first language of globalization' which 'has penetrated societies and impacted upon the lives of individuals to an extent which has no parallel in human history' (O'Regan 2014: 534) is not quite the same as teaching other languages.

What do English teachers have to contend with? It should first be said that teachers as a profession tend towards the practical and pragmatic (see Young and Walsh 2010). They have to contend with paperwork, awkward 'customers', officious or even incompetent managers, limited resources, too many contact hours – we'll take all these as a given. And these are things which English teachers share not just with teachers of other languages but with teachers in general. However, at the level where we talk about things like pedagogy, learning and teaching objectives, self-identity, sense of professional worth, disciplinary focus and so on, it seems to us in our discussions and work with teachers from all over the world (and as teachers ourselves, at different levels and in numerous different contexts) that there are a number of themes which come up again and again, producing a kind of background hum against which the day-to-day business of ELT continues.

10.2.1 ELT has ideological implications

In many societies, English represents, or is perceived to represent, cultural capital. ELT therefore has the *potential*, at least, to perpetuate inequalities just as it has the potential to reduce them. In claiming that English teachers in EFL contexts are 'put in a precarious position of supporting linguistic hegemony and neocolonialism by entering foreign countries and promoting English language attainment', Eslami et al. (2014: 5) are surely overstating the case, as are those who identify English as the primary means by which elites maintain their power in ESL contexts (see e.g. Shamim 2011, Bunce et al. 2016). But still, the link between power and English is a real one, even if it is much more nuanced and unpredictable than either the enthusiasts for the spread of English or its critics suggest. And this implies some degree of enmeshment in ideology, whether the teacher likes it or not, or even *realizes* it or not. Jakubiak (2016) describes the alarming naivety of western native-speaker volunteer teachers (or 'voluntourists') in the developing world. A certain Lauren in South Africa saw her role not mainly as a teacher of

English but as one who 'offers inspiration and excitement to needy people', while Suzanne in Costa Rica explained 'tearfully' that

> I'd like [my students] to believe that if they really want it, that they could go on to college or they could – even if they don't go on to college – they could learn English, or they can at least know that there's somewhere out there... (Jakubiak 2016: 204–5)

As Jakubiak herself observes, this is language teaching seen as content-free, in the way we described in Chapters 1, 5 and 6. And indeed, this is the wretched (and sometimes even dangerous) result of the 'emptying' of TESOL – its removal from the sphere of education proper, with its long traditions of social responsibility and ethical standards, and disconnection from any accompanying academic discipline or core of specialist knowledge. It is tempting, though probably now futile, to wonder how we got here. Who first decided that English language teachers did not really need to be language specialists, or even teachers? In any case, it is plain to see how we get away from here again: the need for a critical pedagogy of TESOL (see e.g. Canagarajah 1999) has never been more urgent. Where ELT is thought of in terms simply of language knowledge on the one hand and methodology on the other, and teacher training involves little or no reflection on the way the English language globally is perceived, represented, distributed, differentially accessed, then ELT practitioners are apt to find themselves in invidious positions, intellectually unprepared and quite likely to do as much harm as good.

Teachers who are armed with critical language awareness and critical pedagogy perspectives, on the other hand, are unlikely either to feel baseless guilt at imposing a neocolonial language or to mistakenly imbue their learners with false hopes. The first, because they understand that English can form part of a speaker's linguistic repertoire without robbing them of agency; the second, because they understand that English comes with particular expectations and feeds into particular narratives, but that it does not alter social structures. Teachers who have embraced the role of critical practitioner use their position to focus on their learners' linguistic and communicative development from an informed perspective. In short, the only hope of finding a path through the thickets and jungles of ideology which have grown up around globalized English – but no other language, to anything remotely like the same degree – is for teachers to be thoroughly confident about their professional identity. And that means being thoroughly confident about their disciplinary expertise.

10.2.2 English is not just a 'foreign language'

One of the more exciting (and challenging, and thought-provoking) responsibilities of the English teacher is that in teaching students English, you are not only inducting them into new discourse communities – though of course, you are doing that to at least some extent, and to a very large extent if you teach EAP. You are inducting them into the enormous community of people who use English to communicate with the rest of the world. In a sense, the English teacher is the conduit through which a learner really begins to experience what it means to live in a globalized world and to have meaningful engagement with other cultures. Many of the teachers who wrote to us to tell us about their work felt this aspect of it very keenly. One African teacher said: '*Since English teaching has just started to be relevant for educational institutions in my country, I feel my classes are showing the students how to interact with peoples from different parts of the world*.' A Latin American, similarly, felt that '*as an English teacher I can show my students a little more about the world in which they live, because sometimes they don't know about other cultures and many things that happen outside their city*'.

If this role is to be taken seriously, taken on in its entirety with all that it reveals about the way English functions in the world, then the implications are clear. *Teachers have to embrace linguistic diversity.* Learners need to know that 'the vast majority of verbal [*sic*] exchanges in English do not involve any native speakers of the language at all' (Seidlhofer 2005: 339). They need to learn that not all native speakers speak standardly (or are white!). They need to be exposed to regional accents, non-standard Englishes, non-native Englishes, even English mixed with other languages, in the way it happens in the real world. They need to learn to think about accommodation, negotiation of meaning, the possibility of transcultural misunderstanding. And if their coursebook does not do this, then teachers must do it. And teachers need to do all this while *still*, in many cases, teaching the standard English which will prepare students to take and pass high-stakes exams – in other words, they need to 'square the circle', as Blair (2017) puts it. A German university teacher whom Fiona met at a conference in London summed it up like this:

> Obviously you need some kind of standard that you teach by at least for production, for reproduction, of course they need to be understandable. . . . We hope that they become craftier in their actual life because they are much more

likely to be talking to people from, I don't know, Spain or China in English than needing a perfect British accent for something.

But we all know that students are capable of focusing on the wrong thing, or misunderstanding the nature of the challenge – like the Chinese students we mentioned in Chapter 4 who were convinced that acquiring a British accent was the key to speaking good English. Put simply, learners of English need to develop critical language awareness, and it is teachers who must help them do it.

This has implications for methodology, too. A lot of the assumptions that still predominate in TESOL have been based on the 1970s paradigm out of which CLT developed. Not that there was anything particularly wrong with the paradigm in itself – but teachers, students and other stakeholders must now acknowledge that it doesn't really match the twenty-first-century reality. Take as an example the 'no-L1-in-the-classroom' rule, which we have had occasion to refer to several times in the course of this book. ELT then was largely conceived of either as taking place in 'home countries' with multilingual classrooms (where the principle of English-only teaching was an obvious one), or as involving monolingual native speakers teaching in EFL contexts, where English-only made some sense as the classroom was quite possibly the only place where English would be encountered. Nowadays, English is available more or less anywhere, if people have the will to access it, and it is used in a lingua franca way as well – therefore the aim of teaching is different, and what can be taught and learned in the classroom is different, too.

At the heart of the matter lies the peculiar position of English. In very large parts of the world, English is not really any more considered a 'foreign' language in the sense of a language primarily used by and associated with a particular population of native speaker foreigners. (Though this is less the case in some places than others – from the perspective of Mexico or Colombia, for instance, English is still identified overwhelmingly with the United States). Rather, it is an additional language for all, and often the default linguistic choice for dealing with people speaking *any* other language. We have no particular view on whether this is a desirable state of affairs or not, and we do not claim that it is unproblematic. But it is the state of play today, and we think that those who are involved in ELT – whether they teach, employ teachers, work in teacher development, design materials or plan the curriculum – may need to rethink their strategies accordingly.

10.2.3 The question of methodology

For some strange reason, English language teaching seems to prioritize methodology over almost any other aspect of the work. It seems to have produced more methodologies than any other subject area, and even sees itself as being in the vanguard of pedagogical technique. This might stem in part from the fact that vast amounts of money are invested in ELT as an industry (see Block et al. 2012), and that a good chunk of this goes to funding pedagogical research. In our experience, many teachers tend to regard mastering the perfect methodology as being the main goal of teacher development programmes, from the four-week CELTA course to an MA. The question 'How can I teach my students better?' almost *always* seems to expect an answer couched in terms of methodology. Our MA students over the years have sometimes been disappointed (at least at first) to find that our answer was couched primarily in terms of subject knowledge. And the subject is language.

Our argument was – and still is – that methodology emerges out of knowledge of language, that is linguistics knowledge, organically. We are not, of course, saying that methodology is useless or irrelevant, or that all language experts are automatically good teachers (sadly, they are not). We are saying that to approach the matter of teaching language from the starting point of methodology is to put the cart before the horse. If you are the kind of language expert who notices, and who likes to encourage students to notice and be curious about the language that surrounds them, then the question of methodology doesn't have to dominate your teaching approach – it can take something of a back seat. Good methodology springs from good language awareness.

10.2.4 The question of power and the question of expertise

When you talk to TESOL teachers around the world, perhaps the most common complaint they have – and it is one that we have touched upon repeatedly through the course of this book – is that nobody really understands their work. Or to be more specific, the people who are in charge of things don't understand. This goes right the way from top to bottom, and is most common of all in mainstream education, whether public or private. A common gripe is that national governments (usually in the form of a ministry of education) have a tendency to issue statements about English language learning and teaching, set objectives, formulate policy and in general make grand plans and pronouncements, all without having much idea at all about language learning and teaching. As one East Asian teacher commented, with delicate understatement, *'In my country, people making decisions on language education are not the most expert in the field.'*

Equally common, and equally resented, is the institutional manager (remember the 'bilingual coordinator' in Chapter 8?), language school director or head teacher who has no background or qualifications in language teaching, but still takes it upon themselves to tell the classroom teacher what they should be doing, and even how. We have come across endless examples of educational managers having utterly unreal expectations for student attainment, and imposing inappropriate teaching and assessment regimes accordingly:

> *Students here (undergraduates at a University) are supposed be at B1 level. But in reality they're often not even close to A1. As we have to follow coursebooks written for B1 level students, things become very difficult.* (British teacher in Middle East)

We have heard of managers patrolling the corridors and peering through classroom windows, making sure that their preferred methodology is being followed. (It quite often involves 'English-only in the classroom', you will not be surprised to hear). As we saw in Chapters 4 and 5, these people, who have a degree of power over teacher recruitment, are also very often in thrall to the ideology of the native speaker and native speaker 'correctness'. They have usually heard of CLT, too, and are much given to instructing their teachers to begin 'teaching communicatively' without delay. One teacher, cited in Machaal's (2012) study exploring the use of mother tongue in the classroom in Saudi Arabia comments, exasperatedly:

> Who are these policy makers? Again, are they acquainted with what teaching is? What English language teaching is? Have they ever been to the classroom? I mean they just mimic in a parrot way what somebody like Krashen said; that the use of L1 is a fatal error . . . So if it's a policy, I mean governments have changed their policies, how on earth can we not change this policy? (Machaal 2012: 207)

We could go on. Why are decisions about language and language teaching so often taken by non-linguists? Or to put a related question: why do English teachers so often lack power and authority in their institutions, even in their own field of expertise, so that they can be overruled (or simply not consulted) with regard to issues that lie within their own professional domain?

Well, everyone has an opinion on language. They don't always have an opinion on particle physics, or entomology, or human geography – but they always have an opinion on language. On 'correctness' or 'speaking properly', on what schools should teach, on what age children should start to learn a second language, on whether texting and social media have a negative effect on literacy, on which accent or variety of a language is the best or most attractive, on which is the easiest language to learn, and on plenty of other things, too. And of course, everyone is entitled to their opinion! But that doesn't mean that everyone's opinion, on a particular specialist subject, is equally good, or right, or worthy of consideration. For instance, Tim has a friend in Boston, Massachusetts, who is a civil engineer: we think that his views on how to build a bridge so that it will stay standing are more valuable than ours, and we imagine that the citizens of Boston would agree. Language teachers should be at the very forefront of shaping and leading debate about language learning and teaching, of helping people to understand how language works, correcting misapprehensions and guiding expectations, in their institutions and beyond. But if they do not own the disciplinary identity of language specialist, do not feel that the study of language is for them, feel perhaps that language teaching is really all about creating a fun atmosphere and 'getting the students to talk', then why should they expect to be listened to on the serious matters? If language teachers see themselves merely as skills providers, not educators (Gray 2000), then why should their opinion have any greater value than that of the unqualified manager or the government bureaucrat?

We have quite often come across EAP teachers working in universities who complain that they are not treated as 'proper' academics, either by their institutional management or by the academics from other disciplines whom they work alongside. This is indeed to be regretted: when EAP specialists genuinely work with other disciplinary specialists, as trusted collaborators in the process of curriculum and materials development, even as co-teachers, the results can be impressive. However, simply demanding the status of an academic peer is not enough. As a general rule, university academics are active researchers in their field. They read the specialist journals, they research and publish, they attend conferences, hold PhDs, and all the rest of it. If EAP teachers do little or none of this, do not think of themselves or position themselves as scholars in their field, then it is no surprise that they are treated as simply 'the English teacher'. As Breen (2018: 5) insists, rightly: 'So long as the label of English teacher is used to define us by our colleagues in the wider university, we will never earn the respect accorded to those who are seen as experts in a more specific subject.' For the unfortunate corollary to this is that quite often, even those EAP specialists who *do* have an academic profile, who research and publish, are not recognized institutionally as 'proper' academics – particularly in university language centres, which are increasingly being outsourced to commercial operations, their teachers rebadged as 'academic-related' or 'instructors'.

It is not just in EAP that the want of status is felt. As one of our ex-students remarked, in the UK particularly, ELT as a whole *'feels more and more like a service industry'*. The 'anyone can do it' view of English teaching is hugely damaging, and affects teachers at every level, in every kind of institution. If it is ever going to change, then teachers themselves, as a whole profession, need to rethink TESOL.

We are not suggesting that everyone who teaches English needs a PhD. We are, though, suggesting that if they wish to be taken seriously, teachers at every level have to own the disciplinary identity of the language specialist. This is clearly the way forward for those multilingual, language-aware native speakers who complain that they are valued *only* as native speakers in the commercial/ educational contexts in which they work (Ellis 2016, Coleman 2012). For non-native speaker teachers, who too often 'tend to be defined by their perceived deficiency in English' (Ellis 2016: 597), the benefits of positioning yourself as the institutional language expert are if anything even clearer. Non-native speakers who concede 'expert' or 'specialist' status to people who are actually just native speakers of English are entering a competition which they have already lost, and *could never possibly have won*. Ellis (2016) finishes her article on teacher linguistic identity on an optimistic and engaging note: 'In the future, the question we ask of a TESOL teacher may be neither "are you a native or non-native speaker?" nor "what variety of English do you speak?" but rather "how rich is your linguistic repertoire and how can this be deployed as a pedagogical resource?" ' (2016: 606). We concur, and we would add another question: 'How much do you understand about language as structure, language as a mode of communication, and language as a social phenomenon – and how can *this* be deployed as a pedagogical resource?'

10.3 Rethinking TESOL as language education

Language knowledge can radically change classroom practice. Consider, for example, the extraordinary explanatory power of the insight that spoken grammar really is different from written grammar (Carter and McCarthy 2017, Carter 1999). A Colombian teacher told us that to assess speaking he generally got his students to write a few paragraphs about themselves and their families and present this orally to the class. They were marked down for hesitation, repetition and so on, as he wanted to encourage a 'cultivated' way of speaking in them. Now, this is a test of plenty of things (grammatical form, structuring a text, memorization, pronunciation, confidence in public speaking, for example) but it is not a test of *speaking* in the sense of 'language for communication' (Widdowson 1983). Some understanding of language, of the spokenness-writtenness distinction we talked about in the last chapter, would have told him that. And remember our Chinese coursebook in Chapter 9, with an activity entitled 'Reading Aloud'. Actually, a similar strategy is still often employed in the UK for GCSE modern foreign languages, and most of us remember 'reading round the class' from our schooldays. We are not saying necessarily that it should not happen, or that it serves no purpose. But what is reading around the class actually *for*? Language-aware, linguistically informed teachers will always think about *why* they are doing things, and what it is that is actually being taught, practised or assessed in any given activity.

In teaching language, we should also be teaching students *about* language: not just how to speak and write, but how to think about speaking and writing in terms of genre, register, mode, and so on (though you might not use these particular terms), and how to choose their words effectively. Given the role of English in the world, we should also be exposing learners to different kinds of Englishes, even at a relatively low level (Sewell 2013). Now, of course there will be problems, and there will be objections. There is the question of coverage and the pressure of time – 'I don't have time to fit everything into the curriculum', and 'I have to finish the book.' This is entirely understandable. However, it assumes that everything in the coursebook is to be taught, and taught just as it is. But a teacher who has a real knowledge of the underlying language framework will have the confidence to select, adapt, replace or just do something different with the available material. The key thing is to make the students aware of what it is you are doing, what they are learning and why (Dow and Ouyang 2006).

Exposing students to non-standard, non-native and lingua franca English may meet with resistance from institutional managers and other stakeholders, such as parents. This is tricky, and teachers might well need to tread carefully. But it is here, of course, where we see the vital importance of language teachers positioning themselves as language experts: the confidence to argue one's case comes from the intellectual confidence of being a disciplinary specialist, rather than someone who happens to speak English. After all, there is obvious merit in showing students the difference between standard and non-standard forms, high register and low, native use and lingua franca use, and enabling them to discuss this in an informed manner: the teacher should be able to explain how all this makes students *more* able, not less, to employ standard English appropriately according to the context and to pass high-stakes exams.

Equally, there are bound to be objections to the use of students' L1 in the classroom. But the crucial point here is not that students talk in their own language, it is the *purpose* of the talk. If the aim is to discuss language, increase awareness, discuss and analyse English language text, then it may well be the case that this is better done in the home language, especially at lower levels. However, if the aim of an activity is to practise English itself, then obviously and of course the students should use English. The key is to have your aims and objectives clear. This goes for teachers as much as students – and for the institutional managers, too.

10.4 Conclusion

Our conception of the language classroom is that it should be a challenging environment – a place where students learn to re-examine their preconceptions about language and language practices. Equally, it should be an environment where students and teachers *exchange* knowledge and insight about language. It should be unsettling rather than soothing (though it can certainly also be that as well, sometimes), a place of active learning rather than one where the teacher delivers content and the students receive it. And this active learning should take place in relation to their L1 as well as to English.

Some people will doubtless argue that the job of the English teacher is to teach English. We agree. However, no language is isolated from the social context in which it is used, and learning another language – whether you like it or not – entails thinking about its relation to your own language, and the way language works more generally. The aim of all this, let it be said once again, is not to turn the unsuspecting learner of English into an academic applied linguist or social semiotician. The point is that if you give students interesting things to do with language, it will have a knock-on effect not only on how they feel about learning the language but also on their knowledge of the English language itself. The English language classroom is an ideal site – quite often the only available site – for exploring and discussing language and developing language awareness.

The answer to the question 'What do I teach when I teach English?' is, of course, 'language'. As we have been saying all along – if you're a language teacher, language should be your thing! The English classroom is first and foremost a language classroom.

Notes

Chapter 1

1   http://www.transitionsabroad.com/listings/work/esl/articles/south-korea-guide-teaching-english-living.shtml [Accessed 4 December 2016].

2   http://www.saudicareers.co.uk/the-roles/teachers-instructors/. http://www.berlitz.co.uk/about_us/employment_opportunities/. https://www.cia.gov/careers/opportunities/support-professional/foreign-language-instructors.html [Accessed 5 September 2017].

3   https://www.teachingenglish.org.uk/blogs/albertrayan/characteristics-highly-effective-teachers-english [Accessed 13 September 2018].

4   http://teachthought.com/pedagogy/6-qualities-of-successful-esl-teachers/.

5   Mario Rinvolucri, 'Humanising Language Teaching' http://www.newhltmag.co.uk/nov05/cse.htm [Accessed 13 October 2018].

6   https://simpleenglishuk.wordpress.com/2014/11/20/do-a-tefl-course-or-not-bother/ [Accessed 27 December 2017]. The question in the title of the webpage rather says it all!

7   https://www.tefl.com/job-seeker/jobpage.html?jobId=116446&countryId=44 [Accessed 11 October 2017].

8   https://www.lalanguefrancaise.com/general/les-30-meilleures-dictees-pour-ameliorer-son-francais/ [Accessed 20 March 2018].

Chapter 2

1   http://ltc-english.com/why-english-language-is-so-popular/ [Accessed 13 September 2018].

2   https://www.moroccoworldnews.com/2015/02/152663/will-english-become-first-foreign-language-morocco/ [Accessed 2 January 2017].

3   This and a number of similar ads can be seen online at http://www.openenglish.com/en/press/tv/ [Accessed 22 November 2016].

4 The Brazilian Portuguese version can be found at https://www.youtube.com/watch?v=H_CkGw8IdKQ [Accessed 22 November 2016].

5 Online at http://english-town-open.weebly.com/blog/open-english-o-englishtown [Accessed 15 November 2016).

6 In saying this, we do not necessarily subscribe to or identify ourselves with all the views of the ELF 'school', various as they are (Jenkins 2015, Seidlhofer 2011). We do, though, note that by its very nature, a language which is used predominantly by NNSs to interact with each other is less likely to own the identity of a systematized variety, and more likely to be made anew (or be 'constantly brought into being' per Canagarajah 2007: 91) in each new context where it is used.

7 http://englishharmony.com/english-is-the-world-language/ [Accessed 13 September 2018].

Chapter 3

1 The words in modern English that we refer to as 'latinate' in fact derive almost in their entirety not directly from Latin, but via Norman French, along with a number deriving via Celtic and Germanic borrowings from Latin (Baugh and Cable 1993). Modern Welsh, though, maintains plenty of words which actually do come direct from Roman Occupation-period Latin: *eglwys*, 'church', from Latin *ecclesia*; *ffenestr*, 'window' from Latin *fenestra* and so on.

2 https://qz.com/962056/by-quietly-expanding-the-role-of-hindi-in-government-narendra-modi-is-playing-with-fire/ [Accessed 22 July 2018].

3 To be fair, it should be noted that Canagarajah in general tends to plough his own distinct furrow on matters pertaining to English used as a lingua franca – and he does acknowledge immediately that this is a 'radical implication' (2007: 925). It certainly is.

Chapter 4

1 https://www.teachingenglish.org.uk/article/english-latin-america-examination-policy-priorities-seven-countries [Accessed 13 September 2018].

2 https://www.uel.ac.uk/Postgraduate/Courses/MA-English-Language-Teaching [Accessed 13 September 2018].

Chapter 6

1 Latin roots are conventionally used to describe the physiological features of the vocal tract just as they are in anatomy more generally. In this case, 'labio' refers to the lips, 'dental' to the teeth and 'fricative' to the action of air passing through a gap where there is some turbulence in the air flow.
2 When referring to the individual sounds represented in the IPA we use square brackets [ ] but when we are using the language-specific phonemic alphabet, we use the double slashes / /.
3 Speakers of varieties which are influenced by other native languages such as Irish or Welsh might use such a form when speaking English, perhaps as a cultural identity marker, but they would be unlikely to write it.
4 Note how some of the initial consonants change, too, as the sentence structure changes. Initial consonant mutation is one of the characteristic quirks of the Celtic languages – and can be a challenging one for the learner.

Chapter 8

1 Available at https://www.youtube.com/watch?v=kUQZifVTIJI&t=3s [Accessed 8 April 2018].
2 An 'academy' school is similar to a 'charter' school in some other countries. They are, essentially, publicly funded independent or private schools which are run by 'academy trusts' sponsored by organizations such as commercial businesses, faith groups or voluntary groups.

References

Alsagoff, L., McKay, S. L., Hu, G., and Renandya, W. (eds) (2012), *Principles and Practices for Teaching English as an International Language*. New York: Routledge.

Álvarez, J. A. (2016), 'English around the Globe and Translocal Flows', in Álvarez, J. A., Amanti, C., and Mackinney, E. (eds), *Critical Views on Teaching and Learning English Around the Globe: Qualitative Research Approaches*. Charlotte, NC: Information Age Publishing, pp. 1–14.

Aneja, G. (2016), '(Non)native Speakered: Rethinking (Non)nativeness and Teacher Identity in TESOL Teacher Education'. *TESOL Quarterly* 50(3): 572–96.

Appleby, R. (2010), *ELT, Gender and International Development: Myths of Progress in a Neocolonial World*. Bristol: Multilingual Matters.

Baker, W. (2012), 'English as a Lingua Franca in Thailand: Characterisations and Implications'. *Englishes in Practice* 1(1): 18–27.

Barnes, D. (1976), *From Curriculum to Communication*. London: Penguin.

Barton, D. and Papen, U. (eds) (2010), *The Anthropology of Writing: Understanding Textually-Mediated Worlds*. London: Continuum.

Bauer, L. and Trudgill, P. (eds) (1998), *Language Myths*. London: Penguin.

Baugh, A. and Cable, T. (1993), *A History of the English Language* (4th edn). Englewood Cliffs, NJ: Prentice Hall.

Bax, S. (2003), 'Authenticity, Culture and Language Learning'. *ELT Journal* 57(3): 278–87.

Befu, H. (2001), *Hegemony of Homogeneity: An Anthropological Analysis of Nihonjinron*. Melbourne: Trans Pacific Press.

Benson, P. and Voller, P. (2013), *Autonomy and Independence in Language Learning*. Abingdon: Routledge.

Berkey, J. (2003), *The Formation of Islam: Religion and Society in the Near East, 600–1800*. Cambridge: Cambridge University Press.

Berns, M. (2003), '(Re)experiencing Hegemony: The Linguistic Imperialism of Robert Phillipson', in Seidlhofer, B. (ed.), *Controversies in Applied Linguistics*. Oxford: Oxford University Press, pp. 33–44.

Bhattacharya, R., Gupta, S., Jewitt, C., Newfield, D., Reed, Y., and Stein, P. (2011), 'The Policy-Practice Nexus in English Classrooms in Delhi,

Johannesburg, and London: Teachers and the Textual Cycle'. *TESOL Quarterly* 41(3): 465–87.

Blair, A. (2017), 'Standard Language Models, Variable Lingua Franca Goals: How Can ELF-Aware Teacher Education Square the Circle?'. *Journal of English as a Lingua Franca* 6(2): 345–66.

Block, D., Gray, J., and Holborow, M. (2012), *Neoliberalism and Applied Linguistics*. London: Routledge.

Blommaert, J. (2005), *Discourse*. Cambridge: Cambridge University Press.

Blommaert, J. (2010), *The Sociolinguistics of Globalization*. Cambridge: Cambridge University Press.

Blommaert, J. (2014), 'Sociolinguistics', in Leung, C. and Street, B. (eds), *The Routledge Companion to English Studies*. London: Routledge, pp. 131–44.

Blommaert, J. (2016), 'Teaching the English That Makes One Happy: English Teaching Could Be Far More Effective If Targeted at Specific Niches of "Integration"'. *English Today* 32(3): 11–13.

Blommaert, J. and Jie, D. (2010), *Ethnographic Fieldwork: A Beginner's Guide*. Bristol: Multilingual Matters.

Blommaert, J. and Rampton, B. (2011), 'Language and Superdiversity'. *Diversities* 13(2): 3–21.

Borg, S. (2006), 'The Distinctive Characteristics of Foreign Language Teachers'. *Language Teaching Research* 10(1): 3–31.

Bourdieu, P. (1991), *Language and Symbolic Power*. Cambridge: Polity Press.

Breen, M. (1985), 'Authenticity in the Language Classroom'. *Applied Linguistics* 6(1): 60–70.

Breen, P. (2018), *Developing Educators for the Digital Age: A Framework for Capturing Knowledge in Action*. London: University of Westminster Press.

British Council (2015), *English in Colombia: An Examination of Policy, Perceptions and Influencing Factors* https://ei.britishcouncil.org/sites/default/files/latin-america-research/English in Colombia.pdf [Accessed 22 March 2017].

British Council (2016), *English in Latin America: An Examination of Policy and Priorities in Seven Countries* https://www.teachingenglish.org.uk/article/english-latin-america-examination-policy-priorities-seven-countries [Accessed 17 January 2018].

Brosch, C. (2015), 'On the Conceptual History of the Term *Lingua Franca*'. *Apples – Journal of Applied Language Studies* 9(1): 71–85.

Bruthiaux, P. (2002), 'Hold Your Courses: Language Education, Language Choice, and Economic Development'. *TESOL Quarterly* 36(3): 275–96.

Brutt-Griffler, J. (2002), *World English: A Study of its Development*. Clevedon: Multilingual Matters.

Bunce, P. (2016), 'Voluntary Overseas English Language Teaching: A Myopic, Altruistic Hydra', in Bunce, P., Phillipson, R., Rapatahana, V., and Tupas, R. (eds), *Why English? Confronting the Hydra*. Bristol: Multilingual Matters, pp. 106–17.

Bunce, P., Phillipson, R., Rapatahana, V., and Tupas, R. (2016), 'Introduction', in Bunce, P., Phillipson, R., Rapatahana, V., and Tupas, R. (eds), *Why English? Confronting the Hydra*. Bristol: Multilingual Matters, pp. 1–20.

Byram, M., Gribkova, B., and Starkey, H. (2002), *Developing the Intercultural Dimension in Language Teaching: A Practical Introduction for Teachers*. Strasbourg: Council of Europe.

Byram, M. and Feng, A. (2005), 'Culture and Language Learning: Teaching, Research and Scholarship'. *Language Teaching* 37(3): 149–68.

Canagarajah, S. (1999), *Resisting Linguistic Imperialism in English Teaching*. Oxford: Oxford University Press.

Canagarajah, S. (2007), 'The Ecology of Global English'. *International Multilingual Research Journal* 1(2): 89–100.

Canagarajah, S. (2013), *Translingual Practice: Global Englishes and Cosmopolitan Relations*. London: Routledge.

Canagarajah, S. (2014), 'In Search of a New Paradigm for Teaching English as an International Language'. *TESOL Journal* 5(4): 767–85.

Canagarajah, S. and Ben Said, S. (2011), 'Linguistic Imperialism', in Simpson, J. (ed.), *The Routledge Handbook of Applied Linguistics*. London: Routledge, pp. 388–400.

Carter, R. (ed.) (1982), *Linguistics and the Teacher*. London: Routledge.

Carter, R. (1999), 'Standard Grammars, Spoken Grammars: Some Educational Implications', in Bex, T. and R. Watts (eds), *Standard English: The Widening Debate*. London: Routledge, pp. 149–66.

Carter, R. (2003), 'Teaching about Talk – What Do Pupils Need to Know about Spoken Language and the Important Ways in Which Talk Differs from Writing?' in Carter, R. and Coffin, C. (eds), *New Perspectives on Spoken English in the Classroom*. London: Qualifications and Curriculum Authority, pp. 5–13.

Carter, R. and McCarthy, M. (2017), 'Spoken Grammar: Where Are We and Where Are We Going?'. *Applied Linguistics* 38(1): 1–20.

Chen, Y. (2017), 'Foreign Languages as Cultural Capital: Empowering UK Students from Disadvantaged Backgrounds through the Learning of Chinese'. Talk given at Goldsmiths, University of London, 6 December 2017.

Cheng, W. and Warren, M. (2006), '// you need to be RUTHless //: Entertaining Cross-Cultural Differences'. *Language and Intercultural Communication* 6(1): 35–56.

Cheshire, J., Kerswill, P., Fox, S., and Torgersen, E. (2011), 'Contact, the Feature Pool and the Speech Community: The Emergence of Multicultural London English'. *Journal of Sociolinguistics* 15(2): 151–96.

Cheskin, A. (2015), 'Identity and Integration of Russian Speakers in the Baltic States: A Framework for Analysis'. *Ethnopolitics* 14(1): 72–93.

Cho, J. (2015), 'Sleepless in Seoul: Neoliberalism, English Fever, and Linguistic Insecurity among Korean Interpreters'. *Multilingua* 34(5): 687–710.

Clayton, T. (2006), *Language Choice in a Nation Under Transition: English Language Spread in Cambodia*. Boston, MA: Springer.

Cogo, A. (2012), 'English as a Lingua Franca: Concepts, Use, and Implications'. *ELT Journal* 66(1): 97–105.

Cogo, A. and Dewey, M. (2012), *Analysing English as a Lingua Franca: A Corpus-Driven Investigation*. London: Bloomsbury.

Cogo, A. and Jenkins, J. (2010), 'English as a Lingua Franca in Europe: A Mismatch between Policy and Practice'. *European Journal of Language Policy* 2(2): 271–94.

Coleman, H. (2010), *The English Language in Development*. London: British Council.

Coleman, H. (2011), 'Developing Countries and the English Language: Rhetoric, Risks, Roles and Recommendations', in Coleman, H. (ed.), *Dreams and Realities: Developing Countries and the English Language*. London: British Council, pp. 9–22.

Coleman, J. (2012), 'Moving beyond an "Instrumental" Role for the First Languages of English Language Learners'. *TESOL in Context* 22(1): 18–37.

Cook, V. (1999), 'Going beyond the Native Speaker in Language Teaching'. *TESOL Quarterly* 33(2): 185–209.

Cook, V. (2001), 'Using the First Language in the Classroom'. *The Canadian Modern Language Review* 57(3): 402–23.

Cook, V. (2016), 'Where Is the Native Speaker Now?'. *TESOL Quarterly* 50(1): 186–89.

Cortina, R. (ed.) (2014), *The Education of Indigenous Citizens in Latin America*. Bristol: Multilingual Matters.

Creese, A. and Blackledge, A. (2010), 'Translanguaging in the Bilingual Classroom: A Pedagogy for Learning and Teaching?'. *Modern Language Journal* 94(1): 103–15.

Crystal, D. (2003), *English as a Global Language* (2nd edn). Cambridge: Cambridge University Press.

Dakhlia, J. (2008), *Lingua Franca*. Arles: Actes Sud.

Darquennes, J. (2016), 'Lingua Francas of Europe', in Linn, A. (ed.), *Investigating English in Europe: Contexts and Agendas*. Berlin: DeGruyter Mouton, pp. 28–33.

Dashti, A. (2015), 'The Role and Status of the English Language in Kuwait'. *English Today* 31(3): 28–33.

Davies, A. (1996), 'Review Article: Ironising the Myth of Linguicism'. *Journal of Multilingual and Multicultural Development* 17(6): 485–96.

Davies, A. (2013), 'Is the Native Speaker Dead?'. *Histoire Épistémologie Langage* 35(2): 17–28.

Davies, A. (2017), 'Commentary on the Native Speaker Status in Pronunciation Research', in Isaacs, T. and Trofimovich, P. (eds), *Second Language Pronunciation Assessment: Interdisciplinary Perspectives*. Bristol: Multilingual Matters, pp. 185–92.

Dekeyser, R. (2009), 'Cognitive-Psychological Processes in Second Language Learning' in Long, M. and Doughty, C. (eds), *The Handbook of Language Teaching*. Chichester: Wiley-Blackwell, pp. 119–38.

de Mejía, A.-M. (ed.) (2005), *Bilingual Education in South America*. Clevedon: Multilingual Matters.

Derwing, T. (2010), 'Utopian Goals for Pronunciation Teaching', in Levis, J. and LeVelle, K. (eds), *Proceedings of the 1st Pronunciation in Second Language Learning and Teaching Conference*. Ames: Iowa State University, pp. 24–37.

de Swaan, A. (2001), *Words of the World: The Global Language System*. Malden: John Wiley.

Dewey, M. (2012), 'Towards a *Post-normative* Approach: Learning the Pedagogy of ELF'. *Journal of English as a Lingua Franca* 1(1): 141–70.

Dewey, M. (2015), 'ELF, Teacher Knowledge and Professional Development', in Bowles, H. and Cogo, A. (eds), *International Perspectives on English as a Lingua Franca*. Basingstoke: Palgrave Macmillan, pp. 176–93.

Dickey, E. (2016), *Learning Latin the Ancient Way: Latin Textbooks from the Ancient World*. Cambridge: Cambridge University Press.

Ding, Y.-R. (2007), 'Text Memorization and Imitation: The Practices of Successful Chinese Learners of English'. *System* 35(1): 271–80.

Dong, H. (2014), *A History of the Chinese Language*. London: Routledge.

Dornyei, Z. (2005), *The Psychology of the Language Learner: Individual Differences in Second Language Acquisition*. Mahwah, NJ: Lawrence Erlbaum.

Dornyei, Z. (2009), *The Psychology of Second Language Acquisition*. Oxford: Oxford University Press.

Dow, E. and Ouyang, H. H. (2006), 'Inside-Out: Student Criticism of "Foreign Experts" in Universities in the PRC'. https://www.llas.ac.uk//resources/gpg/2576 [Accessed 14 April 2018].

EC (European Commission) (2011), *Lingua Franca: Chimera or Reality?*. Brussels: European Commission, Directorate-General for Translation.

Edge, J. (2003), 'Imperial Troopers and Servants of the Lord: A Vision of TESOL for the 21st century'. *TESOL Quarterly* 37: 701–9.

Ellis, R. (2003), *Task-based Language Learning and Teaching*. Oxford: Oxford University Press.

Ellis, E. (2016), '"I May Be a Native Speaker, but I'm Not Monolingual": Reimagining All Teachers' Linguistic Identities in TESOL'. *TESOL Quarterly* 50(3): 597–630.

Ellis, S. and McCarthy, E. (eds) (2011), *Applied Linguistics and Primary School Teaching*. Cambridge: Cambridge University Press.

English, F. (2012), *Student Writing and Genre: Reconfiguring Academic Knowledge*. London: Bloomsbury. [First published in 2011 by Continuum].

English, F. (2015), 'Writing Differently: Creating Different Spaces for Student Learning', in Chik, A., Costley, T. and Pennington, M. (eds), *Creativity and Discovery in University Writing: A Teacher's Guide*. Sheffield: Equinox, pp. 95–114.

English, F. and Marr, T. (2015), *Why Do Linguistics? Reflective Linguistics and the Study of Language*. London: Bloomsbury.

Eslami, Z., Wright, K., and Sonnenburg, S. (2014), 'Globalized English: Power, Ethics and Ideology', in Seawright, L. (ed.), *Going Global: Transnational Perspectives on Globalization, Language, and Education*. Newcastle-upon-Tyne: Cambridge Scholars, pp. 2–17.

Everson, M., Chang, K., and Ross, C. (2016), *Developing Initial Literacy in Chinese*. New York: Asia Society.

Fang, F. (2016), '"Mind Your Local Accent": Does Accent Training Resonate to College Students' English Use?' *Englishes in Practice* 3(1): 1–28.

Far, M. (2008), 'On the Relationship between ESP and EGP: A General Perspective'. *English for Specific Purposes World* 1(17): 1–11.

Figueiredo, D. (2010), 'Context, Register and Genre: Implications for Language Education'. *Revista Signos* 43: 119–41.

Fillmore, L. W. and Snow, C. (2000), *What Teachers Need To Know About Language*. US Dept of Education/Center for Applied Linguistics. https://people.ucsc.edu/~ktellez/wong-fill-snow.html [Accessed 12 September 2017].

Firth, A. (1996), 'The Discursive Accomplishment of Normality. On "Lingua Franca" English and Conversation Analysis'. *Journal of Pragmatics* 26(2): 237–59.

Flores, N. (2013), 'The Unexamined Relationship between Neoliberalism and Plurilingualism: A Cautionary Tale'. *TESOL Quarterly* 47(3): 500–20.

Galloway, N. (2014), '"I Get Paid for My American Accent": The Story of One Multilingual English Teacher (MET) in Japan'. *Englishes in Practice* 1(1): 1–30.

Galloway, N. and Rose, H. (2013), '"They Envision Going to New York, not Jakarta": The Differing Attitudes toward ELF of Students, Teaching Assistants, and Instructors in an English-Medium Business Program in Japan'. *Journal of English as a Lingua Franca* 2(2): 229–53.

Galloway N. and Rose, H. (2017), 'Raising Awareness of Global Englishes in the ELT Classroom'. *ELT Journal* 72(1): doi: 10.1093/elt/ccx010.

García, O. (2009), *Bilingual Education in the 21st Century: A Global Perspective.* Chichester: Wiley-Blackwell.

García, O. (2011), 'Language Spread and Its Study in the 21st Century', in Kaplan, R. (ed.), *Oxford Handbook of Applied Linguistics* (2nd edn). Oxford: Oxford University Press, pp. 398–411.

García, O. and Li, W. (2014), *Translanguaging: Language, Bilingualism and Education.* Basingstoke: Palgrave Macmillan.

Garner, B. (2016), *Garner's Modern English Usage.* Oxford: Oxford University Press.

Garton, S. and Graves, K. (2014), 'Materials in ELT: Current Issues', in Garton, S. and Graves, K. (eds), *International Perspectives on Materials in ELT.* London: Palgrave Macmillan, pp. 1–15.

Gee, J. (1996), *Social Linguistics and Literacies: Ideology in Discourses* (2nd edn). London: Taylor and Francis.

Geng, Y. and Yuan, A. (2015), 'Chinese or English education? A challenge Confronted by Chinese Government'. *US-China Education Review* 5(5): 333–41.

Geyser, J. (2006), *English to the World: Teaching Methodology Made Easy.* Puchong, Malaysia: August Publishing.

Gilmore, A. (2004), 'A Comparison of Textbook and Authentic Interactions'. *ELT Journal* 58(4): 363–74.

Giovanelli, M. (2015), 'Becoming an English Language Teacher: Linguistic Knowledge, Anxieties and the Shifting Sense of Identity'. *Language and Education* 29(5): 416–29.

Giovanelli, M. and Clayton, D. (eds) (2016), *Knowing About Language: Linguistics and the Secondary English Classroom.* London: Routledge.

Goddard, A. (2016), 'Language and Linguistics in Higher Education: Transition and Post-16 English', in Giovanelli, M., and Clayton, D. (eds), *Knowing About Language: Linguistics and the Secondary English Classroom.* London: Routledge, pp. 210–22.

Gorski, P. (2008), 'Good Intentions Are Not Enough: A Decolonizing Intercultural Education'. *Intercultural Education* 19(6): 515–25.

Gray, J. (2000), 'The ELT Coursebook as Cultural Artefact: How Teachers Censor and Adapt'. *ELT Journal* 54(3): 274–83.

Gray, J. (2010a), *The Construction of English: Culture, Consumerism and Promotion in the ELT Global Coursebook.* Basingstoke: Palgrave Macmillan.

Gray, J. (2010b) 'The Branding of the New Capitalism: Representations of the World of Work in English Language Textbooks'. *Applied Linguistics* 31(5): 714–33.

Gray, J. and Morton, T. (2018), *Social Interaction and English Language Teacher Identity.* Edinburgh: Edinburgh University Press.

Grin, F. (2003), 'Economics and Language Planning'. *Current Issues in Language Planning* 4(1): 1–66.

Grosjean, F. (1982), *Life With Two Languages: An Introduction To Bilingualism.* Cambridge, MA: Harvard University Press.

Grosjean, F. (1989), 'Neurolinguists, Beware! The Bilingual Is Not Two Monolinguals in One person'. *Brain and Language* 36(1): 3–15.

Guariento,W. and Morley, J. (2001), 'Text and Task Authenticity in the EFL Classroom'. *ELT Journal* 55(4): 347–53.

Guo, Y. and Beckett, G. (2007), 'The Hegemony of English as a Global Language: Reclaiming Local Knowledge and Culture in China'. *Convergence* 40(1–2): 117–31.

Hadisantosa, N. (2010), 'Insights from Indonesia', in Johnstone, R. (ed.), *Learning Through English: Policies, Challenges and Prospects: Insights From Asia.* London: The British Council, pp. 24–46.

Halliday, M. A. K. (2007), *Language and Education.* London: Continuum.

Halliday, M. A. K. (1985), *An Introduction to Functional Grammar.* London: Edward Arnold

Halliday, M. A. K., McIntosh, A., and Strevens, P. (1964), *The Linguistic Sciences and Language Teaching.* London: Longmans.

Halliday, M. A. K. and Hasan, R. (1989), *Language, Context and Text: Aspects of Language in a Social-Semiotic Perspective* (2nd edn). Oxford: Oxford University Press.

Hann, N. (2010), 'ESOL for Employability Training Materials in the United Kingdom: Contexts and Effects', in Tomlinson, B. and Masuhara, H. (eds), *Research for Materials Development in Language Teaching.* London: Bloomsbury, pp. 172–88.

Harmer, J. (2015), *The Practice of English Language Teaching* (5th edn). Harlow: Longman.

Hasan, R. (1989), 'The Structure of a Text', in Halliday, M. A. K. and Hasan, R. (eds), *Language, Context and Text: Aspects of Language in a Social-Semiotic Perspective.* Oxford: Oxford University Press.

Heller, M. (2007), 'Bilingualism as Ideology and Practice' in Heller, M. (ed.), *Bilingualism: A Social Approach.* Basingstoke: Palgrave, pp. 1–22.

Helms, J. (1998), 'Science and Me: Subject Matter and Identity in Secondary Science School Teachers'. *Journal of Research in Science Teaching* 35(7): 811–34.

Hickey, R. (2012), 'Standard English and Standards of English', in Hickey, R. (ed.), *Standards of English: Codified Varieties Around the World.* Cambridge: Cambridge University Press, pp. 1–31.

Hoffman, K. and Centeno, M. A. (2003), 'The Lopsided Continent: Inequality in Latin America'. *Annual Review of Sociology* 29: 363–90.

Hodge, R. and Kress, G. (1993), *Language as Ideology* (2nd edn). London: Routledge.

Hoey, M. (1991), *Patterns of Lexis in Text*. Oxford: Oxford University Press.

Holliday, A. (2006), 'Native-Speakerism'. *ELT Journal* 6: 385–7.

Honey, J. (1989), *Does Accent Matter? The Pygmalion Factor*. London: Faber and Faber.

Honey, J. (1997), *Language is Power: The Story of Standard English and its Enemies*. London: Faber and Faber.

House, J. (1999), 'Misunderstanding in Intercultural Communication: Interactions in English as a Lingua Franca and the Myth of Mutual Intelligibility', in Gnutzmann, C. (ed.), *Teaching and Learning English as a Global Language*. Tübingen: Stauffenburg, pp. 73–89.

House, J. (2007), 'Communicative Styles in English and German'. *European Journal of English Studies* 10(3): 249–67.

Howard, M. (2008), *Spoken Dialogues in English Language Teaching Text Books: The Speech Genre of Asking for and Giving Directions*. Unpublished MA dissertation, London Metropolitan University.

Hu, G. (2002), 'Potential Cultural Resistance to Pedagogical Imports: The Case of Communicative Language Teaching in China'. *Language, Culture and Curriculum* 15(2): 93–105.

Hu, G. (2005), '"CLT is Best for China" – An Untenable Absolutist Claim'. *ELT Journal* 59(1): 65–8.

Hult, F. (2014), 'How Does Policy Influence Language in Education?', in Silver, R. and Lwin, S. (eds), *Language in Education: Social Implications*. London: Continuum, pp. 159–75.

Hunston, S. and Francis, G. (2000), *Pattern Grammar: A Corpus-driven Approach*. Amsterdam: John Benjamins.

Hyland, K. (2000), *Disciplinary Discourses: Social Interactions in Academic Writing*. London: Longman.

Hyland, K. (2006), *English for Academic Purposes: An Advanced Resource Book*. Abingdon: Routledge.

Hyland, K. (2007), 'Genre Pedagogy: Language, Literacy and L2 Writing Instruction'. *Journal of Second Language Writing* 16: 148–64.

Hymes, D. (1977), *Foundations in Sociolinguistics*. Abingdon: Tavistock Press.

Hymes, D. (1996), *Ethnography, Linguistics, Narrative Inequality: Toward an Understanding of Voice*. London: Taylor and Francis.

Ishikawa, T. (2015), 'Academic Rigour in Criticising English as a Lingua Franca'. *Englishes in Practice* 2(2): 39–48.

Itier, C. (2011), 'What Was the *Lengua General* of Colonial Peru?', in Pearce, A. and Heggarty, P. (eds), *History and Language in the Andes*. New York: Palgrave Macmillan, pp. 63–85.

Ivanic, R., Edwards, R., Satchwell, C., Mannion, G., Smith, J. and Fowler, Z. (eds) (2009), *Improving Learning in College: Rethinking Literacies Across the Curriculum*. London: Routledge.

Jakubiak, C. (2016), 'A Pedagogy of Enthusiasm: A Critical View of English-Language Voluntourism', in Álvarez, J. A., Amanti, C., and Mackinney, E. (eds), *Critical Views on Teaching and Learning English Around the Globe: Qualitative Research Approaches*. Charlotte, North Carolina: Information Age Publishing, pp. 193–209.

Janks, H. (2004), 'The Access Paradox'. *Literacy Learning: The Middle Years* 12(1)/*English in Australia* 139: 33–42.

Jaworski, A. and Thurlow, C. (eds) (2010), *Semiotic Landscapes: Language, Image, Space*. London: Bloomsbury.

Jenkins, J. (2006a), 'Current Perspectives on Teaching World Englishes and English as a Lingua Franca'. *TESOL Quarterly* 40(1): 157–81.

Jenkins, J. (2006b), 'Global Intelligibility and Local Diversity: Possibility or Paradox?', in Rubdy, R. and Saraceni, M. (eds), *English in the World: Global Rules, Global Roles*. London: Continuum, pp. 32–9.

Jenkins, J. (2007), *English as a Lingua Franca: Attitude and Identity*. Oxford: Oxford University Press.

Jenkins, J. (2015), 'Repositioning English and Multilingualism in English as a Lingua Franca'. *Englishes in Practice* 2(3): 49–85.

Jenkins, J. (2017), 'Trouble with English?', in Kelly, M. (ed.), *Languages after Brexit: How the UK Talks to the World*. Basingstoke: Palgrave Macmillan, pp. 25–34.

Jenkins, J., Cogo, A., and Dewey, M. (2011), 'Review of Developments in Research into English as a Lingua Franca'. *Language Teaching* 44(3): 281–315.

Jensen, C. (1999), 'Tupí-Guaraní', in Dixon, R. and Aikhenvald, A. (eds), *The Amazonian Languages*. Cambridge: Cambridge University Press, pp. 125–63.

Jewitt, C., Bezemer, J., and O'Halloran, K. (2016), *Introducing Multimodality*. Abingdon: Routledge.

Johnson, A. (2009), 'The Rise of English: The Language of Globalization in China and the European Union'. *Macalester International* 22(12): 131–68.

Jørgensen, J. and Møller, J. (2014), 'Polylingualism and Languaging', in Leung, C. and Street, B. (eds), *The Routledge Companion to English Studies*. London and New York: Routledge, pp. 67–83.

Joseph, M., and Ramani, E. (2006), 'English in the World Does Not Mean English Everywhere: The Case for Multilingualism in the ELT/ESL Profession', in Rubdy, R. and Saraceni, M. (eds), *English in the World: Global Rules, Global Roles*. London: Continuum, pp. 186–99.

Kachru, B. (1985), 'Standards, Codification and Sociolinguistic Realism: The English Language in the Outer Circle', in Quirk, R. and Widdowson,

H. (eds), *English in the World: Teaching and Learning the Language and Literatures*. Cambridge: Cambridge University Press, pp. 11–30.

Kamwangamalu, N. (2016), *Language Policy and Economics: The Language Question in Africa*. London: Palgrave Macmillan.

Kettemann, B. (1995), 'Concordancing in English Language Teaching'. *TELL and CALL* 4: 4–15.

Kim, H. and Elder, C. (2009), 'Understanding Aviation English as a Lingua Franca: Perceptions of Korean Aviation Personnel'. *Australian Review of Applied Linguistics* 32(3): 23.1–23.17.

Kimura, D. (2017), 'L1 English Speaker Participation in ELF Interaction: A Single Case Analysis of Dyadic Institutional Talk'. *Journal of English as a Lingua Franca* 6(2): 265–86.

King, B. (2008), '"Being Gay Guy, That Is the Advantage": Queer Korean Language Learning and Identity Construction'. *Journal of Language, Identity and Education* 7: 230–52.

Kirkpatrick, A. (2006), 'Which Model of English? Native-Speaker, Nativized or Lingua Franca?', in Rubdy, R. and Saraceni, M. (eds), *English in the World: Global Rules, Global Roles*. London: Continuum, pp. 71–83.

Kirkpatrick, A. (2009), 'Learning English and Other Languages in Multilingual Settings: Myths and Principles'. Hong Kong: Hong Kong Institute of Education.

Kirkpatrick, A. (2010), *English as a Lingua Franca in ASEAN: A Multilingual Model*. Hong Kong: Hong Kong University Press.

Kirkpatrick, A. (2011), 'English as an Asian Lingua Franca and the Multilingual Model of ELT'. *Language Teaching* 44(2): 212–24.

Kirkpatrick, A. (2012), 'English in ASEAN: Implications for Regional Multilingualism'. *Journal of Multilingual and Multicultural Development* 33(4): 331–44.

Kirkpatrick, A. (2015), 'ELF in Asia: Implications for Pedagogy'. Talk given at Goldsmiths, University of London, 29 October 2015.

Knapp, K. and Meierkord, C. (eds) (2002), *Lingua Franca Communication*. Frankfurt am Main: Peter Lang GmbH.

Knell, E. and West, H. (2015), 'Writing Practice and Chinese Character Recognition in Early Chinese Immersion Students'. *Journal of the Chinese Language Teachers Association* 50(3): 45–61.

Kramsch, C. (2009), *The Multilingual Subject: What Foreign Language Learners Say about their Experience and Why it Matters*. Oxford: Oxford University Press.

Kress, G. (2003), *Literacy in the New Media Age*. London: Routledge.

Kress, G. (2010), *Multimodality: A Social Semiotic Approach to Contemporary Communication*. London: Routledge.

Kress, G. and van Leeuwen, T. (1996), *Reading Images – The Grammar or Visual Design*. London: Routledge

Kubota, R. and Okuda, T. (2016), 'Confronting Language Myths, Linguicism and Racism in English Language Teaching in Japan', in Bunce, P., Phillipson, R., Rapatahana, V., and Tupas, R. (eds), *Why English? Confronting the Hydra*. Bristol: Multilingual Matters, pp. 159–76.

Kumaravadivelu, B. (2003), *Beyond Methods: Macrostrategies for Language Teaching*. New Haven: Yale University Press.

Kumaravadivelu, B. (2012), *Language Teacher Education for a Global Society: A Modular Model for Knowing, Analyzing, Recognizing, Doing, and Seeing.* Abingdon: Routledge.

Kumaravadivelu, B. (2016), 'The Decolonial Option in English Teaching: Can the Subaltern Act?'. *TESOL Quarterly* 50(1): 66–85.

Labov, W. (1972), *Sociolinguistic Patterns*. Philadelphia: University of Pennsylvania Press.

Lee, S. (2012), *Japanese Learners' Underlying Beliefs Affecting Foreign Language Learners' Motivation: New Perspectives of Affective Factors Mechanism.* Shiga: Afrasian Research Centre, Ryukoku University. Studies on Multicultural Societies Working Papers Series No. 4.

Lee, W. (1995), 'Authenticity Revisited'. *ELT Journal* 49(4): 323–8.

Lefevre, R. (2015), 'The Coming of North Africa's "Language Wars"'. *Journal of North African Studies* 20(4): 499–502.

Lenhart, A., Arafeh, S., Smith, A., and Macgill, A. (2008), 'Writing Technology and Teens', Report for The National Commission on Writing, Washington, DC: Pew Internet & American Life Project. Available at http://www.pewinternet.org/Reports/2008/Writing-Technology-and-Teens.aspx.

Leung, C. (2005), 'Convivial Communication: Recontextualizing Communicative Competence'. *International Journal of Applied Linguistics* 15(2): 119–44.

Lewis, G., Jones, B., and Baker, C. (2012), 'Translanguaging: Origins and Development from School to Street and Beyond'. *Educational Research and Evaluation* 18(7): 641–54.

Li, W. (2016), 'New Chinglish and the Post-Multilingualism Challenge: Translanguaging ELF in China'. *Journal of English as a Lingua Franca* 5(1): 1–25.

Li, W. (2018), 'Translanguaging as a Practical Theory of Language'. *Applied Linguistics* 39(1): 9–30.

Lillis, T. (2013), *The Sociolinguistics of Writing*. Edinburgh: Edinburgh University Press.

Linn, A. (2016), *Investigating English in Europe: Contexts and Agendas*. Berlin: DeGruyter Mouton.

Lock, G. (1996), *Functional English Grammar: An Introduction for Second Language Teachers*. Cambridge: Cambridge University Press.

López, D. and Bartlett, L. (2014), 'Language and Identities', in Leung, C. and Street, B. (eds), *The Routledge Companion to English Studies*. London: Routledge, pp. 344–58.

Lopriore, L. and Vettorel, P. (2015), 'Promoting Awareness of Englishes and ELF in the English Language Classroom', in Bowles, H. and Cogo, A. (eds), *International Perspectives on English as a Lingua Franca*. Basingstoke: Palgrave Macmillan, pp. 13–34.

Machaal, B. (2012), 'The Use of Arabic in English Classes: A Teaching Support or a Learning Hindrance?'. *Arab World English Journal* 3(2): 194–232.

Margić, B. (2016), 'Communication Courtesy or Condescension? Linguistic Accommodation of Native to Non-Native Speakers of English'. *Journal of English as a Lingua Franca* 6(1): 29–55.

Mar-Molinero, C. (2000), *The Politics of Language in the Spanish-speaking World*. London: Routledge.

Mar-Molinero, C. and Paffey, D. (2015), 'Who Owns Global Spanish?', in Díaz-Campos, M. (ed.), *The Handbook of Hispanic Sociolinguistics*. Chichester: Wiley-Blackwell, pp. 747–64.

Marr, T. (2005), 'Language and the Capital: A Case Study of English "Language Shock" among Chinese Students in London'. *Language Awareness* 14(4): 239–53.

Marr, T. (2011), '"*Ya no podemos regresar al quechua*": Modernity, Identity and Language Choice among Migrants in Urban Peru', in Pearce, A. and Heggarty, P. (eds), *History and Language in the Andes*. New York: Palgrave Macmillan, pp. 215–38.

McCarthy, M. and Carter, R. (2012), 'Size Isn't Everything: Spoken English, Corpus, and the Classroom'. *TESOL Quarterly* 35(2): 337–40.

McDonald, M., Badger, R., and Dasli, M. (2006), 'Authenticity, Culture and Language Learning'. *Language and Intercultural Communication* 6(3/4): 250–61.

McKay, S. L. (2012), 'Teaching Materials for English as an International Language', in Matsuda, A. (ed.), *Principles and Practices of Teaching English as an International Language*. Bristol: Multilingual Matters, pp. 70–83.

McKenzie, R. (2008), 'Social Factors and Non-Native Attitudes towards Varieties of Spoken English: A Japanese Case Study'. *International Journal of Applied Linguistics* 18(1): 63–88.

McNamara, T. (2012), 'English as a Lingua Franca: The Challenge for Language Testing'. *Journal of English as a Lingua Franca* 1(1): 199–202.

Mezirow, J. (2000), 'Learning to Think Like an Adult: Core Concepts of Transformation Theory' in Mezirow, J. and Associates (eds), *Learning as Transformation*. San Francisco: Jossey-Bass, pp. 3–34.

Moore, P. (2017), 'Becoming Bilingual in the EFL Classroom'. *ELT Journal*. DOI: https://doi.org/10.1093/elt/ccx045.

Mora, R., Pulgarín, C., Ramírez, N., and Mejía-Vélez, M. (2018), 'English Literacies in Medellín: The City as Literacy', in Nichols, S. and Dobson, S. (eds), *Learning Cities. Multimodal Explorations and Placed Pedagogies*. Singapore: Springer, pp. 37–60.

Mugford, G. and Rubio-Mitchel, C. (2018), 'Racial, Linguistic and Professional Discrimination Towards Teachers of English as a Foreign Language: Mexican Context'. *Journal of Language and Discrimination* 2(1): 32–57.

Mullen, A. (2016), 'Sociolinguistics', in Millett, M., Revell, L., and Moore, A. (eds) *The Oxford Handbook of Roman Britain*. Oxford: Oxford University Press, pp. 573–98.

Munro, M. and Derwing, T. (2011), 'The Foundations of Accent and Intelligibility in Pronunciation Research'. *Language Teaching* 44: 316–27.

Murphy, J. (2014), 'Intelligible, Comprehensible Non-Native Models in ESL/EFL Pronunciation Teaching'. *System* 42: 258–69.

Myhill, D. (2016), 'The Effectiveness of Explicit Language Teaching: Evidence from the Research', in Giovanelli, M. and Clayton, D. (eds), *Knowing About Language: Linguistics and the Secondary English Classroom*. London: Routledge, pp. 36–49.

Newbold, D. (2017), ' "Co-certification": A Close Encounter with ELF for an International Examining Board'. *Journal of English as a Lingua Franca* 6(2): 367–88.

Niño-Murcia, M. (2003), ' "English Is like the Dollar": Hard Currency Ideology and the Status of English in Peru'. *World Englishes* 22(2): 121–42.

Norton, B. (2000), *Identity and Language Learning: Gender, Ethnicity and Educational Change*. Harlow: Longman.

Norton, B. (2010), 'Identity, Literacy, and English-Language Teaching'. *TESL Canada Journal* 28: 1–13.

Norton, B. and Kamal, F. (2003), 'The Imagined Communities of English Language Learners in a Pakistani school'. *Journal of Language, Identity and Education* 2: 301–17.

Nunan, D. (2003), 'The Impact of English as a Global Language on Educational Policies and Practices in the Asia-Pacific Region'. *TESOL Quarterly* 37(4): 589–613.

O'Keefe, A., McCarthy, M., and Carter, R. (2007), *From Corpus to Classroom*. Cambridge: Cambridge University Press.

O'Regan, J. (2014), 'English as a Lingua Franca: An Immanent Critique'. *Applied Linguistics* 35(5): 533–52.

Ostler, N. (2005), *Empires of the Word: A Language History of the World*. London: HarperCollins.

Ostler, N. (2010), *The Last Lingua Franca: English Until the Return of Babel*. New York: Walker.

Otsuji, E. and Pennycook, A. (2010), 'Metrolingualism: Fixity, Fluidity and Language in Flux'. *International Journal of Multilingualism* 7(3): 240–54.

Paikeday, T. (1985), *The Native Speaker Is Dead!* Toronto: Paikeday Publishing.

Painter, C. (2001), 'Understanding Genre and Register: Implications for Language Teaching', in Burns, A. and Coffin, C. (eds), *Analysing English in a Global Context: A Reader*. London: Routledge/Macquarie University/The Open University, pp. 167–80.

Paradowski, M. (2013), Review of Seidlhofer, B. (2011), Understanding English as a Lingua Franca. *The Interpreter and Translator Trainer* 7(2): 312–20.

Park, J.-K. (2009), '"English Fever" in South Korea: Its History and Symptoms'. *English Today* 97: 50–7.

Pedrazzini, L. (2015), 'Raising Trainee Teachers' Awareness of Language Variation through Data-Based Tasks', in Vettorel, P. (ed.), *New Frontiers in Teaching and Learning English*. Newcastle-upon-Tyne: Cambridge Scholars, pp. 77–99.

Pennycook, A. (1994), *The Cultural Politics of English as an International Language*. London: Longman.

Pennycook, A. (1998), *English and the Discourses of Colonialism*. London: Routledge.

Pennycook, A. (2010), *Language as a Local Practice*. London: Routledge.

Phillipson, R. (1992), *Linguistic Imperialism*. Oxford: Oxford University Press.

Phillipson, R. (2003), *English-Only Europe? Challenging Language Policy*. London: Routledge.

Phillipson, R. (2008), 'Lingua Franca or Lingua Frankensteinia? English in European Integration and Globalisation'. *World Englishes* 27(2): 250–67.

Phillipson, R. (2009a), *Linguistic Imperialism Continued*. London: Routledge.

Phillipson, R. (2009b), 'English in Globalization, a Lingua Franca or a Lingua Frankensteinia?'. *TESOL Quarterly* 43(2): 335–9.

Phillipson, R. (2014), 'English, the Lingua Nullius of Global Hegemony'. Online at: http://www.linguistic-rights.org/robert-phillipson/ Robert_Phillipson_English_in_global_ hegemony. pdf [Accessed 25 December 2016].

Pinner, R. (2016), *Reconceptualising Authenticity for English as a Global Language*. Bristol: Multilingual Matters.

Prabhu, N. S. (1990), 'There Is No Best Method. Why?'. *TESOL Quarterly* 24(2): 161–75.

Rajagopalan, K. (1999), 'Of EFL Teachers, Conscience and Cowardice'. *ELT Journal* 53(3): 200–6.

Rampton, B. (1990), 'Displacing the Native Speaker: Expertise, Affiliation and Inheritance'. *ELT Journal* 44(2): 97–101.

Rao, H. (2002), 'Chinese Students' Perceptions of Communicative and Non-communicative Activities in EFL Classroom'. *System* 30: 85–105.

Roach, P. (2009), *English Phonetics and Phonology* (4th edn). Cambridge: Cambridge University Press.

Samarin, W. (1972), 'Lingua Francas of the World', in Fishman, J. (ed.), *Readings in the Sociology of Language*. The Hague: Mouton, pp. 660–72.

Samarin, W. (1987), 'Lingua Franca', in Ammon, U., Dittmar, N. and K. Mattheier (eds), *Sociolinguistics: An International Handbook of the Science of Language and Society*. Berlin: De Gruyter, pp. 371–4.

Sarno-Pedreira, K. (2004), *Speaking English, Behaving Brazilian*. Unpublished MA dissertation, London Metropolitan University.

Sayer, P. (2010), 'Using the Linguistic Landscape as a Pedagogical Resource'. *ELT Journal* 64(2): 143–54.

Schwyter, J. (2016), *Dictating to the Mob. The History of the BBC Advisory Committee on Spoken English*. Oxford: Oxford University Press.

Scollon, R. and Scollon, S. (2003), *Discourses in Place: Language in the Material World*. London: Routledge.

Seidlhofer, B. (2001), 'Closing a Conceptual Gap: The Case for a Description of English as a Lingua Franca'. *International Journal of Applied Linguistics* 11: 133–58.

Seidlhofer, B. (2003), *A Concept of International English and Related Issues: From 'Real English' to 'Realistic English'?*. Strasbourg: Council of Europe.

Seidlhofer, B. (2005), 'English as a Lingua Franca'. *ELT Journal* 59(4): 339–41.

Seidlhofer, B. (2006), 'English as a Lingua Franca in the Expanding Circle: What It Isn't', in Rubdy, R. and Saraceni, M. (eds), *English in the World: Global Rules, Global Roles*. London: Continuum, pp. 40–50.

Seidlhofer, B. (2010), 'Lingua Franca English: The European Context', in Kirkpatrick, A. (ed.), *The Routledge Handbook of World Englishes*. Abingdon: Routledge, pp. 355–71.

Seidlhofer, B. (2011), *Understanding English as a Lingua Franca*. Oxford: Oxford University Press.

Sewell, A. (2013), 'English as a Lingua Franca: Ontology and Ideology'. *ELT Journal* 67(1): 3–10.

Shamim, F. (2011), 'English as the Language for Development in Pakistan: Issues, Challenges and Possible Solutions', in Coleman, H. (ed.), *Dreams and Realities: Developing Countries and the English Language*. London: British Council, pp. 297–315.

Shohamy, E. (2006), *Language Policy: Hidden Agendas and New Approaches*. London: Routledge.

Sifakis, N. (2014), 'ELF Awareness as an Opportunity for Change: A Transformative Perspective for ESOL Teacher Education'. *Journal of English as a Lingua Franca* 3(2): 317–35.

Singleton, D. and Ryan, L. (2004), *Language Acquisition: The Age Factor*. Clevedon: Multilingual Matters.

Smotrova, T. (2009), 'Globalisation and English Language Teaching in Ukraine'. *TESOL Quarterly* 43(4): 727–32.

Soleil, S. (2004), 'L'Ordonnance de Villers-Cotterêts, Cadre Juridique de la Politique Linguistique des Rois de France?' in proceedings of the colloquium *Langue(s) et Constitution(s)*. Aix-en-Provence: Economica/ Presses Universitaires d'Aix-Marseille, pp. 19–34.

Song, J. (2016), 'Emotions and Language Teacher Identity: Conflicts, Vulnerability, and Transformation'. *TESOL Quarterly* 50(3): 631–54.

Sousanis, N. (2015), *Unflattening*. Cambridge, MA: Harvard University Press.

Stanley, P. (2013), *A Critical Ethnography of 'Westerners' Teaching English in China: Shanghaied in Shanghai*. Abingdon: Routledge.

Stanley, P. (2016), 'Economy Class? Lived Experiences and Career Trajectories of Private-Sector English-Language School Teachers in Australia', in Haworth, P. and Craig, C. (eds), *The Career Trajectories of English Language Teachers*. Oxford: Symposium Books, pp. 185–99.

Starr, D. (2012), *China and the Confucian Education Model*. Universitas 21 Teaching and Learning Position Paper.

Stern, H. H. (1983), *Fundamental Concepts of Language Teaching*. Oxford: Oxford University Press.

Street, B. (1984), *Literacy in Theory and Practice*. Cambridge: Cambridge University Press.

Subtirelu, N. (2013), 'What (Do) Learners Want (?): A Re-examination of the Issue of Learner Preferences regarding the Use of 'Native' Speaker Norms in English Language Teaching'. *Language Awareness* 22(3): 270–91.

Subtirelu, N. and Lindemann, S. (2016), 'Teaching First Language Speakers to Communicate across Linguistic Difference: Addressing Attitudes, Comprehension, and Strategies'. *Applied Linguistics* 37(6): 765–83.

Suzuki, A. (2011), 'Introducing Diversity of English into ELT: Student Teachers' Responses'. *ELT Journal* 65(2): 145–53.

Swan, A., Aboshiha, P., and Holliday, A. (eds) (2015), *(En-)Countering Native-speakerism: Global Perspectives*. Basingstoke: Palgrave Macmillan.

Swan, M. (2017), 'EFL, ELF, and the Question of Accuracy'. *ELT Journal* 71(4): 511–15.

Tan, P., Ooi, V., and Chiang, A. (2006), 'World Englishes or English as a Lingua Franca? A View from the Perspective of Non-Anglo Englishes', in Rubdy, R. and Saraceni, M. (eds), *English in the World: Global Rules, Global Roles*. London: Continuum, pp. 84–94.

Tan, P. and Rubdy, R. (eds) (2008), *Language as Commodity: Global Structures, Local Marketplaces*. London: Bloomsbury.

Thompson, A. (2017), 'Diversity of Users, Settings, and Practices: How are Features Selected into ELF Practice?'. *Journal of English as a Lingua Franca* 6(2): 205–35.

Thompson, G. (1996), 'Some Misconceptions about Communicative Language Teaching'. *ELT Journal* 50(1): 9–15.

Thornbury, S. (2001), 'The Unbearable Lightness of EFL'. *ELT Journal* 55(4): 391–96.

Trappes-Lomax, H. and Ferguson, G. (eds) (2002), *Language in Language Teacher Education*. Amsterdam: John Benjamins.

Tupas, R. and Rubdy, R. (2015), 'Introduction: From World Englishes to Unequal Englishes', in Tupas, R. and Rubdy, R. (eds), *Unequal Englishes: The Politics of Englishes Today*. Basingstoke: Palgrave Macmillan, pp. 1–17.

Trudgill, P. (1998), Review of Honey, J. (1997), 'Language Is Power: The Story of Standard English and Its Enemies'. *Journal of Sociolinguistics* 2(3): 457–61.

Tsui, A. (2007), 'Complexities of Identity Formation: A Narrative Inquiry of an EFL Teacher'. *TESOL Quarterly* 41(4): 657–80.

Turner, J. (2011), *Language in the Academy: Cultural Reflexivity and Intercultural Dynamics*. Bristol: Multilingual Matters.

Ullman, C. (2010), 'Consuming English: How Mexican Transmigrants Form Identities and Construct Symbolic Citizenship through the English-Language Program *Inglés Sin Barreras* [English Without Barriers]'. *Linguistics and Education* 21: 1–13.

Vang, N. (2003), 'English Language Teaching in Vietnam Today: Policy, Practice and Constraints', in Ho, W. and Wong, R. (eds), *English Language Teaching in East Asia Today: Changing Policies and Practices*. Singapore: Eastern Universities Press, pp. 455–74.

Vikør, L. (2004), 'Lingua Franca and International Language', in Ammon, U. (ed.), *Sociolinguistics: An International Handbook of the Science of Language and Society*, vol. 1. Berlin: De Gruyter, pp. 328–35.

Vu, N. and Burns, A. (2014), 'English as a Medium of Instruction: Challenges for Vietnamese Tertiary Lecturers'. *Journal of Asia TEFL* 11(3): 1–31.

Wang, Y. (2015), 'Chinese University Students' ELF Awareness: Impacts of Language Education in China'. *Englishes in Practice* 2(4): 86–106.

Wang, X. and Li, Y. (2014), '"English Fever" in China Has Reached a Watershed'. *International Higher Education* 75: 13–14.

Warriner, D. (2007), 'Language Learning and the Politics of Belonging: Sudanese Women Refugees Becoming and Being "American"'. *Anthropology and Education Quarterly* 38(4): 343–59.

Wedell, M. (2011), 'More than Just "Technology": English Language Teaching Initiatives as Complex Educational Changes', in Coleman, H. (ed.), *Dreams and Realities: Developing Countries and the English Language*. London: British Council, pp. 269–90.

Wei, R. and Su, J. (2012), 'The Statistics of English in China'. *English Today* 28: 10–14.

Widdowson, H. (1978), *Explorations in Applied Linguistics*. Oxford: Oxford University Press.

Widdowson, H. (1983), *Learning Purpose and Language Use*. Oxford: Oxford University Press.

Widdowson, H. (1994), 'The Ownership of English'. *TESOL Quarterly* 28(2): 377–89.

Wigglesworth, G. and Yates, L. (2007), 'Mitigating Difficult Requests in the Workplace: What Learners and Teachers Need to Know'. *TESOL Quarterly* 41(4): 791–803.

Wilson, R. (2016), *The PTE Academic and Outer Circle Students: Assessing Proficiency in English, Ownership of English, and Academic Performance at UK Universities*. Doctoral Thesis, University of Warwick. Available at http://wrap.warwick.ac.uk/90065.

Wright, S. (2009), 'The Elephant in the Room'. *European Journal of Language Policy* 1(2): 93–120.

Wright, T. (2002), 'Doing Language Awareness: Issues for Language Study in Language Teacher Education', in Trappes-Lomax, H. and Ferguson, G. (eds), Language in Language Teacher Education. Amsterdam: John Benjamins, pp. 113–30.

Young, T. and Walsh, S. (2010), 'Which English? Whose English? An Investigation of 'Non-native' Teachers' Beliefs about Target Varieties'. *Language, Culture and Curriculum* 23(2): 123–37.

Yu, X. (2013), 'Learning a Foreign Language through Text and Memorisation: the Chinese Learners' Perceptions'. *Journal of Language Teaching and Research* 4(4): 731–40.

Zhang, D., Li, Y., and Wang, Y. (2013), 'How Culturally Appropriate Is the Communicative Approach with Reference to the Chinese Context?'. *Creative Education* 4(10A): 1–5.

Index